WORKS ISSUED BY

THE HAKLUYT SOCIETY

THE JAMESTOWN VOYAGES
UNDER THE FIRST CHARTER
1606–1609

VOLUME I

SECOND SERIES
No. CXXXVI

ISSUED FOR 1969

HAKLUYT SOCIETY

PATRON:
H.R.H. THE DUKE OF GLOUCESTER, K.G., P.C., K.T., K.P.

COUNCIL AND OFFICERS, 1968-69

PRESIDENT
SIR GILBERT LAITHWAITE, G.C.M.G., K.C.B., K.C.I.E., C.S.I.

VICE-PRESIDENTS

J. N. L. BAKER, M.A., B.Litt. Sir ALAN BURNS, G.C.M.G.
Professor C. R. BOXER, F.B.A. Dr E. S. DE BEER, F.B.A.
Professor D. B. QUINN

COUNCIL (with date of election)

W. E. D. ALLEN, O.B.E. (1967) Rear-Admiral G. S. RITCHIE, D.S.C.
Dr K. R. ANDREWS (1966) (1965)
Professor C. F. BECKINGHAM (1964) Royal Commonwealth Society (1966,
Dr J. S. CUMMINS (1967) D. H. SIMPSON)
Sir PHILIP HAY, K.C.V.O., T.D. (1968) Royal Geographical Society (G. R.
Dr C. I. JACKSON (1967) CRONE)
Sir HARRY LUKE, K.C.M.G. (1967) A. N. RYAN (1968)
B. F. MACDONA, C.B.E. (1967) R. A. SKELTON (1966)
J. F. MAGGS (1966) Dr J. W. STOYE (1968)
Mrs DOROTHY MIDDLETON (1966) Lieut-Cdr D. W. WATERS, R.N. (1965)

TRUSTEES
J. N. L. BAKER
Sir GILBERT LAITHWAITE, G.C.M.G., K.C.B., K.C.I.E., C.S.I.
The Right Hon. LORD RENNELL of RODD, K.B.E., C.B.

HONORARY TREASURER
J. N. L. BAKER

HONORARY SECRETARIES
Miss E. M. J. CAMPBELL, Birkbeck College, London, W.C. 1
Dr T. E. ARMSTRONG, Scott Polar Research Institute, Cambridge

HON. SECRETARIES FOR OVERSEAS
Australia: G. D. RICHARDSON, The Public Library of New South Wales, Macquarie Street, Sydney, N.S.W. 2000
Canada: Professor J. B. BIRD, McGill University, Montreal
India: Dr S. GOPAL, Ministry of External Affairs, 3 Man Singh Road, New Delhi
New Zealand: C. R. H. TAYLOR, Box 5102, Tawa
South Africa: Professor ERIC AXELSON, University of Cape Town, Rondebosch, South Africa
U.S.A.: Dr W. M. WHITEHILL, Boston Athenaeum, $10\frac{1}{2}$ Beacon Street, Boston, Massachusetts 02108

CLERK OF PUBLICATIONS AND ASSISTANT TREASURER
Mrs ALEXA BARROW, Hakluyt Society, c/o British Museum, London, W.C. 1

PUBLISHER AND AGENT FOR SALE AND DISTRIBUTION OF VOLUMES
Cambridge University Press, Bentley House, 200 Euston Road, London, N.W. 1

Published by the Syndics of the Cambridge University Press
Bentley House, 200 Euston Road, London, N.W.1
American Branch: 32 East 57th Street, New York, N.Y. 10022

Library of Congress Catalogue Card Number: 68-23173
Standard Book Number: 521 01027 6 (set of 2 vols)

*Printed in Great Britain
by Robert MacLehose & Company Limited
at The University Press, Glasgow*

The Jamestown Voyages Under the First Charter 1606—1609

VOLUME I

Documents relating to the foundation of
Jamestown and the history of the
Jamestown colony up to the
departure of Captain John Smith,
last president of the council in Virginia
under the first charter,
early in October, 1609

Edited by

PHILIP L. BARBOUR

CAMBRIDGE
Published for the Hakluyt Society
AT THE UNIVERSITY PRESS
1969

The original fleet of 1606. A reconstruction of the *Discovery*, *Godspeed* and *Susan Constant*, built in West Norfolk, Virginia, in 1956–57. The ships made a ceremonial landing at Cape Henry on 26 April 1957. They are permanently moored at Jamestown Festival Park.

TO THE MEMORY OF
SIR WALTER RALEGH
1861–1922

PREFACE

THE Jamestown colony was the first permanent English colony founded on the American continent. As such, it was not only the mother colony of Virginia, but indirectly also the ancestress of New England. Indeed, it was Jamestown that showed that a colony could survive on far from hospitable shores with its lifeline ever subject to the threat of inimical action from the lord of the western hemisphere, Philip III of Spain (and II of Portugal). Even Newfoundland, Nova Scotia and eventually all Canada became British only after – not to say because of – the historical fact of the permanence of the Jamestown colony.

The voyages which established Jamestown are therefore of prime interest in any study of the origins of the British Empire, as well as of the world powers known as the Commonwealth and the United States today. The documents which authorized the first voyages and the narratives, letters and reports which have survived are basic material for such study. Yet no-one has collected and interpreted, so to speak, these documents in the present century, and the only previous general collection (that of Alexander Brown, in his *Genesis of the United States*), while lacking a handful of items only recently found or made available, suffers from a historical bias that cannot but vitiate in some measure the value of the documentation.

The narrative and descriptive material relative to the early Jamestown voyages is voluminous, despite the loss or disappearance of much valuable information which is known to have been available at one time. For that reason, the editor has thought it proper to limit the present volume to the discovery, settlement, and early troubles of the Jamestown colony only during the life of the original charter, of 10 April 1606. Nevertheless, because communications were slow and uncertain, it is not a simple matter to cut off the narrative with the entry into

PREFACE

force of the second charter, of 23 May 1609 – which changed the legal nature of the nascent colony at the same time that it provided more effective means to nourish and expand it. It would have taken weeks for the effect of the new charter to be felt in Virginia under any circumstances, but a greater power than the Spanish monarch, the Caribbean storm-god *Huracán*, delayed the matter even more. Unwisely voyaging together, all three chiefs of the colonization fleet sent out under the second charter were caught by an early hurricane on the same ship, and blown on to the reefs of Bermuda. With them were the only official copies of the charter itself, and of the orders intended to implement it.

The energy and ability of the new governor of Virginia (the first to bear that title), Sir Thomas Gates, found a way to ferry his colonists to the mainland, but it was nearly a year before they arrived. Meanwhile, the headless residue of the same expedition reached Jamestown with no orders, no charter, and no-one in undisputed command. The president of the Virginia council, Captain John Smith, refused to obey word-of-mouth orders from London, persuaded as he was that the objective of the newcomers was largely to usurp his power.

Although Smith's position was legally right, and from a practical point of view more than right, it proved impossible to carry on the established government after his own term of office expired one month after the arrival of the new group. Disabled by an accident (of what real seriousness will probably never be known), Smith let the second-charter colonists take over, and sailed for London by the first available ship.

The misfortune to the ship bearing Gates and his associates, Somers and Newport, provides the closing point for this volume on the Virginia voyages under the first charter. Obviously, there is a certain amount of overlap in time, because the second charter could not take full effect in Virginia without any legally appointed governor. With Smith's departure, however, the last vestige of management under the

PREFACE

first charter was gone. Only such documents as have bearing on that final episode have consequently been included. If a supplementary volume should be needed, dealing with the disastrous winter of 1609–1610 and the final cementing of English permanence in Virginia toward the close of 1611, the intentional overlap will provide clear continuity to the narrative.

In broad lines, the arrangement of this volume follows that so successfully initiated by Professor David Beers Quinn in his *The Roanoke voyages, 1584–1590* (Hakluyt Society, 2nd ser., CIV–CV (1952)), without any attempt to imitate. Nevertheless, it may be said with Professor Quinn that, while an attempt has been made here to include all the material that is pertinent, there may well be more documents awaiting the collector in England, and certainly much work of investigation and consolidation needs still to be done on the continent, particularly in Spain (see Document no. 62 and notes).

It is a pleasure here to acknowledge the wide and enthusiastic help which has been accorded the editor during the preparation of this book. Professor Quinn himself stands first in place, not only for his willingness, and his knowledge of the field, but also because of his insatiable curiosity for information that might throw light on the earliest period of English colonial history – a term virtually equivalent to early American history. Next him stands Mr R. A. Skelton, who has encouraged and helped the editor both while he was Honorary Secretary of the Society, and even after his regretted resignation.

For the individual documents herein published, the editor wishes to thank many institutions and individuals for their help, and for permission to publish documents in their possession. The Duke of Portland and the Duke of Northumberland have graciously consented to the appearance here of several letters belonging to them, as have the Marquess of Salisbury and the Marquess of Downshire. Miss Clare Talbot, Librarian at Hatfield House, has been particularly kind about locating a handful of items which, though not directly used, have thrown

PREFACE

light on the narratives. Similarly, Mr William J. Smith, County Archivist of the Royal County of Berkshire, has been most helpful, and Mr F. G. Emmison, County Archivist, Essex County Council, has cleared up at least one point of doubt. Dr M. A. P. Meilink-Roelofsz, Keeper of the First Section, Algemeen Rijksarchief, The Hague, has kindly supplied a transcript from their records. The Trustees of the British Museum have graciously permitted xerox and photostatic copies of printed books and manuscripts for inclusion, while a number of transcripts of Crown-copyright records in the Public Record Office appear by permission of the Controller of H.M. Stationery Office. Both the Lambeth Palace Library and the India Office Library have authorized the use of documents, as well. In Spain, the Dirección General de Archivos y Bibliotecas, Madrid, and Don Ricardo Magdaleno, Director, Archivo General de Simancas, have graciously granted permission for the publication of translations of a number of manuscript letters preserved there, and Don José de la Peña, Director, Archivo General de Indias, Seville, has permitted the translation and publication of a long extract from a document in their archives. Also, the editor is indebted to the staff of the Plymouth Municipal Records, Plymouth, for their cooperation, and to the Bodleian Library, Oxford, and The Huntington Library, San Marino, California, for permission to print manuscripts in their possession.

Mr Lewis M. Stark, Chief, Rare Book Division, the New York Public Library, has helped greatly with rare copies of John Smith's early works, and both that Library and the Library of the New York Historical Society are to be thanked for permission to copy and use a few pages from volumes in their possession. In Washington, D.C., the Folger Shakespeare Library was kind enough to grant to the editor a fellowship to permit careful study and analysis of both printed books and manuscripts belonging to them. Also, the Library of Congress has authorized the use of several early transcripts of documents

PREFACE

formerly belonging to President Thomas Jefferson. Mr William J. Van Schreeven, State Archivist, Virginia State Library, has supplied further early transcripts from the Virginia Land Office Patents. Mr Howard A. MacCord, Sr, Treasurer of the Archaeological Society of Virginia, and Mr Edward F. Heite, of the Virginia State Library, have supplied invaluable information regarding the potential location of Indian villages mentioned in various documents. Especial acknowledgment is due to Mr T. C. Skeat, Keeper of Manuscripts, British Museum, for expert advice on the transcription and reconstruction of the trimmed marginal notes, Document no. 33. And lastly, the editor wishes to thank Mr Wolfgang Rennert, of Newtown, Connecticut, for his great help in comparing texts and in other details of preparation.

Philip L. Barbour

NEWTOWN, CONNECTICUT,
AND LONDON
September 1966

CONTENTS
VOLUME I

Illustrations	*page* xxi
Abbreviations used in the footnotes	xxii
On editing	xxiii
Table of Jamestown voyages	xxiv
Combined list of original planters	xxv

Introduction: Brief review of sources   1

I The Preliminaries

NARRATIVE   13

1   10 April 1606. Letters patent to Sir Thomas Gates and others   24
P.R.O., Patent Roll, 4 James I, C.66/1709

2   20 November 1606. Instructions for Government   34
Virginia State Library, Land Office Patent Book 2, 1643–1651

3   10 December 1606. Order of the Council for Virginia   45
L.C., Bland MS, pp. 19–23

4   [Between 20 November and 19 December, 1606.] The London Council's 'Instructions given by way of Advice'   49
L.C., Bland MS, pp. 14–18

5   13 December 1606. Examination Concerning Damage to the *Susan Constant*   55
Extract. P.R.O., H.C.A., 13/38

6   20 November 1606. Robert Hunt's Will   60
Extract. Somerset House, P.C.C. 72 Windebank

7   24 November 1606. Dispensation for Richard Hakluyt and Robert Hunt   62
P.R.O., Patent Roll, 4 James I, pt. 14, C.66/1708

II The Original Voyage

NARRATIVE 65

8 [14/]24 January 1607. Pedro de Zúñiga to Philip III 69
Decoded. Extract, translated. Archivo General de Simancas, Legajo E 2585, 78–79

9 9 March 1607. Ordinance and Constitution enlarging the Council 71
P.R.O., C.O. 5/1354, 49–53, collated with V.S.L., Patents No. 2, 1643–1651

10 29 July 1607. Newport's Letter to Lord Salisbury 76
Northumberland Papers, Syon House MSS, fo. 268

11 [12/]22 August 1607. Pedro de Zúñiga to Philip III 77
Decoded. Extract, translated. Archivo General de Simancas, Legajo E 2586, 66

12 22 June 1607. Letter from the Council in Virginia 78
Northumberland Papers, Syon House MSS, fo. 263

13 21 May–21 June 1607. A relatyon... written... by a gent. of ye Colony 80
P.R.O., S.P. Colonial, C.O. 1/1, folios 46^r–52^r

14 21 May–21 June 1607. Description of the River and Country 98
P.R.O., S.P. Colonial, C.O. 1/1, folios 53^r–55^r

15 21 May–21 June 1607. Description of the People 102
P.R.O., S.P. Colonial, C.O. 1/1, folios 55^r–56^v

16 22 June 1607. Robert Tindall, Gunner, to Prince Henry 104
B.M., Harl. MS 7007, (Plut. LXVI, I.F.), Letters to and from Prince Henry, fo. 139

17 Between 27 May and 22 June, 1607. Undated letter from William Brewster 107
Hatfield House, Cecil Papers, 124/17

18 12 August 1607. Sir Walter Cope to Lord Salisbury 108
Hatfield House, Cecil Papers, 124/18

19 13 August 1607. Sir Walter Cope to Lord Salisbury 111
Extract. Hatfield House, Cecil Papers, 117/29

VI Spain Investigates

NARRATIVE 291

62 After 24 September 1609, with postscript of 28 November. Report of Francisco Fernández de Écija 293
   Extract, translated. Archivo General de Indias, Seville, Patronato 261, Ramo 11

VII Captain John Smith's Summary: *A Map of Virginia*

NARRATIVE 321

63 Completed between 25 March and late autumn, 1612. *A map of Virginia*, by Captain John Smith and others 327
   Printed at Oxford, 1612. Text from B.M. copy C. 33. c. 18, with inserted dedication to the Earl of Hertford from a copy in the New York Public Library.

Appendices 465

Bibliography 483

Indexes 495

LIST OF ILLUSTRATIONS AND MAPS

Jamestown settlers' ships *frontispiece*
Photograph courtesy of the Jamestown Foundation, Williamsburg, Virginia

'Bound for Virginia': the full-scale reconstruction of the
Susan Constant *facing page* 22
Photograph courtesy of the Jamestown Foundation, Williamsburg, Virginia

Robert Tindall's 'Draughte of Virginia' *page* 105
Redrawn from the original in the British Museum, Cotton MS, Aug. I, ii, 46

Chesapeake Bay *page* 169
Based on a map first published in Philip L. Barbour's *The Three Worlds of Captain John Smith*. Courtesy of Houghton Mifflin Company, Boston

The so-called 'Zúñiga Map', 1608 *facing page* 239
Courtesy of the Archivo General de Simancas

Écija's voyage of reconnaissance *page* 294
Based on U.S. Coast and Geodetic Survey, Chart JN-45, scale 1 : 2,000,000. 1965

Detail from the Velasco map (1611), showing the Virginia of the Jamestown voyages *page* 336
Courtesy of the Archivo General de Simancas

John Smith's map of 1612 *facing page* 374
Copy bound in with William Strachey's *Historie*, British Museum, Sloane MS 1622. Courtesy of the Trustees

Abbreviations used in the footnotes

Shortened titles of printed books will be easily identified
by reference to the Bibliography

B.M.	British Museum
H.C.A.	High Court of Admiralty
H.M.C.	Historical Manuscripts Commission (Calendars)
L.C.	Library of Congress
OED	*Oxford English Dictionary*
P.R.O.	Public Record Office
S.P.	State Papers
VMHB	*Virginia Magazine of History and Biography*
WMQ	*William and Mary Quarterly*

CONTENTS

20 17 August 1607. Sir Thomas Smythe to Lord Salisbury   112
    Hatfield House, Cecil Papers, 122/23

21 18 August 1607. Dudley Carleton to John Chamberlain   113
    Extract. P.R.O., S.P. 14/28

22 4 September 1607. Court Minute of the East India Company   114
    India Office Library, London. Court Minute Book, 4 September 1607, fo. 50ᵛ

23 [12/]22 September 1607. Pedro de Zúñiga to Philip III   114
    Decoded. Translated. Archivo General de Simancas, Legajo E 2586, 65

24 [25 September/]5 October 1607. Pedro de Zúñiga to Philip III   116
    Decoded. Translated. Archivo General de Simancas, Legajo E 2586, 64

25 [28 September/]8 October 1607. Pedro de Zúñiga to Philip III   117
    Decoded. Extract, translated. Archivo General de Simancas, Legajo E 2586, 68

26 [6/]16 October 1607. Pedro de Zúñiga to Philip III   120
    Decoded [?]. Extract, translated. Archivo General de Simancas, Legajo E 2586, 69

27 [18/]28 October 1607. Philip III to Don Pedro de Zúñiga   122
    Instruction to code. Extract, translated. Archivo General de Simancas, Legajo E 2571, 215

III In Virginia, from Newport's Departure to the Arrival of the First Supply

NARRATIVE   125

28 1608 [?]. [Before 12 April 1612.] George Percy's *Discourse*   129
    Purchas, *Pilgrimes*, IV, 1685–90

29 1608 [?]. [Before 12 April 1612.] George Percy, Fragment published in 1614   146
    Purchas, *Pilgrimage* (1614), 768

CONTENTS

30   1608 [?]. [Before 1614.] William White, Fragments published in 1614   147
Purchas, *Pilgrimage* (1614), 766–67

31   1 July 1610. Francis Magnel's Relation of the First Voyage and the Beginnings of the Virginia Colony   151
Translated. Archivo General de Simancas, Legajo E 2587, 98

32   28 March 1608. Francis Perkin[s] in Jamestown to a Friend in England. Accompanied by letter of transmission from Zúñiga, dated [16/] 26 June   158
Translated. Archivo General de Simancas, Legajo E 2586, 111–14

33   Before 2 June 1608. Captain John Smith, *A true relation.* . . .   165
Text from British Museum copy, C. 33. c. 5, supplemented by address, New York Historical Society Library copy

IV   Events in England, 1608

NARRATIVE   209

34   1508. [Finished after 21 May.] Edward Maria Wingfield, Discourse   213
Lambeth Palace Library, MSS, 250, folios 382–96

35   1608. [Published in 1611.] News from Paris   234
Extract, translated. *Le Mercure François* . . . [1605–1610]. Paris, 1611. Sigs. Bb3ᵛ–Bb4

36   24 April 1608. Resolution of the States General   235
Translated. St. Gen., inv. nr. 33 (1608), fo. 57

37   7 July 1608. John Chamberlain to Dudley Carleton   236
Extract. P.R.O., S.P. Dom., S.P. 14/35

38   [5/]15 September 1608. Pedro de Zúñiga to Philip III   236
Translated. Archivo General de Simancas, Legajo E 2586, 145

39   Prior to 5/15 September 1608. Anonymous account of Virginia   237
Translated. Archivo General de Simancas, Legajo E 2586, 146

40   Prior to 5/15 September 1608. Anonymous map of Virginia   238
Archivo General de Simancas, Legajo E 2586, 148

xvi

CONTENTS

41 Between 10 September and early December, 1608. Captain John Smith to the Treasurer and Council of Virginia, London   241
   Extract. Captain John Smith, *The generall historie*. . . . London, 1624, pp. 70–72

42 26 November 1608. Peter Winne to Sir John Egerton   245
   Holograph. Huntington Library, Jamestown colony, EL 1683

43 23 January 1609. John Chamberlain to Dudley Carleton   246
   Extract. P.R.O., S.P. Dom., S.P. 14/43

44 14 February 1609. John Chamberlain to Dudley Carleton   247
   Extract. P.R.O., S.P. Dom., S.P. 14/43

VOLUME II

V Dissatisfaction, and the Second Charter

NARRATIVE   249

45 [23 February/]5 March 1609. Pedro de Zúñiga to Philip III   254
   Decoded. Translated. Archivo General de Simancas, Legajo E 2587, 12

46 [22 March/]1 April 1609. Pedro de Zúñiga to Philip III   258
   Decoded. Extract, translated. Archivo General de Simancas, Legajo E 2587, 18

47 [2/]12 April 1609. Pedro de Zúñiga to Philip III   259
   Decoded. Translated. Archivo General de Simancas, Legajo E 2587, 19

48 3 May 1609. Lord Salisbury to His Majesty's Customs, London   260
   Holograph. P.R.O., S.P. Dom., S.P. 14/45

49 [10/]20 May 1609. Pedro de Zúñiga to Philip III   261
   Decoded. Extract, translated. Archivo General de Simancas, Legajo E 2587, 29

B   xvii   J.V. I

CONTENTS

50 Before 15 May 1609. Instructions to Sir Thomas Gates 262
    Extract. Bodleian Library, Ashmolean MSS, 1147, folios 175–90

51 [25 June/]5 July 1609. Pedro de Zúñiga to Philip III 269
    Decoded. Translated. Archivo General de Simancas, Legajo E 2587, 37

52 [1610.] Emanuel van Meteren, *Commentarien Ofte Memorien.* . . . 270
    Extracts, translated. Text from 1610 edition, printed in London

53 31 August 1609. Gabriel Archer, from Virginia, to an unknown friend 279
    Purchas, *Pilgrimes*, IV, 1733–4

54 4 October 1609. John Ratcliffe to Lord Salisbury 283
    P.R.O., [Colonial Papers, General Series], C.O. 1/1, fo. 66

55 9 November 1609. John More to William Trumbull 285
    Extract. Trumbull MSS, XXXII. More, 1609–1622, 5. [Berkshire Record Office, Reading.]

56 [13/]23 November 1609. Pedro de Zúñiga to Philip III 285
    Decoded. Translated. Archivo General de Simancas, E 2587, 49

57 [30 November/]10 December 1609. Pedro de Zúñiga to Philip III 286
    Translated. Archivo General de Simancas, Legajo E 2587, 52

58 30 November 1609. John Beaulieu to William Trumbull 287
    Extracts. Trumbull MSS, IV.Beaulieu, 1606–1611, fo. 70. [Berkshire Record Office, Reading.]

59 7 December 1609. John Beaulieu to William Trumbull 287
    Extract. Trumbull MSS, IV. Beaulieu 1606–1611, fo. 71

60 15 December 1609. The Earl of Southampton to the Earl of Salisbury 288
    Extract. P.R.O., S.P. Dom., S.P. 14/50

61 [21/]31 December 1609. Pedro de Zúñiga to Philip III 289
    Translated. Archivo General de Simancas, Legajo E 2587, 59

xviii

Table of Jamestown Voyages under the First Charter

		Sailed	Arrived	Time
Original				
Newport	Outbound	19–20 Dec. 1606	26 Apr. 1607	18 wks. 2 ds.
	Return	22 June 1607	29 July 1607	5 wks. 2 ds.
First Supply				
Newport	Outbound	8 Oct. 1607	2 Jan. 1608	12 wks. 2 ds.
Nelson	Outbound	8 Oct. 1607	20 Apr. 1608	Wintered in West Indies
Newport	Return	10 Apr. 1608	21 May 1608	5 wks. 6 ds.
Nelson	Return	2 June 1608	pre-7 July 1608	Under 5 wks.
Second Supply				
Newport	Outbound	c. 15 July 1608	[?] Sep. 1608	10–11 wks. [?]
	Return	[?] Dec. 1608	pre-16 Jan. 1609	

Exploratory Voyage under the Second Charter and Initial Supply

Argall	Outbound	5 May 1609	13 July 1609	9 wks. 6 ds.
	Return	c. 1 Sep. 1609	pre-9 Nov. 1609	c. 9 weeks
Gates	Outbound	8 June 1609	21 May 1610	Shipwrecked on Bermuda
Others	Outbound	8 June 1609	11 Aug. 1609	9 wks. 1 d.
Smith et. al.	Return	c. 4 Oct. 1609	23–30 Nov. 1609	Under 8 wks.

On editing

Texts printed from manuscripts are as faithful to the letter as possible, with a few alterations in punctuation added in brackets. Contractions have been expanded and italicized, but in the case of the virtually universal contractions for 'with' and 'which' the expansion has been made silently. This has also been done with a few mistakes of the kind called 'misprints' in printed books. The latter, also, have been corrected silently. Brackets are further used to indicate both words added (which may well have existed in the original text, where this is lost), and some editorial clarifications.

The dates are 'old style' throughout, except in the Spanish documents. In these, the English date has been prefixed in square brackets. In a very few cases, a notation has been made as to which style it is. (In both the 1500s and 1600s the 'new style' was ten days in advance of the old.) The English legal year used to begin on March 25, but this has been silently corrected to the year beginning on January 1. In any cases of possible doubt, both years have been entered; namely, 8 February 1607/8.

It should be noted that the name *Virginia* generally corresponds in these documents more closely with modern usage than was the case at the time of the Roanoke colony. But again, where there might be doubt, the modern political divisions are indicated in brackets.

Combined list of original planters and those who followed in the first and second relief voyages
(Up to c. 1 October, 1608)

Abbay, Thomas, gent.
Abbot, Jeffrey, gent.
Acrig(ge), George
Adling, Henry, gent.
Alberton, Robert, perfumer
Alicock, Jeremy, gent.
Ap Hugh, David, artisan
Archer, Gabriel, Captain
Asbie, John, gent.

Bagnall (Baggly), Anthony, surgeon (sergeant?)
Barnes, Robert, gent.
Bayley, William, gent.
Beadle (Bedell), Gabriel, gent.
Beadle (Bedell), John, gent.
Beast (Best), Benjamin, gent.
Beckwith, William, tailor
Beheathland, Robert, gent.
Belfield, Richard, goldsmith
Bell, Henry, artisan
Bentley, William, labourer
Bourne, James, gent.
Bouth, John, labourer
Bradley, Thomas, artisan
Brinton, Edward, mason
Bristow, Richard, labourer
Brookes, Edward, gent.
Brookes, John, gent.
Browne, Edward, gent.
Brumfield, James, boy
Bruster (Brewster), William, gent.
Buckler, Andrew, Master
Burket, Richard, labourer

Burras (Burroughs), Anne (married Laydon, below)
Burras (Burroughs), John, artisan
Burton, George, gent.

Callicut (Caldicot), William, refiner
Cantrill, William, gent.
Capper, John
Cassen, George, labourer
Cassen, Thomas, labourer
Cassen, William, labourer
Causey, Nathaniel, gent.
Clarke, John, artisan
Clovill, Eustace, gent.
Coderington (Cudderington), John, gent.
Coe, Thomas, gent.
Collier, Samuel, boy
Collings, Henry, gent.
Collson (Cotson), John, mariner
Cooke, Roger, gent.
Cotton, Robert, tobacco-pipe maker
Cowper, Thomas, barber
Coxe, William, (boy?)
Crashaw, Raleigh, gent.
Crofts, Richard, gent.
Cutler, Robert, gent.

Dauxe, John, gent. (Dawkes?)
Dawse, Thomas, labourer (Dowse, Douse?)
Dawson, William, refiner
Dier (Dyer), William, gent.
Dixon, Richard, gent.
Dods, John, labourer

COMBINED LIST OF ORIGINAL PLANTERS

Dole (Dowle), Richard, blacksmith
Dowman, William, gent.

Ellis, David, artisan
Emry, Thomas, carpenter

Fenton, Robert, gent.
Fetherstone, Richard, gent.
Fettiplace (Phettiplace), Michael, gent.
Fettiplace (Phettiplace), William, gent.
Field, Thomas, apothecary
Fitch, Matthew, mariner
Floud, ——, labourer
Flower, George, gent.
Ford, Robert, gent.
Forest, George, gent.
Forest, Thomas, gent.
Forest, Mistress Thomas
Fox, Thomas, labourer
Frith, Richard, gent.

Galthorpe (Calthorpe), Stephen, gent.
Garret, William, bricklayer
Gibson, Thomas, artisan
Gittnat (Ginnet), Post, chirurgeon
Goodison, Raymond, labourer
Gore, Thomas, gent. (Gower?)
Gosnold, Anthony, gent.
Gosnold, Anthony (a cousin), gent.
Gosnold, Bartholomew, gent.
Goulding (Golding), George, labourer
Gradon, Richard, labourer
Graves, Thomas, gent.
Grevill (Grivill), William, gent.
Gurganay, Edward, gent.

Hancock, Nicholas, labourer
Hardwin, ——, labourer
Harford, John, apothecary

Harper, John, gent.
Harrington, Edward, gent.
Harrison, Harman, gent.
Herd, John, bricklayer
Hill, George, gent.
Hilliard, ——, boy
Holt, John, gent.
Hope, Thomas, tailor
Houlgrave (Holgrave), Nicholas, gent.
Hunt, Master (Thomas?), gent.
Hunt, Master Robert, preacher

Jacob, Thomas, gent.
Johnson, William, goldsmith
Johnson, William, labourer

Keale, Richard, fishmonger
Keffer, Peter, gunsmith
Kendall, George, gent.
Killingbeck, Richard, gent.
Kingston, Ellis, gent.

Lambert, Thomas, (?)
Lavander, Thomas, artisan
Laxon, William, carpenter
Laydon, John, labourer
Leds (Leeds), Timothy, gent.
Leigh (Ley, Lee), Henry, gent.
Lewes, John, cooper
Love, William, tailor
Lowicke, Michael, gent.

Magnel (Magner?), Francis
Mallard, Thomas, labourer
Martin, George, gent.
Martin, John, gent. (Captain)
Martin, John, gent.
Maxes, Thomas, gent.
May, William, labourer
'Michael', labourer
Midwinter, Francis, gent.
Milman, ——, boy

COMBINED LIST OF ORIGINAL PLANTERS

Milmer, Richard, labourer
Molyneux, Richard, gent.
Momford (Mountford?), Thomas, gent.
Morrell, ——, labourer
Morris, Edward, gent.
Morton, Ralfe, gent.
Mounslic, Thomas, (?)
Mouton, Thomas, gent.
Mutton, Richard, boy (possibly a relative)

Nelson, Master Francis, mariner
Nelstrop, Rowland, labourer
Nichols, John, gent.
Norton, Thomas, gent.

O Conor, Dionis, artisan

Peacock, Nathaniel, boy
Pennington, Robert, (?) (His name *may* be John)
Perce (Pearce?), William, labourer
Percy, George, esq.
Perkins, Francis, gent.
Perkins, Francis, labourer (his son)
Phelps, Thomas, artisan
Phettiplace, see Fettiplace
Philpot, Henry, gent.
Pickhouse (Piggas), Drue, gent.
Pising, Edward, carpenter ('Sergeant' in 1608)
Pory, Peter, gent.
Pots, Richard, gent.
Powell, Master (Henry), artisan
Powell, John, tailor
Powell, Nathaniel, gent.
Prat, John, artisan
Pretty, George, gent.
Profit, Jonas, sailor fisherman
Proger (Prodger), Richard, gent.

Ransacke, Abram, refiner

Ratcliffe, see Sicklemore
Read, James, blacksmith
Robinson, Jehu (John?), gent.
Rodes, Christopher, labourer ⎫
Roods, William, labourer ⎬ The same family?
Rose, ——, labourer ⎭
Russell, John, gent.
Russell, Dr Walter, gent.
Russell, William, gent.

Sambage, William, gent.
Sands (Sandys?), Thomas, gent.
Savage, Richard, labourer
Savage, Thomas, boy, labourer, ensign
Scot, ——, labourer
Scrivener, Matthew, gent.
Short, Edward, labourer ('ould Edward', 'old Short')
Short, John, gent.
Shortridge, Jeffrey, artisan
Sicklemore, alias Ratcliffe, Capt. John
Sicklemore, Michael, gent. (apparently unrelated)
Simons, Richard, gent.
Simons, William, labourer
Skot, Nicholas, drummer
Small, Robert, carpenter
Smethes, William, gent.
Smith, Capt. John, gent.
Snarsbrough, Francis, gent.
Speareman, John, labourer
Spence, William, gent.
Stalling, Daniel, jeweller
Stevenson, John, gent.
Studley, Thomas, gent.

Tankard, William, gent.
Taverner, John, gent.
Tavin, Henry, labourer
Tayler (Taler), William, labourer

COMBINED LIST OF ORIGINAL PLANTERS

Taylor, Richard
Throgmorton, Kellam (Kenelm), gent.
Tindall, Robert, gunner
Todkill, Anas, soldier (Capt. Martin's 'servant')
Towtales, Lawrence, tailor
Tucker, Daniel, gent.

Unger, William, labourer

Ven, Nicholas, labourer
Vere, ——, labourer
Volday (Waldo, Faldoe), William (Henry), a Swiss

Waldo, Capt. Richard, gent.
Walker, ——, labourer
Walker, George, gent.
Waller, John, gent.
Ward, William, tailor
Watkins, James, labourer
Webbe, Thomas, gent.

West, Francis, esq.
White, William, labourer
Wiffin, David, (?)
Wiffin, Richard, gent.
Wiles, Bishop, labourer
Wilkinson, William, surgeon
Williams, ——, labourer
Wingfield, Edward Maria, esq.
Winne, Hugh, artisan
Winne (Wynne), Capt. Peter, gent.
Wollestone (Willestone), Hugh, gent.
Worley (Worsley?), Richard, gent.
Wotton, Thomas, surgeon

Yarington, George, gent.
Young, William, tailor

'Dutchmen':
Adam
Francis
Samuel

Of a total of about 295 individuals, these represent 239 whose names are known, or 80%.

Introduction

BRIEF REVIEW OF SOURCES

Samuel Purchas and John Smith

Richard Hakluyt, supreme propagandist of English colonial expansion, dedicated *The third and last volume of the Voyages, Navigations, Traffiques, and Discoueries of the English Nation* to Sir Robert Cecil on 1 September 1600.

That same year, Samuel Purchas, aged twenty-two, son of George Purchas, yeoman, of Thaxted, Essex, took the degree of M.A. at St John's College, Cambridge. In 1601, as Curate of Purleigh, ten miles east of Chelmsford, he married Jane Lease, and on 24 August 1604 he was instituted to the vicarage of Eastwood, a village two miles from the thriving seaport of Leigh, but today virtually absorbed by the resort town of Southend-on-Sea.

Whether it was the accident of brushing shoulders with sailors home from the sea, or of a copy of Hakluyt's 'Voyages' resting between his elbows, or a combination of both, mingled with a cosy Christianity, the Reverend Samuel Purchas soon got the idea of undertaking a transcendental compilation, remotely similar to Hakluyt's, which would have 'a theologicall and geographicall historie of Asia, Africa, and America' for its theme.

Perhaps such events as his meeting with George Barkeley in 1605 and, a little later, with a prodigal son of Leigh named Andrew Battel supplied the immediate stimulus – and the examples are not unique.[1] But whatever the spur, and whenever precisely it took effect, Purchas set to work early during his ten year stay at Eastwood on the volume which eventually bore the title *Purchas his pilgrimage or Relations of the World and*

---

[1] Purchas, *Pilgrimes*, XIII, 450, for Barkeley; VI, 406, for Battel, who appears to have returned in April, 1608. Others were Thomas Turner, Anthony Knivet, John Vassall (later of the Virginia Company) and Thomas Byam.

the Religions observed in all ages and places discouered, from the Creation to this Present. Patently he had chosen a far vaster field for his writings than had interested Richard Hakluyt.

Yet Purchas' rôle in relation to the Jamestown voyages is similar to Hakluyt's first treatment of the earlier American expeditions under the aegis of Sir Humphrey Gilbert and Sir Walter Ralegh, though not so full at the start. And as Hakluyt gradually veered from recounting English voyages in general to personal endorsement of American colonization, so Purchas in time came to stress the American side of his work and to interest himself, also personally, in such Jamestown colonists as returned to London, to visit or to stay.

At first, Purchas' writings on America laboured under a handicap. Hakluyt had devoted Volume III of his *Principal Navigations*, comprising eight hundred and sixty-eight folio pages, to the documentation of a vast number of expeditions that sailed north-west, west and south-west – toward America. The subject was exhausted. Furthermore, although activity continued, and colonial plans were on the eve of rebirth when Hakluyt laid down his pen, the few years elapsed since then had provided little for Purchas. One small quarto had been published (on Gosnold's exploratory trip of 1602) while Purchas was at Purleigh.[1] Then, the year after his arrival at Eastwood another small volume had appeared with the story of George Waymouth's voyage, more or less in Gosnold's wake.[2] Of the activities of privateers, mostly in the Caribbean, there was news by word of mouth only. Indeed, by Purchas' thirtieth birthday precious little about America could have reached his ears.

The publication of the *Pilgrimage*, however, was still a long way off when another 'American' quarto was entered for publication in London, on 13 August 1608: 'A booke called

---

[1] *A Briefe and true Relation of the Discouerie of the North part of Virginia:* . . . by M. John Brereton (London, 1602).

[2] *A true Relation of the most prosperous voyage made this present yeere 1605, by Captaine George Waymouth,* . . . by James Rosier (London, 1605).

INTRODUCTION

A true relation of suche occurrences and accidentes of note as haue happened in Virginia synce the first plantinge of that Colonye which is nowe resident in the south parte of Virginia till master Nelsons comminge away from them, &c. vjd.' The author was Captain John Smith, 'one of the said Collony,' and there was a foreword by a still unidentified I. H., which explained that the same I. H. 'happening vpon this relation by chance (as I take it, at the second or third hand) [,] induced thereunto by diuers well willers of the action, ... I thought good to publish it.' Captain Smith being still in Virginia, I. H. also admitted that he had left out some passages which he thought 'fit to be private'.[1]

In this way, John Smith entered his career as a writer, blue-pencilled to an unknowable extent. Even so, that he should have written such an account is notable – not to mention the fact that it was printed. The colony numbered several men of considerably better education than Smith, any one of whom might have been expected to publish the first book on their voyage and the land where they had settled. Gabriel Archer, Bartholomew Gosnold, George Percy, and Edward Maria Wingfield, for example, had all been admitted to one or another of the Inns of Court, while Smith had had no schooling after he was fifteen. But Gosnold wrote nothing, so far as is known, Archer is the putative author of the 'official report' brought back by Captain Newport and first published in 1860, Wingfield drew up a defence of his administration which included notes on the colonists' petty bickering, and Percy seems to have limited himself to a sort of diary *cum* necrology unfortunately somewhat cut by Purchas, and that is all. Even if Purchas had eliminated as much as one third of Percy's 'Discourse,' all three accounts would only amount to half again as much as Smith wrote (and his was also 'edited').

[1] On the entry for publication, see *A Transcript of the Registers of the Company of Stationers of London, 1554–1640 A.D.*, edited by E. Arber (London, 1876), III, 388. For a bibliographical survey of the *True Relation*, see Joseph Sabin *et al.*, *A Dictionary of Books Relating to America* (29 vols., New York, 1868–1936), XX, 254–8, prepared by Wilberforce Eames. On Smith, see Barbour, *Smith*.

3

In any event, when Smith appeared in London in person, late in November 1609 it may be surmised that it was not long before he and Samuel Purchas met. Which sought out the other is not known, but it is evident that the returning colonist had quite a considerable collection of manuscript notes (not to mention recollections) to supplement, if not even to supplant, his published book, and surely was soon looking for a publisher.

At that same time, Purchas was at work on his encyclopedic volume. As the printed book shows, he borrowed some of Smith's material. But Smith's contribution turned out to be less than six pages, out of a total of over seven hundred, and in all likelihood represented only a small part of the information he (Smith) had amassed. Since the details of what took place can be supplied only by conjecture, they need not be suggested here.[1] Suffice it to say that Smith assembled his notes and published his second book in 1612 – that is, sometime between 25 March 1612, and 24 March 1613.[2] Its title was *A map of Virginia, with a description of the countrey, the commodities, people, government and religion* and Captain Smith himself was referred to as 'sometimes Governour of the Countrey'.

This small quarto, of 8+39 pages was published by Joseph Barnes, in Oxford, becoming immediately a bibliographical oddity amongst Barnes' religious tracts and books in Greek and Hebrew type. Simultaneously with it, and in identical format, there appeared a second part, as announced on Smith's title page, called *The proceedings of the English Colonie in Virginia since their first beginning from England in the yeare of our Lord 1606, till this present 1612.* . . .

This second part is stated to have been 'taken . . . out of the writings' of some nine 'diligent observers, that were residents in Virginia', by W. S. – William Symonds (or Simons), curate

[1] Barbour, *Smith*, pp. 299–301.
[2] The English *legal year* began on 25 March, the date of the vernal equinox re-established by Julius Caesar. Although most of Europe, including Scotland, had adopted the year beginning on 1 January, the English legal year continued to follow the old Julian calendar until the middle of the eighteenth century.

INTRODUCTION

of Halton Holgate, Lincolnshire (by courtesy of Smith's friend Robert Bertie, Lord Willoughby), and later preacher of St Saviour's Church, Southwark. It would seem, however, that Symonds was merely a sort of general editor, for the preface by Thomas Abbay (a returned colonist) says that it 'first was compiled by Richard Pots', who had also returned to England, probably not before September, 1610. This historical addendum to Smith's geographical and ethnological treatise (the *Map*) ran to 4+110 pages. Despite the absence of Smith's name as the author of any part of it, there can be little doubt that here, too, he contributed materially.[1]

While this double work was in the hands of the printer in Oxford, Samuel Purchas was finishing his much larger book. It was entered for publication on 7 August 1612, and the dedication (to George Abbot, Archbishop of Canterbury) was dated November 5 of the same year. As not infrequently happened, however, several months elapsed before the book was published, and the title-page gives the year as 1613. There are marginal notes in the chapters devoted to Virginia which mention not only John Smith ('M.S.' – in manuscript), but also W. S. (William Symonds), and one note lists the initials of seven of the contributors to the *Proceedings*. In addition, there are references to Richard Hakluyt and to other sources both antedating and postdating the first Jamestown voyages. Among the latter is one reference to 'Cap. Argoles boy his name was Henry Spilman', nephew of Sir Henry Spelman (the correct spelling), who returned to England with Captain Samuel Argall and Lord De La Warr on 28 March 1611.[2]

---

[1] The title page of the first part lists eight 'diligent observers'; that of the second, nine. Of the eight, Geoffrey Abbot is not mentioned as author of any part of the complete work, nor is he mentioned among the nine listed for the *Proceedings*. Of the two added to the latter, one (Thomas Abbay) wrote a foreword to both volumes, and the other (Thomas Hope) signed nothing. It would appear, then, that the seven listed by Purchas actually contributed something. The seven were: Anas Todkill, named four times; Thomas Studley and William Phettiplace [preferably, Fettiplace], each named twice; and Dr. Walter Russell, Nathaniel Powell, Richard Wiffin and Richard Pots, each once.

[2] Purchas used Henry Spelman's account of the creation myth of the Virginia

Lastly, there are one or two references which hint that Purchas had read contemporary publications which he did not see fit to quote or directly to acknowledge. The phrase 'A New Britanian Common-wealth' seems to refer to Robert Johnson's *Nova Britannia* of 1609, while the marginal note, 'The New Life of Virginia', certainly refers to the same author's book of that name which was entered for publication on 1 May 1612.

By then, Smith's *Map* had made a name for Smith. Purchas' *Pilgrimage* did even more for Purchas. It was a work, as Professor E. G. R. Taylor has said, 'well calculated to delight Hakluyt'; and the famous geographer went to seek out the unknown Vicar of Eastwood, taking 'a grave pleasure in displaying his treasures', maps, manuscripts, and all.[1] So before long Purchas became convinced that Hakluyt regarded him as his successor in the work of glorifying England and her sailors, and even as the legitimate heir to Hakluyt's collections. The immediate outcome of this was a new edition of the *Pilgrimage* in 1614, expanded in volume by about one-fifth.

Meanwhile, undoubtedly due to the first edition, Purchas had found favour in the eyes not only of George Abbot, Archbishop of Canterbury, who made him his chaplain, but also of John King, Bishop of London, who appointed him rector of St Martin's, Ludgate – both in 1614. The preferment to London afforded him contacts, books, and that indispensable news-centre which was St Paul's Cathedral.

By the time Purchas set to work to revise the *Pilgrimage* it is clear that Captain Smith's *Map of Virginia* was on the market, since the second edition refers to the second part as by Richard Pots (mentioned as the compiler on leaf A2^r therein) and

---

Indians, which he seems to have rewritten in part. Spelman's 'Relation of Virginia', not printed until 1872, is in crude English, while Purchas' quotation is clear and straightforward. Spelman had spent some time among the Powhatan and Potomac Indians, had been rescued by Samuel Argall in September, 1610, and had presumably sailed for England with Argall (and Lord De La Warr) on 28 March 1611.

[1] See *The original writings & correspondence of the two Richard Hakluyts*, ed. by E. G. R. Taylor (Hakluyt Society, 2nd ser., LXXVI–VII, (1935)), 64–5.

INTRODUCTION

Thomas Studley (the first in the list of names on the title page). Smith himself is named as well, partly as 'M.S.' and partly without qualification, as if Purchas had borrowed from the printed copy in those instances.

Although there is evidence in the 1614 edition of the *Pilgrimage* that Hakluyt began to supply Purchas with additional material (e.g., p. 743), it was not long before they drifted apart, and when the former died on 23 November 1616, Purchas' hopes of being named heir to the great manuscript collection were disappointed. In fact, he obtained it only with great trouble and expense.[1] Nevertheless, obtain it he did, and in 1617 he issued a still larger edition of the *Pilgrimage* – its final form. (The 1626 'edition' is merely a reprint, with only a few variations in spelling and the like.) The bulk of the material he obtained from Hakluyt, however, did not see the light until 1625, when his magnum opus, *Hakluytus Posthumus or Purchas his Pilgrimes*, was published. John Smith's chief work, *The Generall Historie of Virginia, New-England, and the Summer Isles . . . to this present 1624*, had come out the year before.

The *Pilgrimes* runs to nearly four thousand folio pages and almost doubles Hakluyt's *Principal Navigations* in size, but it is far from being as well co-ordinated a whole. Purchas was often capricious and showed less reportorial sense than Hakluyt. Perhaps the shortcomings of Purchas can best be summed up in the lack of fixity of purpose which characterized Hakluyt. Then, although it is likely that modern readers without his *Pilgrimage* would be without many of the accounts they need, yet we could wish that his industry or interest had not failed him so often, and led him to make serious cuts in the documents he copied. All too often a glowing report is abruptly snipped short, with the statement in the margin that he fears to bore his readers, or that some other account tells the same story better.

Nevertheless, in the end, Purchas and Smith remain the

---

[1] Taylor, *Hakluyts*, II, 64–5.

primary existing sources for the early history of the Jamestown voyages. There was originally a third great source as well, but this was never printed and is now no longer at hand. This was the Virginia Company's 'first Court booke beginning the Eighte & Twentith day of January, 1606, and ending the Fourteenth day of February in the yeare 1615.'[1] Had it survived, it unquestionably would have provided an immense amount of detail regarding the Virginia venture, although modern scholars might have found it difficult to determine to what extent that detail was coloured by partisanship. As it is, all we have today, in addition to the reports and other documents in Smith's and Purchas' works, are the manuscript 'Discourse' of Edward Maria Wingfield (in Lambeth Palace Library), the 'Relations' of Captain Newport (attributed to Gabriel Archer, in the P.R.O.), and a fairly large collection of assorted items, well scattered in England and the United States, and in the Archivo General de Simancas and the Archivo General de Indias (Seville), in Spain.

SCATTERED SOURCES, AND MODERN COLLECTIONS

The original patent of 10 April 1606 has disappeared, but the chancery warrant (slightly damaged) and the copy engrossed in the Patent Roll are both housed in the Public Record Office, London. Samuel Purchas printed a few lines more than one-third of the document in his *Pilgrimes*, with only minor variations in spelling, wording, and punctuation, and later manuscript copies are to be found, some of them damaged, in other archives in England, and in the United States.

The three documents which supply the *modus operandi* of the 'two severall Colonies and Companies' authorized by the letters patent are available only in less satisfactory copies (see p. 19, below). These, as well as the letters patent, or first

---

[1] Kingsbury, IV, 123. (Transcription corrected by comparison with the origina document, Ferrar Papers, Misc. 2, 1368 bis.)

INTRODUCTION

charter, have been printed more than once during the past two centuries, as will be seen in the notes to each of them. And other pertinent material has been collected over the same period of time, and published with more or less fidelity. It is therefore worth while referring briefly here to the most significant of these collections.

At the outset, it must be mentioned that nine of these were assembled and printed for purely documentary purposes. (Purchas' *Pilgrimes*, for all its shortcomings, perhaps comes closest to that ideal. Smith was too involved personally to present a detached picture.) Furthermore, several of them were histories, rather than documentary anthologies, and the line is not always simple to draw.

As early as 1609, William Strachey, a Virginia settler who was appointed secretary of the council in Virginia (1610–1611), began a manuscript 'Historie of Travell into Virginia Britania' which was never finished, and was not printed until 1849. Though the part relating to the Jamestown colony was largely taken from Smith's *Map*, augmented by Strachey's own observations, there is at least one considerable passage on New England, taken from a manuscript now lost which adds a small amount to the documentation of the 'second colony'. Strachey's value for the early Jamestown voyages lies principally in the light he throws on the Indians.[1]

---

[1] Strachey had three copies of his *Historie* made, the most accurate of which seems to be the copy he presented to Henry Percy, ninth Earl of Northumberland, which is now in the possession of Princeton University. This copy was first published as *The Historie of Travell into Virginia Britania*, ed. by Louis B. Wright and Virginia Freund (Hakluyt Society, 2nd ser., CIII (1953)). A century before, however, the Hakluyt Society had published another copy, *The Historie of Travaile Into Virginia Britannia*, ed. by R. H. Major (1st ser., VI (1849)), which was given by the author to Francis Bacon, newly created Baron Verulam, in 1618. The manuscript is in the British Museum. The third known copy has not been printed, but is available for study in the Bodleian Library. Although the basic text is nearly the same in all three copies, there are omissions and additions here and there. Strachey's original manuscript has not been found, although notes in the copies appear to be in his own handwriting. On Strachey in general, see S. G. Culliford, *William Strachey 1572–1621* (see bibliography), which has this to say regarding Strachey and John Smith: 'One third of this first book consists of extracts from John Smith's *Map* . . .' (p. 178).

No-one approached the subject then until Virginia-born Robert Beverley published *The History and Present State of Virginia* in 1705, in London. His sources for the period from 1606 to 1609 were John Smith and, in a lesser degree, Samuel Purchas. The same applies for the same period to the *History of the First Discovery and Settlement of Virginia* of the Reverend William Stith, printed at Williamsburg, Virginia, in 1747.

Two generations later, Thomas Jefferson collected a number of transcripts, but little was printed until the middle of the nineteenth century, when Peter Force published a few early 'tracts', followed shortly by the Reverend Edward D. Neill with several sizable works on early Virginia history. A handful of papers not previously printed appeared in one or another of these.

It remained, however, for Alexander Brown to make an exhaustive investigation and to compile his *Genesis of the United States* (Boston, 1890), with its eight hundred-odd pages of documents of all kinds relating to the history of Virginia 'from 1605 to 1616', supplemented by two hundred and fifty pages of biographies and index. This signal publication was regrettably inspired by a *parti pris* which supplied both industry and persistence but which, coupled with a consuming dislike of Captain John Smith, left Brown open to justifiable charges of occasional distortion. Besides, Brown was torn between accuracy and popularity in his transcriptions, to the detriment of the former. And finally, his diligence in locating long neglected Spanish documents was embarrassed by his lack of knowledge of Spanish. Although he entrusted the translation to the ablest philologist then available in Virginia, Professor Maximilian Schele de Vere, essential reference works on the Spanish of Cervantes' day either did not exist or were not at hand, and Schele de Vere's translations suffered accordingly.

Shortcomings of this sort in Brown's *Genesis* are the basic justification for the presentation of *The Jamestown Voyages under the First Charter*, to which may be added in second place

INTRODUCTION

the desirability of essential annotation and other concomitants of modern documentation.

Since Brown's day, Susan Myra Kingsbury has published her *Records of The Virginia Company of London* (4 vols., Washington, 1906–1935), some new material has turned up, and a host of scholarly articles and reprints have appeared. Advantage has been taken of these, within the bounds of space. The presentation of accurate transcriptions and translations, however, has always been the prime consideration – notwithstanding the hardiness of the plant called error. Commentary has consequently been held to a minimum, and reference has been made wherever possible to other available works containing fuller explanations.

As to the original sources themselves, the pertinent English letters are distributed among the Cecil Papers at Hatfield House and the archives of the Duke of Northumberland, the Duke of Portland, and the Marquess of Downshire, as well as the more public collections in the Manuscript Room of the British Museum, the Public Record Office, London, and the Huntington Library in California. The correspondence of the Spanish ambassador with Philip III is in the Archivo General de Simancas. And the remaining single items are to be found as indicated for each document. Indeed, beyond the P.R.O. and the Simancas Archives, there is no single collection where any considerable number of documents can be found.

I

The Preliminaries

NARRATIVE

The Charter of 1606 and Allied Documents

After Sir Walter Ralegh abandoned all colonial plans in 1590, a dozen years passed before anyone renewed the attempt.[1] Then in 1602, about the same time that Ralegh sent Captain Samuel Mace to Virginia, two young cousins, Captain Bartholomew Gosnold and Captain Bartholomew Gilbert, ventured a plantation in what is now New England.[2] William Strachey claimed that the Earl of Southampton 'lardgly contrybuted' to the latter, but there is no confirmation of this.[3] Certainly others must have been associated with the Earl.

In any event, the project was abandoned during Gosnold's brief stay off Cape Cod, Massachusetts, and the entire expedition returned to England. The following year Gilbert (no relation to Sir Humphrey) ventured toward Virginia, only to be killed by Indians, while the very young shipmaster, Martin Pring, followed Gosnold's route on an exploratory voyage. By then, Queen Elizabeth had died, and for a year essays at exploring and colonizing were halted until the attitude of the new monarch could be determined.

Although this was clearly indicated when James I signed a peace treaty with Spain in 1604, early in 1605 Captain George Waymouth, veteran of an attempted search for the Northwest Passage, was sent to probe the coast of North America. Less than four months later, on 18 July, he returned, bringing a handful of aborigines. This seems to have been the catalytic

---

[1] See Quinn, *Roanoke*, II, 579.
[2] See Gookin and Barbour, *Gosnold*.
[3] Strachey, *Historie*, pp. 150–1.

agent, for before the end of the legal year (24 March 1606) Sir John Popham, Lord Chief Justice of England, had heard about it, took some sort of 'great pains' about the plantation of a colony in Virginia, and declared himself ready to call all interested parties before him and 'by their advices set down the best manner of project'.[1]

The next step was undoubtedly the drafting of a charter, in which Sir John himself may have taken the lead, aided or influenced by Sir Robert Cecil, newly created Earl of Salisbury and His Majesty's principal secretary, and possibly Sir Edward Coke, attorney general, and John Doddridge, solicitor general. There were prototypes for the proposed colonial organization, such as the fifty-year-old Muscovy Company and the infant East India Company. And there were conflicting notions regarding its financing and administration, for the objectives were different from those of the prototypes. Yet in a short space of time not only had two widely divergent plans been developed, but a compromise had been reached which incorporated features of both.

The two extremes were the proposal for private settlement, advanced by Lord Arundell of Wardour in 1605 (for Waymouth's voyage) and shortly thereafter by Sir John Zouche of Codnor (who signed a contract with Waymouth on his return), and the governmental plan proposed by Sir John Popham. Popham believed that the North American coast between the areas claimed or occupied by Spain (to the south) and France (to the north) should be taken under King James' protection and removed from private exploitation. In between, there was the suggestion of Edward Hayes, long a pioneer in colonial proposals, for a joint public and private enterprise with the consent of Parliament involved. The idea of Parliamentary hands poking about in the Virginia project would evidently not appeal to the King, so a compromise was reached through the modification of Popham's royal company into a hybrid

[1] Hist. MSS Comm., *Cecil Papers*, XVIII, 84.

organization which has usually been labelled a 'public joint-stock company'.[1]

More specifically, both old and new enthusiasts for American colonization were brought together in the persons of greater and lesser magnates in London, Bristol and Plymouth.[2] North America (or Virginia, as it was then called) was divided for the purpose of plantation into a northern and a southern colony, but funds were made available for the project as a whole. Investment was solely by individuals, in the corporate form of joint-stock companies, one for each colony, to be privately managed under the supervision of a council in London composed of thirteen persons directly responsible to the Crown. With these basic principles established and approved, it was but a step to the preparation of the final petition, followed by the issuance of the chancery warrant and the letters patent as already mentioned.

Eight individuals were named in the charter as suitors, along with 'divers others' who remained unidentified. Four of the eight were conspicuously representative of the group which intended to colonize 'southern' Virginia, while the remaining four equally conspicuously were interested in the more northerly region, now known as New England. Of the first four, the most prominent was Richard Hakluyt, whose interest in colonies dated back at least to 1584.[3] Hakluyt undoubtedly was one of the chief influences in bringing together the divergent groups working toward the charter and the Jamestown voyage of 1606.

Two of Hakluyt's associates as patentees, Sir Thomas Gates and Edward Maria Wingfield, were old soldiers, trained in the Netherlands, where Gates still was. Obscure though they were,

[1] See D. B. Quinn, 'Edward Hayes, Liverpool colonial pioneer', *Transactions of the Historic Society of Lancashire and Cheshire*, CXI (1959), 25–45, and Kingsbury, *Records*, I, 17–18.

[2] This group has been appropriately and picturesquely labelled the 'greater England clique' by Professor Darrett B. Rutman in his 'The Historian and the Marshal', *VMHB*, LXVIII (1960), 293, n. 39.

[3] See Quinn, *Roanoke*, I, 118, and Taylor, *Hakluyts*, II, 211–326.

Gates had probably already been considered as a potential future governor in the nascent colony, and Wingfield was ready to go in person with the first shipment. In addition, it may be considered that his relationship with Captain Bartholomew Gosnold, though distant, had something to do with Wingfield's presence. Gosnold played a hidden but evidently important part in organizing the first Jamestown voyage.

The fourth patentee for Virginia, as opposed to New England, represented a different element. Sir George Somers, M.P. for Lyme Regis, Dorset, had a not inconsiderable career in privateering behind him, having obtained letters of reprisal with John Young as far back as 1585. A ship-captain, Somers was a 'professional, mixing naval service with private enterprise', while demonstrating his ability as a land-soldier on the 1595 expedition against Caracas which was headed by Sir Amyas Preston.[1] Somers and Sir John Popham's nephew, George Popham, were two of the ex-privateers whose success contributed so largely to their value in the establishment of England as a colonial power in America.

The four patentees for the northern colony may be mentioned parenthetically here, although their activities lie outside the scope of this volume. They were Raleighe (Ralegh) Gilbert, son of Sir Humphrey; William Parker, like Somers an ex-privateer and one-time servant of Sir Walter Ralegh; George Popham, nephew of the Lord Chief Justice, also an ex-privateer; and Thomas Hannam (Hanham), a lawyer and grandson of Popham.

It is only necessary to point out that, while these eight were the 'humble suitors' for the patent, they were neither the only suitors nor, probably, even the most significant. The Lord Chief Justice himself was certainly intimately involved, and there can be little doubt that Lord Salisbury was also. Others

---

[1] K. R. Andrews, *Elizabethan Privateering* (Cambridge, 1964), p. 92, and see *English Privateering Voyages to the West Indies 1588–1595* (Hakluyt Society, 2nd ser., CXI (1959)), 377–98.

may be guessed at by consulting the list of councillors appointed eight months later.[1]

After naming the patentees, the charter defines the geographical bounds for the proposed colony. The southernmost limit was 34° north latitude, which was roughly the point where Spanish exploration and occupation north from Florida had died out. (A short-lived colony in Chesapeake Bay and occasional reconnoitring were ignored.) At the other extreme, France had no permanent settlement as yet in Canada, but King James did not wish to disturb the summer fishery at Newfoundland. The northern limit was therefore set at 45° north latitude, almost precisely at Passamaquoddy Bay – today's boundary between the United States and Canada.

Having determined this, the charter provided for the division of the entire coastal strip between two colonies, at the same time allowing each colony to spread somewhat over the other's territory, depending on which got there first. To accomplish this, the northern limit for the southern colony was set at 41°, while the southern limit for the northern one was put at 38°. This was presumably to permit the more energetic, or more successful, colony to expand at the other's expense.

It is curious to note to how great an extent these limits are reflected in modern political divisions. The southern tip of North Carolina is less than ten miles below 34°. The Maryland-Virginia line across the Delmarva Peninsula, established by magnetic compass, is at 38°. The southernmost point in New England, at Greenwich, Connecticut, is but a couple of miles south of 41°. And the 'international boundary' set by the charter not only persists today at the southernmost point of New Brunswick, as already mentioned, but still forms the northern boundaries of the states of Vermont and New York, within a matter of less than a mile.

To return to the charter, after an exhortation to the patentees to propagate the Christian religion to 'the infidels and salvages

[1] See Document no. 2, p. 35, below.

living in those partes', it turns to full and legal explanation of where the colonists may settle and build, in both colonies, how they shall be governed locally and how an overall control shall be organized in London, and every conceivable detail of life in the colonies, economic, financial, and legal.[1]

Two days after the promulgation of the charter, according to Samuel Purchas, 'Articles and instruction' were 'dated, signed and sealed, with the Privie Seale for the government of the said Plantation'.[2] But, although it would seem logical that such a document, providing for the government of the colonies, would have followed immediately upon signing the charter, there is no further reference to the matter for eight months, and it may be that Purchas erred. In any event, one month later both the deputy mayor of Plymouth, Walter Mathewe, and the governor of Plymouth Castle, Sir Ferdinando Gorges, were complaining to Salisbury about the establishment of the King's council for Virginia in London.[3] Then all is silent regarding the colonies until 20 November 1606.

Parenthetically, it should be noted that on the same day on which the charter was signed the companies of English merchants known as the Russia Company and the East India Company jointly issued a pass to Captain John Knight for the discovery of the Northwest Passage, which resulted in his death in Labrador.[4] The survivors returned to Dartmouth on 24 September 1606. In addition, before long, the Plymouth group of 'northern' colonists apparently learned that their complaints had not fallen on deaf ears, and on 12 August sent out a 'small ship of the burthen of fiftie five Tunnes or thereabout', under Master Henry Challons, 'intended for the North Plantation of Virginia', which was 'immediately' followed by

[1] See Document no. 1, pp. 25–34, below.
[2] Purchas, *Pilgrimes*, XVIII, 359–60.
[3] Hist. MSS Comm., *Cecil Papers*, XVIII, 133–4.
[4] See *The Register of Letters &c.* . . . (of the East India Company), ed. by Sir George Birdwood assisted by William Foster (London, 1893), 86–7; Purchas, *Pilgrimes*, XIV, 353–65; and the appendix to *The Voyages of Sir James Lancaster, Knt., to the East Indies*, ed. by Clements R. Markham (Hakluyt Society, 1st ser., LVI (1877)).

another ship under Thomas Hanham, bound for the same destination.¹ Challons ran afoul of the Spaniards and was taken prisoner on 10 November. He did not see England again for twelve months. Hanham reached the coast of what is now Maine, wintered there, and, not having seen nor heard from Challons, abandoned his post and returned home early in 1607.

Meanwhile, the London group went ahead with their plans for the first Jamestown voyage. Prospective colonists were sought and found, as well as ships to transport them, and supplies of all kinds assembled. It was all done quietly, almost surreptitiously, as if men were afraid that the pious young King of Spain would somehow prevent the voyage if he heard about it. Philip III fell too far short of his father in enterprise and push to be a source of danger, but the entrepreneurs of the Jamestown voyage were probably not in a position to be certain of this. In any case, the Spanish ambassador, Don Pedro de Zúñiga, beyond reporting (misreporting would be more accurate) on the gossip prevalent as early as March 1606 seems to have had little that was concrete to write about until the voyage was actually under way.²

At length, on 20 November, the 'Articles and instruction' already mentioned were 'made, sett down and established' by James I under the title 'Articles Instructions and orders'. A roughly contemporary copy of this has survived, in an abbreviated version, in the Plymouth City Archives (W. 363/89, f. 2), but the oldest of the apparently complete copies are from the late seventeenth or early eighteenth century (Virginia State Library and the Library of Congress). There are no differences of substance between any of these copies.³

While these instructions were clearly necessary for overall management, their chief interest for the modern reader is the

[1] Purchas, *Pilgrimes*, XIX, 284–96; and see Henry S. Burrage, *The Beginnings of Colonial Maine 1602–1658* (Portland, Maine, 1914), 58–61.
[2] See below, pp. 65–6.
[3] The Plymouth copy of the 'Articles' was discovered by Professor and Mrs David B. Quinn in 1965, and the information sent in a personal communication dated 19 June 1966, for which the editor is grateful.

light they throw on the elements that went to make up the body of entrepreneurs. Fourteen men were appointed to the Royal (or London) council for Virginia (as it can be called to distinguish it from the subsidiary, local councils), not thirteen as provided by the charter. Seven of them evidently represented the London group, seven were West Country men. The division seems to reflect the complaints from Plymouth, and token service to Edward Hayes' recommendations regarding Parliament may be found in the fact that ten of the fourteen were members of Parliament, and an eleventh had been.

The London group was composed of three great merchants, Sir Thomas Smythe and Sir William Romney, both prominent in the East India Company, and John Eldred, an ex-privateer also of the East India Company; and four public figures, Sir Walter Cope (close to Lord Salisbury), Sir George More, Sir William Waad (or Wade), lieutenant of the Tower, and Sir Henry Montagu, recorder of the City of London, both of the latter lawyers.

The second group was more closely knit: three ex-privateers, James Bagg and Thomas James, merchants, and John Doddridge, solicitor general; three ardent colonialists, Sir Ferdinando Gorges (with valuable connexions), and the son and grandson of the Lord Chief Justice, Sir Francis Popham and Thomas Warre; and Sir John Trevor, a West Country counterpart of Sir George More.

While it was generally conceded that the patron *par excellence* of the 'northern' (West Country) colony was the Lord Chief Justice, Lord Salisbury's rôle as patron of the 'southern' (London) colony was less overtly acknowledged only because of his position as the King's principal secretary of state. By the same token as Sir Francis Popham may be said to have represented his father on the newly appointed council, so Lord Salisbury's close and trusted friend, Sir Walter Cope, may be said to have been his representative. Indeed, there are hints in the surviving records at Hatfield House that Cope was on occasion a channel for Lord Salisbury's 'adventure', or investment in the Virginia project.[1]

Three weeks after the signing of the 'Articles, Instructions and orders', the council issued the first of its own orders on 10 December.[2] These 'Orders and Directions' appear to exist only in the manuscript copy in the Library of Congress. They inform us that Captain Christopher Newport, an ex-privateer, has been chosen 'to have the sole charge and command ... until such time as they shall fortune to land upon the said coast of Virginia' and that Captain Bartholomew Gosnold is his second in command. The two names are significant.

Christopher Newport, born c. 1560, had been active as a privateer since 1590, and undoubtedly knew the West Indian waters better than any Englishman then alive.[3] Gosnold, born c. 1572, had made one privateering voyage in 1595, and had led the 1602 expedition to Cape Cod and Martha's Vineyard, both thus named by him.[4] The third ship-captain named in the document, Captain John Ratcliffe, later identified as John Sicklemore alias Ratcliffe, is otherwise a completely obscure figure – though it must be noted that both Newport and Gosnold were virtually unknown until recently.

Along with the captains, the three ships are named: the *Sarah Constant* (an error in transcription, for *Susan Constant*), the *Godspeed* (or *God Speed*), and the pinnace called the *Discovery*. Details regarding the *Susan Constant* may be found in Document 5, below. The *Godspeed* was very likely the ship used by Waymouth in his search for the Northwest Passage in 1602, and probably again in 1604 to 1606 by Thomas Weldon, merchant, sponsored by 'Master Russell' of the Muscovy

---

[1] Information contained in a personal letter from Miss Clare Talbot, Librarian, Hatfield House, dated 28 April 1966. The editor is again grateful for the courtesy.

[2] See Document no. 3, pp. 45–8, below.

[3] See David B. Quinn, 'Christopher Newport in 1590', *The North Carolina Historical Review*, XXIX (1952), 305–16; K. R. Andrews, 'Christopher Newport of Limehouse, Mariner,' *WMQ*, 3rd ser., XI (1954), 28–41; and K. R. Andrews, ed., *English Privateering Voyages* (see above, p. 16, n.), consult index.

[4] See Gookin and Barbour, *Gosnold*.

Company. The *Discovery* in turn, less certainly identified than the other two, may have been the unnamed pinnace which accompanied Weldon's *Godspeed*, in 1606. If so, the chief point of interest lies in the fact that the known ship and pinnace were operated by members of the Muscovy and East India companies, a select few of the directors of both of which were also entrepreneurs of the Jamestown voyage. The elusive and often insignificant details add up to a demonstration of the determination of the entrepreneurs not to fail this time, as Ralegh had failed.

Hand in hand with the 'Orders and Directions', so to speak, an undated document was issued by the Company, under the title 'Instructions given by way of advice . . . for the intended voyage to Virginia.' From its general tenor and several of the specific points mentioned, this document is usually considered to have been prepared with the assistance of or in collaboration with Richard Hakluyt.[1]

While these final formal authorizations and instructions were being prepared, the flag-ship of the Virginia fleet, the *Susan Constant*, was brought to a mooring 'over against Ratcliffe Crosse', at the end of the second week in November 1606. By then it was fully laden. About a week later, there was a collision between the *Susan Constant* and another ship already on the scene, and both ships suffered some damage. This led to an examination before the High Court of Admiralty, which in turn resulted in the filing of a number of documents, which were discovered by a happy chance by Mrs Alison M. Quinn in the summer of 1965. Particularly pertinent are those passages which give the correct name of the ship, as well as the names of the owners.[2]

At about the same time final arrangements were also made regarding the spiritual responsibilities for the voyage. Since Richard Hakluyt had been one of the patentees, it may have

[1] Document no. 4, pp. 49–54, below. See also Taylor, *Hakluyts*, II, 492–6 and notes.
[2] Document no. 5, pp. 55–60, below.

'BOUND FOR VIRGINIA'. The *Susan Constant* rides in Hampton Roads. The reconstruction was based on the most reliable sources for the period, but a later discovery (Document no. 5) shows her to be 20 tons too light. She flies the English Cross of St George and the new Union Flag of England and Scotland.

been thought that he would go to Virginia in person. His age and position in London, however, discouraged such ideas, and a deputy was sought, possibly through the efforts of another patentee, Edward Maria Wingfield.[1]

Just when the search started is not known, but the choice seems to have been made by 20 November, for on that date Robert Hunt, vicar of Heathfield, Sussex, signed a significant will.[2] Its terms are such that it is almost impossible not to feel that Hunt's family life was not entirely happy and that this may well have provided the immediate reason for his decision to leave the safety and comfort of his Sussex parish for the unknown dangers of the *terra incognita* on the shores of Chesapeake Bay.

The identity of Hunt and the reason for the will become clear on 24 November, when a warrant was issued wherein he is specifically named with Richard Hakluyt as authorized to go to Virginia. The intent is obvious. While Hakluyt held the prior right, but would not go, a younger man who would go had been found. To protect either or both of them from loss of position, rights, income and all the rest, in England, James I signed a dispensation, in the quaint and pompous Latin of the age.[3]

With repairs finished on the *Susan Constant* and all foreseeable exigencies provided for, the colonists went aboard (apparently on Friday, 19 December) and by 20 December had begun their epochal voyage. There was no fanfare. There was apparently not even any announcement – in fact, only two of the colonists have left mention of the date.[4] Yet that sailing laid the foundation for the British Empire, now transmuted into the voluntary association of nations called the British Commonwealth.

[1] See Document no. 34, p. 233, below.
[2] Document no. 6, pp. 60–2, below.
[3] Document no. 7, pp. 62–4, below.
[4] See Documents nos. 28 and 63, pp. 129 and 378, below.

1. *10 April 1606.*
Letters patent to Sir Thomas Gates and others.[1]

James by the grace of God &c Whereas our loving and well disposed subiectes Sir Thomas Gates and Sir George Somers Knightes Richard Hackluit Clarke prebendarie of Westminster and Edwarde Maria Winghfeilde Thomas Hannam and Raleighe Gilberde Esquiers William Parker and George Popham Gentlemen and divers others of our lovinge subiects haue been humble sutors vnto vs that wee woulde vouchsafe vnto them our licence to make habitacion plantacion and to deduce a Colonie of sondrie of our people into that parte of America commonly called Virginia and other parts and territories in America either appertaining vnto vs or which are not nowe actuallie possessed by anie Christian Prince or people scituate lying and being all along the sea Coastes beteweene fower and Thirtie degrees of northerly latitude from the equinoctiall lyne and Fyve and Fortie degrees of the same latytude and in the mayne lande beteweene the same Fower and Thirtie and Fyve and Fourtie degrees and the Ilandes thereunto adiacente or within one hundred myles of the Coaste thereof and to that ende and for the more speedy accomplishemente of theire saide intended plantacion and habitacion there are desirous to devide themselues into two severall Colonies and Companies the one consisting of certaine Knightes Gentlemen marchauntes and other Adventurers of our Cittie of London and elsewhere

[1] Patent Roll, 4 James I, P.R.O., C.66/1709. The Chancery Warrant, dated 5 April 1606 is P.R.O., C.82/1729 m.1. There is an early, but damaged, copy of this in the Plymouth City Archives, W. 360/57, and a much later copy in the Library of Congress (the 'Bland Manuscript', pp. 1–13, see bibliography), neither of which differs in substance from the patent roll copy. (In a personal letter to the editor, dated 10 June 1966, the chief of the manuscript division of the Library of Congress, Mr David C. Mearns, said: 'The writing of the charters you mention appears to us to be a late seventeenth or early eighteenth century hand. We have no documentation to support this opinion, however.') The patent, commonly called the *First Charter*, has been printed, with greater or less fidelity, by William Stith (1747), William W. Hening (1809), Alexander Brown (1890), Samuel M. Bemiss (1957), and others.

which are and from tyme to tyme shalbe ioined vnto them which doe desyre to begin theire plantacions and habytacions in some fitt and conveniente place betweene Fower and Thirtie and one and Fortie degrees of the said latitude all alongest the Coaste of virginia and Coastes of America aforesaide and the other consisting of sondrie Knightes Gentlemen merchauntes and other Adventurers of our Cities of Bristoll and Exeter and of our towne of Plymouthe and of other places which doe ioyne themselues vnto that Colonie which doe desire to begynn theire plantacions and habitacions in some fitt and convenient place betweene Eighte and thirtie degrees and Five and Fortie degrees of the saide latitude all alongst the saide Coaste of Virginia and America as that Coaste lyeth[1]

wee greately commending and graciously accepting of theire desires to the furtherance of soe noble a worke which may by the providence of Almightie God hereafter tende to the glorie of hys divyne maiestie in propagating of Christian religion to suche people as yet live in darkenesse and myserable ignorance of the true knowledge and worshippe of god and may in tyme bring the infidels and salvages lyving in those partes to humane civilitie and to a setled and quiet govermente doe by theise our lettres Patentes graciously accepte of and agree to theire humble and well intended desires

And doe therefore for vs our heires and successors graunte and agree that the saide Sir Thomas Gates Sir George Sumers Richarde Hackluit and Edwarde Maria Winghfeilde Adventurers of and for our Cittie of London and all suche others as are or shalbe ioyned vnto them of that Colonie shalbe called the firste Colonie And they shall and may begynne theire saide firste plantacion and seate of theire firste aboade and habitacion at anie place vpon the

---

[1] To facilitate reading, long unbroken texts such as this charter have been divided by the simple expedient of dropping one line where modern punctuation would require a full stop, new paragraph, and capital letter. In this way, the original text is 'unmodernized', at the same time as the reader is aided.

saide Coaste of virginia or America where they shall thincke fytt and conveniente betweene the saide fower and thirtie and one and Fortie degrees of the saide latitude And that they shall haue all the landes woodes soyle Groundes havens portes Ryvers Mynes Myneralls Marshes waters Fyshinges Commodities and hereditamentes whatsoever from the said first seate of theire plantacion and habytacion by the space of Fyftie miles of Englishe statute measure all alongest the saide Coaste of Virginia and America towardes the Weste and southeweste as the Coaste lyeth with all the Islandes within one hundred myles directlie over againste the same sea Coaste And alsoe all the landes soyle Groundes havens portes Ryvers Mynes Myneralls woodes Marrishes waters Fyshinges Commodities and hereditamentes whatsoever from the saide place of theire firste plantacion and habitacion for the space of Fiftie like Englishe miles all alongest the saide Coaste of Virginia and America towardes the Easte and Northeaste as the Coaste lyeth together with all the Islandes within one hundred Miles directlie over againste the same sea Coaste And alsoe all the landes woodes soyle Groundes havens portes Ryvers Mynes Myneralls Marrishes waters Fishinges Commodities and hereditamentes whatsoever from the same Fyftie Miles everie waie on the Sea Coaste directly into the mayne lande by the space of One hundred like Englishe myles and shall and may inhabyt and remaine there and shall and may alsoe buylde and fortifie within anie the same for theire better safegarde and defence according to theire best discrecions and the direction of the Counsell of that Colonie and that noe other of our subiectes shalbe permitted or suffered to plante or inhabyt behinde or on the backside of them towardes the mayne lande without the expresse lycence or consente of the Counsell of that Colonie thereunto in writing firste had or obtained

And wee . . .

[The following thirty-seven and a half lines of the patent contain an all but verbatim repetition of the same provisions for the 'Seconde Colonie', under 'Thomas Hannam and Raleighe Gilberde William Parker and George Popham' and others, 'betweene Eighte and Thirtie degrees of the saide latitude and Fyve and Fortie degrees.']

Prouided alwaies and our will and pleasure herein ys that the plantacion and habytacion of suche of the saide Colonies as shall laste plante themselues as aforesaid shall not be made within one hundred like Englishe miles of the other of them that firste beganne to make theire plantacion as aforesaide

And wee doe alsoe ordaine establishe and agree for vs our heires and successors that eache of the saide Colonies shall haue a Counsell which shall governe and order all matters and Causes which shall arise growe or happen to or within the same severall Colonies according to such lawes ordynaunces and Instructions as shalbe in that behalfe given and signed with our hande or signe manuell and passe vnder the privie seale of our Realme of Englande Eache of which Counsells shall consist of Thirteene parsons [i.e., persons] and to be ordained made and removed from tyme to tyme according as shalbe directed and comprised in the same Instructions and shall haue a severall seale for all matters that shall passe or concerne the same severall Counsells Eache of which seales shall haue the Kinges Armes engraven on the one syde thereof and hys pourtraiture on the other And that the seale for the Counsell of the saide first Colonie shall haue engraven rounde about on the one side theise wordes Sigillum Regis Magne Britanie Francie & Hibernie on the other side this Inscripture rounde about *pro Consillio Prime Colonie virginie* And the seale for the Counsell of the saide seconde Colonie shall alsoe haue engraven rounde about the one side thereof the foresaide wordes Sigillum Regis Magne Britanie Francie & Hibernie and on the other side *pro Consilio secunde Colonie Virginie*

And that alsoe ther shalbe a Counsell established here in Englande which shall in like manner consist of thirteene parsons to be for that purpose appointed by vs our heires and successors which shalbe called our Counsell of Virginia And shall from tyme to tyme haue the superior mannaging and direction onelie of and for all matters that shall or may concerne the govermente aswell of the said seuerall Colonies as of and for anie other parte or place within the aforesaide precinctes of Fower and thirtie and Fyve and Fortie degrees abouemencioned which Counsell shall in like manner haue a seale for matters concerning the Counsell with the like Armes and purtraiture as aforesaide with this inscripcion engraven rounde about the one side Sigillum Regis Magne Britanie Francie & Hibernie and rounde about the other side pro Consilio Suo Virginie

And moreover wee doe graunte and agree for vs our heires and successors that the saide severall Counsells of and for the saide severall Colonies shall and lawfully may by vertue hereof from tyme to tyme without intervpcion of vs our heires or successors giue and take order to digg myne and searche for all manner of Mynes of Goulde Silver and Copper aswell within anie parte of theire saide severall Colonies as of the saide Mayne landes on the backeside of the same Colonies and to haue and enioy the Goulde Silver and Copper to be gotten thereof to the vse and behoofe of the same Colonies and the plantacions thereof yeilding therefore yerelie to vs our heires and successors the Fifte parte onelie of all the same Goulde and Silver and the Fifteenth parte of all the same Copper soe to be gotten or had as ys aforesaide without anie other manner of profytt or Accompte to be given or yeilded to vs our heires or successors for or in respecte of the same

And that they shall or lawfullie may establishe and cawse to be made a coyne to passe currant there betweene the people of those severall Colonies for the more ease of traffique and bargaining betweene and amongest them and the natives there of such mettall and in suche manner and forme as the same severall Counsells there shall lymitt and appointe And wee doe likewyse for vs and our heires and successors by theise presents give full power and auctoritie to the said Sir Thomas Gates Sir George Sumers Richarde Hackluit Edwarde Maria Winghfeilde Thomas Hannam Raleighe Gilberde William Parker and George Popham and to everie of them and to the saide seuerall Companies plantacions and Colonies that they and everie of them shall and may at all and everie tyme and tymes hereafter haue take and leade in the saide voyage and for and towardes the saide severall plantacions and Colonies and to travell thitherwarde and to abide and inhabit there in everie of the saide Colonies and Plantacions such and somanie of our subiectes as shall willinglie accompanie them or anie of them in the saide voyages and plantacions with sufficiente shipping and furniture of Armour Weapon ordonnance powder victuall and all other thinges necessarie for the saide plantacions and for theire vse and defence there Prouided alwaies that none of the said parsons be such as hereafter shalbe speciallie restrained by vs our heires or successors

Moreover wee doe by theise presentes for vs our heires and successors giue and graunte licence vnto the said Sir Thomas Gates Sir George Sumers Richarde Hackluite Edwarde Maria Winghfeilde Thomas Hannam Raleighe Gilberde William Parker and George Popham and to everie of the said Colonies that they and everie of them shall and may from tyme to tyme and at all tymes for ever hereafter for their severall defences incounter or expulse repell and resist aswell by sea as by lande by all waies and meanes whatsoever all and everie suche parson and parsons as without especiall licence of the said severall Colonies and plantacions shall attempte to inhabit within the saide seuerall precinctes and lymittes of the saide severall Colonies and plantacions or anie of them or that shall enterprise or attempt at anie tyme hereafter the hurte detrymente or annoyance of the saide severall Colonies or plantacions

Gyving and graunting by theise presentes vnto the saide Sir Thomas Gates Sir George Somers Richarde Hackluite and Edwarde Maria Winghfeilde and theire Associates of the saide firste Colonie and vnto the saide Thomas Hannam Raleighe Gilberde William Parker and George Popham and theire Associates of the saide Seconde Colonie and to everie of them from tyme to tyme and at all tymes for ever hereafter power and auctoritie to take and surprize by all waies and meanes whatsoever all and everie parson and parsons with theire shipps Vessells Goods and other furniture which shalbe founde traffiqueing into anie harbor or harbors Creeke Creekes or place within the lymittes or precinctes of the saide seuerall Colonies and plantacions not being of the same Colonie vntill such tyme as they being of anie Realmes or Domynions vnder our obedience shall paie or agree to paie to the handes of the Tresorer of that Colonie within whose lymittes and precinctes theie shall soe traffique twoe and a halfe vpon anie hundred of anie thing soe by them traffiqued boughte or soulde and being straungers and not subiectes vnder our obeysaunce vntill they shall paie Fyve vpon everie hundred of suche wares and Commodities as theie shall traffique buy or sell within the precinctes of the saide severall Colonies wherein theie shall soe traffique buy or sell as aforesaide which sommes of money or benefitt as aforesaide for and during the space of one and twentie yeres nexte ensuing the date hereof shalbe whollie ymploied to the vse benefitt and behoofe of the saide severall plantacions where such traffique shalbe made And after the saide one and twentie yeres ended the same shalbe taken to the vse of vs our heires and successors by such officer and Mynister as by vs our heires and successors shalbe thereunto assigned or appointed

And wee doe further by theise presentes for vs our heires and successors giue and graunte vnto the saide Sir Thomas Gates Sir George Sumers Richarde Hackluit and Edwarde Maria Winghfeilde and to theire Associates of the saide firste Colonie and plantacion and to the saide Thomas Hannam Raleighe Gilberde William Parker and George Popham and theire Associates of the saide Seconde Colonie and plantacion that theie and everie of them by theire Deputies Mynisters and Factors may transporte the Goodes Chattells Armor munition and furniture needfull to be vsed by them for theire saide Apparrell defence or otherwise in respecte of the saide plantacions out of our Realmes of Englande and Irelande and all other our domynions from tyme to tyme for and during the tyme of seaven yeres nexte ensuing the date hereof for the better releife of the said seuerall Colonies and plantacions without anie Custome subsidie or other dutie vnto vs our heires or successors to be yeilded or paide for the same

Alsoe wee doe for vs our heires and successors declare by theise presentes that all and everie the parsons being our subiectes which shall dwell and inhabit within everie or anie of the saide severall Colonies and plantacions and everie of theire children which shall happen to be borne within the lymittes and precinctes of the said severall Colonies and plantacyons shall haue and enioy all liberties Franchises and Immunities within anie of our other domynions to all intentes and purposes as yf they had been abyding and borne within this our Realme of Englande or anie other of our saide Domynions

Moreover our gracyous will and pleasure ys and wee doe by theise presentes for vs our heires and successors declare and sett forthe that yf anie person or parsons which shalbe of anie of the said Colonies and plantacions or anie other which shall trafficque to the saide Colonies and plantacions or anie of them shall at anie tyme or tymes hereafter transporte anie wares Marchandize or Commodities out of our Domynions with a pretence and purpose to lande sell or otherwise dyspose the same within anie the lymittes and precinctes of anie of the saide Colonies and plantacions And yet nevertheles being at the sea or after he hath landed the same within anie of the said Colonies and plantacions shall carrie the same into any other forraine Countrie with a purpose there to sell or dyspose of the same without the licence of vs our heires or successors in that behalfe first had or obtained That then all the Goodes and Chattells of the saide parson or parsons soe offending and transporting together with the said shippe or vessell wherein suche transportacion was made shall be forfeyted to vs our heires and successors

Prouided alwaies and our will and pleasure ys and wee doe hereby declare to all Christian Kinges Princes and estates that yf anie parson or parsons which shall hereafter be of anie of the said severall Colonies and plantacions or anie other by his theire or anie of theire licence or appointement shall at anie tyme or tymes hereafter robb or spoile by sea or by lande or doe anie Acte of vniust and vnlawfull hostilitie to anie the subiectes of vs our heires or successors or anie of the subiectes of anie King Prince Ruler Governor or State being then in league or Amitie with vs our heires or successors and that vpon suche Iniurie or vpon iuste complainte of such Prince Ruler Governor or State or theire subiectes wee our heires or successors shall make open proclamacion within anie the portes of our Realme of Englande commodious for that purpose that the saide parson or parsons having committed anie such Robberie or spoyle shall within the tearme to be lymitted by suche Proclamacions make full restitucion or satisfaction of all suche Iniuries done soe as the saide Princes or others soe complained may houlde themselues fully satisfied and contented and that yf the saide parson or parsons having comitted such robberie or spoyle shall not make or cause to be made satisfaction accordingly with[in] such tyme soe to be lymitted That then yt shalbe lawfull to vs our heires and successors to put the saide parson or parsons having comitted such robberie or spoyle and theire procurers Abbettors or Comfortors out of our allegeaunce and protection and that yt shalbe lawefull and free for all Princes and others to pursue with hostilitie the saide Offenders and everie of them and theire and everie of theire procurors Ayders Abbettors and comforters in that behalfe

And finallie wee doe for vs our heires and successors graunte and agree to and with the saide Sir Thomas Gates Sir George Sumers Richarde Hackluit and Edwarde Maria Winghfeilde and all others of the saide firste Colonie That wee our heires or successors vpon peticion in that behalfe to be made shall by lettres Patentes vnder the greate [seal] of Englande giue and graunte vnto such parsons theire heires and Assignees as the Counsell of that Colonie or the most parte of them shall for that purpose nommynate and assigne all the landes tenementes and hereditamentes which shalbe within the precinctes lymitted for that Colonie as aforesaid To be houlden of vs our heires and successors as of our Mannor of Eastgreenwiche in the Countie of Kente in free and Common Soccage onelie and not in Capite

And doe in like manner graunte . . .

[Twelve lines of repetition of the same provisions for the second colony follow.]

All which landes tenementes and hereditamentes soe to be passed by the saide seuerall lettres Patentes shalbe by sufficient Assurance from the same patentees soe distributed and devided amongest the undertakers for the plantacion of the said seuerall Colonies and such as shall make theire plantacion in either of the saide seuerall Colonies in such manner and forme and for such estates as shalbe ordered and sett downe by the Counsell of the same Colonie or the most part of them respectively within which the same landes tenementes and hereditamentes shall ly or be Althoughe expresse mencion &c [of known and recognized legal provisions are omitted]. In witnesse whereof &c witnesse our selfe at Westm*inster* the xth day of Aprill [illegible] p*er* bre*ve* de privato sigillo

> [*From the Chancery Warrant:*] Gyven vnder our Privie Seale at our Pallace of westm*inster* the fyfte daye of Aprill in the fowrth yeare of our Reigne of England Fraunce and Ire[land . . . and of Scotland the] nyne and thirtieth.

2. *20 November 1606.*
   Instructions for Government.[1]

Articles, Instructions and orders made, sett down and established by Vs the twentieth day of Nouember in ye year of our raigne of England, France and Ireland the fourth, and of Scotland the fortieth, for ye good order and Gouernment of the two seueral Colonies and Plantations to be made by our Louing Subjects, in the Country commonly called Virginia and America, between 34 and 45 degrees from the æquinoctial Line.

Whereas Wee by our Letters Pattents, under our great seale of England, bearing date att Westminster the tenth day of Aprill, in the year of our raigne of England, France and Ireland the fourth, and of Scotland ye 39th haue giuen lycence to sundry our Louing subjects named in ye said Letters Pattents and to

---

[1] These seem to be the 'Instructions' mentioned in the charge brought against Sir Thomas Smythe in 1623 (probably in April), 'That his Ma*i*esties Instructions first giuen for gou*er*nment were not obserued, nor so much as published' (Kingsbury, *Records*, IV, 83). As mentioned above (p. 19), three copies of this document are known, two of them apparently complete. The text here given is that of the Virginia State Library, Land Office, Patent Book 2, 1643–51, recopied at the end of the seventeenth century. The copy in the Library of Congress (Bland MS, pp. 25–33) has numerous variant readings, as shown below, but has been relied on where the V.S.L. copy has been damaged. The entire text has been printed, with some modernization, by Hening, Alexander Brown, and Mr Samuel M. Bemiss (in 1957).

their Associates, to deduce and conduct two seueral Collonies or Plantations of sundry our Louing people[1] willing to abide and Inhabit in certaine parts of Virginia and America, with diuers preheminences, priuiledges, authorities, and other things, as in and by the same Letters Pattents more particularly it appeareth, Wee according to ye effect, and true meaning of ye same Letters Pattents doe by these Presents signed with our hand, signe manual and sealed with our Privy seale of our realme of England establish and ordaine, that our Trusty and Welbeloued Sir William Wade Knight our Leiuetenant of our Tower of London, Sir Thomas Smith Knight, Sir Walter Cope Knight, Sir George Moor[2] Knight, Sir Francis Popeham Knight, Sir Ferdinando Gorges Knight, Sir John Treuor Knight, Sir Henry Mountague[3] Knight Recorder of ye City of London, Sir William Rumney Knight, John Dodderidge Esq. Sollicitor General, Thomas Warr Esq., John Eldred of ye Citty of London merchant, Thomas James of the Citty [of] Bristol merchant and James Bagge[4] of Plymouth in ye County of Deuonshire merchant shall be our Councel for all matters, which shall happen in Virginia or any the Territories of America between 34 and 45 deg: from y^e æquinoctial line northward, and the Islands to the seueral Collonies limitted, and assigned and that they shal be called the Kings Councel of Virginia, which Councel or the most part of them shal haue full power and authority, att our pleasure, in our name, and under us, our heires and successors to giue directions to the Councels of the seueral Colonies, which shal be within any part of the said Country of Virginia and America, within ye degrees first aboue mentioned, with [y^e] Islands aforesaid, for ye good Gouernment of ye people to be planted in those part[s] and for the good ordering and disposing of all causes happening within ye same[,] ye same[5] to be done for ye substance thereof, as neer to the Common Lawes [of] England, and the equity thereof,

[1] L.C. copy, 'subject'. [2] L.C. copy, 'More'.
[3] L.C. copy, 'Mountagu'. [4] L.C. copy, 'Bagg'.
[5] Repetition of 'ye same' omitted in L.C. copy.

as may be, and to passe under our seale app[ointed] for that Councel, which Councel and euery, or[1] any of them shall from time to [time] be encreased, altered or changed, and others put in their places, att the n[omi]nation of us, our heires and successors, and att our and their will & plea[sure] and the same Councel of Virginia, or the more[2] part of them, for the time bei[ng] shall nominate and appoint the first seueral Councellours of those seuera[l] Councells, which are to be appointed for those two seueral Colonies, whi[ch are] to be made Plantations in Virginia and America, between ye degrees be[fore] mentioned, according to our said Letters Pattents in that behalfe made[,] and that each of the same Councels of the same seueral Colonies shal by ye major part of them choose one of ye same Councel, not being ye minister of Gods word, to be President of ye same Councel, and to continue in that office, by ye space of one whole year, unlesse he shall in ye mean time dye or be remoued from that office;

and Wee doe further hereby establish & ordaine, that it shal be lawful for ye major part of either of ye s[ai]d Councells upon any just cause, either absence of otherwise to remoue the President or any other of that Councel, from being either President, or any of that Councel,[3] and upon ye deathes or remoual of any of ye Presidents or Councel it shal be lawfull for the major part of that Councel to elect another in the place of ye party soe dying or remoued, soe alwaies, as they shal not be aboue thirteen of either ye said Councellours,

and Wee doe establish & ordaine, that ye President shal not continue in his office of Presidentship aboue ye space of one year; and wee doe specialy ordaine, charge, and require the said Presidents and Councells and ye ministers of ye said seueral Colonies respectiuely within their seueral limits and precincts, that they with all diligence care

---
[1] L.C. copy, 'and'.   [2] L.C. copy, 'most'.
[3] L.C. copy omits 'from being either President, or any of that Councel,' places a full stop at this point, and continues: 'And upon the Death and Removal of any. . . .'

and respect, doe prouide, that the true word and seruice of God and Christian Faith be preached, planted and used, not only within euery of ye said seueral Colonies and Plantations, but alsoe as much as they may, amongst ye saluage people, which doe or shall adjoine unto them, or border upon them, according to ye doctrine, rights and religion now professed and established within our realme of England, and that they shall not suffer any person or persons to withdraw any of ye subjects or people inhabiting, or which shall inhabit within any of ye said seueral Colonies and Plantations, from ye same or from their due allegiance, unto us, our heires and successors, as their immediate Soueraigne under God; and if they shall find; within any of ye said Colonies, and Plantations any person or persons, soe seeking to withdrawe any of ye subjects of Vs, our heires, or successors, or any of ye People of those lands or territories, within ye Precincts aforesaid, they shall with all diligence him or them soe offending cause[1] to be apprehended, arrested and imprisoned, until he shall fully and throughly reforme himselfe, or otherwise, when ye cause soe requireth, that he shall withall conuenient speed be sent into our realme of England here to receiue condigne punishment for his or their said offence or offences;

and moreouer Wee doe hereby ordaine and establish for us, our heires and successors, that all the lands, tenements and hereditaments to be had and enjoyed by any of our subjects, within ye Precincts aforesaid, shal be had and inherited[2] and enjoyed, according as in ye like estates they be had & enjoyed by ye Lawes, within this realme of England: and that ye offences of tumults, rebellion, Conspiracies, mutiny and seditions in those parts which maybe dangerous to the estates[3] there, together with murther, manslaughter, Incest, rapes, and adulteries committed in those parts within ye Precincts of any ye degrees aboue mentioned (and noe other

---

[1] L.C. copy omits 'cause'. [2] L.C. copy, 'inhabited'.
[3] L.C. copy, 'States'.

offences) shal be punished by death, and that without yᵉ benefit of yᵉ Clergy, except in case of manslaughter, in which Clergie is to be allowed, and that the said seueral Presidents and Councells, and yᵉ greater number of them, within euery of yᵉ seueral limits and precincts shall haue full power and authority to hear and determine all and euery the offences aforesaid within yᵉ precinct[1] of their seueral Colonies, in manner and forme following that is to say by twelue hones[t] and indifferent persons sworne upon the Euangelists to be returned by such ministers and officers, as euery of yᵉ said Presidents and Councells, or the most part of them respectiuely shall assigne, and yᵉ twelue persons soe returned and sworne shall according to their euidence to be giuen unto them upon oath, and according to the truth in their consciences either conuict or acquit euery of the said persons soe to be accused & tried by them, and that all and euery person or persons, which shall uoluntarily confesse any of yᵉ said offences to be committed by him, shall upon such his confession thereof be conuicted of yᵉ same, as if he had been found guilty of yᵉ same[2] by ye verdict of any such twelue Jurors, as is aforesaid, and that euery person and persons which shall be accused of any of yᵉ said offences, and which shall stand mute [or refuse to make direct answer thereunto the said person so standing mute][3] or refusing to make direct answer thereunto shall be and he[4] held conuicted of the said offence, as if he had been found guilty by yᵉ verdict of such twelue Jurors, as aforesaid, and that euery person and persons soe conuicted either by verdict, his own confession or by standing mute,[5] or by refusing directly to answer as aforesaid of any yᵉ offences before mentioned, the said Presidents or Councells or yᵉ greatest number of them within their seueral Precincts and limitts,

---

[1] L.C. copy, 'precincts'.
[2] L.C. copy has 'thereof' for 'of yᵉ same'.
[3] The passage in square brackets has been supplied from the L.C. copy.
[4] The words 'and he' appear in both copies, although they appear superfluous.
[5] L.C. copy inserts 'or' before 'his own confession or' and omits the word 'by' which follows 'or'.

where such conuiction shall be had and made as[1] aforesaid shall haue full power and authority by these Presents to giue Judgement of death upon euery such offender, without ye benefit of ye Clergy, except only in cause of manslaughter, and noe person soe adjudged attainted[2] or condemned shall be repriued from ye execution of ye said Judgement, without ye consent of ye said President and Councel or ye most part of them, by whom such Judgement shall be giuen; and that noe person shal receiue any pardon, or be absolutely discharged of any ye said offences, for which he shall be condemned to death as aforesaid, but by pardon of us, our heires and successors, under our great seale of England;

and Wee doe in like manner establish and ordaine, if any either of ye said Collonies shall offend in any ye offences before mentioned, within any part between ye degrees aforesaid, out of ye Precincts of[3] his or their Collony, that then euery such offendor or[4] offendors shall be tried and punished as aforesaid, within his or their proper Collony; and that euery of ye said Presidents and Councells within their seueral limits and precincts, and ye more part of them shall haue power and authority by these presents to hear and determine all and euery other wrongs, trespasses, offences, and misdemeanours whatsoeuer, other then those before mentioned upon accusation of any person and proofe thereof made, by sufficient witnesse upon oath, and that in all those cases, the said President and Councel, and ye greater number of them shall haue power and authority, by these presents respectiuely, as is aforesaid, to punish ye offender or offenders, either by reasonable corporal punishment and imprisonment, or else by a conuenient fine, awarding damages, or other satisfaction to ye party[5] greiued, as to ye said President & Councel, or to the more part of them shall be thought fitt and conuenient,

---

[1] L.C. copy inserts 'is' after 'as'. [2] L.C. copy, 'adjudg'd attain'd'.
[3] L.C. copy supplies 'of' for incorrect 'or'.
[4] L.C. copy omits 'offendor or'. [5] L.C. copy, 'parties'.

hauing regard to yᵉ quality of yᵉ offence, or state of yᵉ cause, and that alsoe yᵉ said President & Councel shall haue power and authority by virtue of these presents to punish all manner of excesse, through drunkennesse or otherwaies,[1] and all idle loytering and uagrant persons, which shall be found within their seueral limits and precincts, according to their best discretions, and with such conuenient punishment, as they or yᵉ most part of them shall think fitt; alsoe our Will and pleasure concerning yᵉ Judicial proceedings aforesaid, [is] that yᵉ same shall be made and done summarily, and uerbally without writing, untill it come to yᵉ Judgement or sentence, and yet neuerthelesse our will and pleasure is, that euery Judgement and sentence hereafter to be giuen in any yᵉ causes aforesaid, or in any other of yᵉ said seueral Presidents and Councells, or the greater number of them, within their seueral limits and precincts shall be breifely and summarily registred into a book to be kept for that purpose, together with yᵉ cause, for which yᵉ said Judgement or sentence was giuen; and that yᵉ said Judgement and sentence soe registred and written shall be subscribed with yᵉ hands or names of the said President and Councel, or such of them, as gaue yᵉ Judgement or sentence;

alsoe our will and pleasure is, and wee doe hereby establish and ordaine, that the said seueral Collonies and Plantations, and euery person and persons of yᵉ same seuerally and respectiuely shall within euery of their seueral precincts for yᵉ space of fiue yeares next after their first landing upon yᵉ said Coast of Virginia and america trade together all in one stocke, or deuideably, but in two, or three stocks att yᵉ most, and bring not only all the fruits of their labours there, but alsoe all such other goods and commodities, which shall be brought out of England or any other place into yᵉ same Collonies, into seuerall magazines or storehouses for that purpose to be made, and erected there and that in such order, manner and forme as yᵉ Councel of that Collony

---

[1] L.C. copy, 'otherwise'.

THE PRELIMINARIES

or the more part of them shall sett downe and direct;

and our will and pleasure is, and wee doe in like manner ordaine, that if[1] in euery of yᵉ said Collonies and Plantations there shall be chosen three[,] elected[2] yearely by yᵉ President and Councel of euery of yᵉ said seueral Colonies and Plantations, or the more part of them, one person of yᵉ same Colony and Plantation to be Treasurer or Cape merchant of yᵉ same Colony and Plantation to take yᵉ charge and mannageinge ot all such goods, wares and commodities, which shall be brought into, or taken out of yᵉ seuerall magazines or storehouses, The same Treasurer or Cape merchant to continue in his office by yᵉ space of one whole year next after his said election, unlesse he shall happen to dye within yᵉ said year, or uoluntarily giue ouer the same, or be remoued for any just or reasonable cause; and that thereupon the same President and Councel, or yᵉ most part of them shall haue power and authority to elect him againe or any other or others in his room or stead to continue in yᵉ same office as aforesaid; and that alsoe there shall be two or more persons of good discretion within euery of yᵉ said Colonies and Plantations elected and chosen yearely, during the said terme of fiue yeares by yᵉ President and Councel of yᵉ same Collony, or yᵉ most part of them respectiuely, within their seueral limits and precincts, yᵉ one, or more of them to keep a book, in which shall be registred and entred all such goods, wares and merchandizes, as shall be receiued into yᵉ seueral magazines or storehouses, within that Colony, being appointed for that purpose, and yᵉ other to keep a like book, wherein shall be registred all goods, wares and merchandizes which shall issue or be taken out of any yᵉ seueral magazines or storehouses of that Collony; which Clarks shall continue in their said places but att the will of yᵉ President and Councel of that Colony, whereof he is, or of the major part of

---

[1] L.C. copy, 'is'. Either word seems superfluous.
[2] L.C. copy, 'chosen or elected'.

them, and that euery person of Euery the said seueral Colonies and Plantations shall be furnished with all necessaries out of those seueral magazines or[1] storehouses, which shal belong to ye said Colony and Plantation, in which that person is, for and during ye terme and time of fiue yeares, by ye appointment, direction and order of ye President and Councel there, or of ye said Cape merch*ant* and two Clerks or of ye most part of them, within the said seueral limits and precincts of ye said Colonies and Plantations;

alsoe our will and pleasure is, and wee doe hereby ordaine, that ye aduenturers of ye said first Colony, and Plantation shall and may during ye said terme of fiue yeares elect and choose out of themselues one or more Companies, each Company consisting of three persons att ye least, who shall be resident att or neer London, orsuch [*sic*] other place, and places, as ye Councel of y^t Colony for ye time being, or ye most part of them, during ye said fiue yeares, shall think fitt, who shall there from time to time take charge of the trade, and accompt of all such goods, wares, merchandizes, and other things, which shall be sent from thence, to ye Company of ye same Colony or Plantation in Virginia, and likewise of all such wares, goods and merchandizes, as shall be brought from ye said Colony, or Plantation, unto y^t [*sic*] place within our realme of England, and of all things concerning ye mannaging of ye affaires and profits concerning ye aduenturors of that Company, which shall soe passe out of, or come into that place or port:

> [thirteen and a half lines of virtually identical provisions for the 'second Colony' follow, with Plymouth substituted for London];

alsoe our will and pleasure is, that noe person or persons shall be admitted into any of ye said Colonies and Plantations there to abide and remaine, but such as shall take not only ye usual oath of obedience to us, our heires, and successors, but alsoe y^e

---

[1] L.C. copy, 'and'.

oath which is limitted in ye last session of Parliament holden att Westminster, in ye fourth year of our raigne, for their due obedience unto us, our heires and successors, that ye trade to, and from any the Colonies aforesaid may be mannaged to, and from such ports & places, within our realme of England, as is before in these articles intended, any thing set down heretofore to ye contrary notwithstanding[,] and that ye said President and Councel of each of ye said Colonies and ye more part of them respectiuely shall and may lawfully from time to time constitute, make and ordaine such constitutions, ordinances and officers, for ye better order, gouernment and peace of ye people of their Seueral Collonies, soe alwaies as the same ordinances, and constitutions doe not touch any party in life or member, which constitutions & ordinances shall stand and continue in full force, untill ye same shall be otherwise altered or made uoid, by us, our heires, or successors, or our or their Councel of Virginia, soe alwaies as ye same alterations be such as may stand with, and be in substance, consonant unto ye Lawes of England, or the equity thereof:

Furthermore our will and pleasure is, and wee doe hereby determine and ordaine, that euery person and persons being our subjects of euery the said Collonies and Plantations shall from time to time well entreate those saluages in those parts, and use all good meanes to draw the saluages and heathen people of ye said seueral places and of the territories and Countries adjoining to the true seruice and knowledge of God, and that all just, kind and charitable courses shall be holden with such of them, as shall conforme themselues to any good and sociable traffique and dealing with ye subjects of us, our heires and successors, which shall be planted there, whereby they may be ye sooner drawne to the true knowledge of God, and ye Obedience of us, our heires and successors, under such seuere paines and punishments as shal be inflicted by ye same seueral Presidents and Councells of ye said seueral Colonies, or the most part of them, within their seueral limits & precincts on such as shall offend therein, or doe ye contrary, and that as ye said Territories and Countries of Virginia and America, within ye degrees aforesaid shall from time to time encrease in Plantation, by our subjects, Wee, our heires and successors will ordeine and giue such order and further Instructions, Lawes, Constitutions and ordinances for ye better rule, order and Gouernment of such, as soe shall make plantations there, as to us, our heires and successors shall from time to time be thought fitt & conuenient, which alwaies shall be such, as may stand with, or be in substance consonant unto ye Lawes of England, or ye equity thereof:

and lastly Wee doe ordaine, and establish, for us, our heires, and successors that such oath shall be taken by each of our Councellors here for Virginia concerning their place and office of Councel, as by ye Priuy Councel of us, our heires and successors of this our realme of England, shall be in that behalfe limited & appointed; and that each Councellor of ye said Colonies shall take such oath for ye execution of their place and office of Councel, as by ye Councel of us, our heires and successors here in England, for Virginia shall in that behalfe be limited and appointed, and aswell [sic] those seueral articles and Instructions herein mentioned and conteined as alsoe all such, as by uirtue hereof shall hereafter be made and ordained, shall as need shall require, by ye aduice of our Councel here for Virginia be transcripted ouer unto ye said seueral Councells of the said seueral Colonies, under ye seale to be ordained for oursaid [sic] Councell here for Virginia; In Witnesse &c

3. *10 December 1606.*
Orders for the Council for Virginia.[1]

Certain Orders and Directions Conceived and Set Down the tenth Day of December in the Year of the Reign of Our Soverain Lord King James of England France & Ireland the fourth and of Scotland the fortieth by his majesties Counsel for Virginia for the better Government of his Majesties Subjects both Captains Soldiers Marriners and Others that are now bound for that Coast to Settle his Majesties first Colony in Virginia there to be by them Observed as Well in their passages thether by Sea as after their arrival and Landing there –

Whereas Our said Soverain Lord the king by Certain Articles Signed by his Ma*j*estie and Sealed with his highness privy Seal hath appointed us whose names are Underwritten with Some Others to be his Ma*j*esties Counsel for Virginia Giving unto us by his Ma*j*esties Warrant under the said Privy Seal full power and authority in his Ma*j*esties name to nominate the first several Councellors of the Several Colonies which are to be planted in Virginia and to Give Directions unto the Several Councellors for their better Government there we having Such Due respect as is requisite to a Service of Such importance being assembled together for the better Ordering and Directing of the Same Do by this Our Writing Sealed With his Ma*j*esties Seal appointed for this Coun[s]el Ordain Direct & Appoint in manner and form following –

First Whereas the Good Ship Called the Sarah Constant[2]

---

[1] Library of Congress, Bland MS, pp. 19–23. First printed by Edward D. Neill in his *History of the Virginia Company of London* (Albany, N.Y., 1869), pp. 4–8, with many changes in capitalization, and some in punctuation. Reprinted without alteration in Brown, *Genesis*.

[2] Apparently the scribe's error. The correct name of the ship was the *Susan Constant* (see Document 5, pp. 55–60, below). This is the only instance of the mistake known

and the Ship Called the Godspeed[1] with a pinnace called the Discovery are now ready Victualed riged and furnished for the said Voyage We think it fit and So Do Ordain and Appoint that Cap*tain* Christopher Newport Shall have the Sole Charge to appoint Such Captains Soldiers and Marriners as Shall Either Command or be Shiped to pass in the said Ships or pinnace and Shall also have the Charge and Oversight of all Such munitions victuals and Other provisions as are Or Shall be Shiped at the publick Charge of the Adventurers in them or any of them And further that the said Cap*tain* Neweport shall have the Sole charge and Command of all the Captains Soldiers and marriners and Other persons that Shall Go in any the Said Ships and pinnace in the said Voyage from the Day of the Date hereof until Such time as they Shall fortune to Land upon the Said Coast of Virginia and if the said Captain Newport should happen to Dye at Sea then the Masters of the said Ships and pinnace Shall Carry them to the Coast of Virginia aforesaid. And

Whereas We have Caused to be Delivered unto the said Captain Newport Captain Barthol[omew] Gosnold and Captain John Ratcliffe Several instruments Close Sealed with the Counsels Seal aforesaid Containing the names of Such Persons as we have appointed to be of his Majesties Counsel in the said Country of Virginia we Do Ordain and Direct that the said Captain Christopher Newport Captain Bartholomew Gosnold and Captain John Ratcliffe or the Survivor Or Survivors of them Shall Within four and twenty hours next after the said Ships Shall arrive upon the said Coast of Virginia and not before Open and Unseal the said Instrument and Declare and publish unto all the Company the names therein Set down and that the persons by Us therein named are and Shall be known and taken to be his Maje*s*ties Counsel of his first Colony

to the editor, but because of the number of times it has been reproduced there has been a needless amount of discussion.

[1] *Godspeed* was miscopied by Neill as *Goodspeed*, giving rise to further solemn 'weighing of evidence'.

in Virginia aforesaid. And further that the said Counsel So by us nominated Shall upon the publishing of the said Instrument proceed to the Election and nomination of a President of the said Counsel and the said President in all matters of Controversy and Question that Shall arise During the Continuance of his Authority where there shall fall Out to be Equality of Voices shall have two Voices and Shall have full power and Authority with the advice of the Rest of the said Counsel or the Greatest part of them to Govern Rule and Command all the Captains and Soldiers and all Other his Majesties Subjects of his Colony according to the true meaning of the Orders and Directions Set Down in the articles Signed by his Majestie and of these presents And that immediately upon the Election and nomination of the Said President the President himself Shall in the presence of the said Counsel and Some twenty of the Principal Persons adventurers in the said Voyage to be by the Said President and Counsel Called thereunto take his Corporal Oath upon the holy Evangelists of Alleageance to Our Soverain Lord the king and for performance of this Duty in his Place in manner and form following.

I, N[,] Elected President for his Majesties Counsel for the first Colony to Virginia Do Swear that I Shall be a true and faithfull Servant unto the Kings majestie as A Councellor & President of his Majesties Counsel for the first Colony planted or to be Planted in any the territories of America between the Degrees of 34 and 41 from the Equinoctial Line Northward and the trades thereof and that I Shall faithfully and truely Declare my mind and Opinion according to my heart and Conscience in all things treated of in that Counsel and Shall keep Secreet all matters Committed and Revealed unto me Concerning the same Or that Shall be treated of Secreetly in that Counsel until [such] time as by the Consent of his Majesties Privy Counsel or the Counsel of Virginia or the more part of them publication Shall be made thereof and of all matters of Great importance or Difficulty I Shall make his Majesties

General Counsel for Virginia acquainted therewith and follow their Directions therein I Shall to the best of my Skill and Knowledge uprightly and Duely Execute all things committed to my Care and Charge according to Such Directions as are or Shall be Given unto me by or from his Majestie his heirs or Successors or his or their Privy Counsel or his or their Councel for Virginia according to the tenour Effect and true meaning of his Majesties Letters Patents and of Such articles and instructions as are Set Down by his highness under his Majesties Privy Seal for and Concerning the Government of the said Colony and my uttermost bear faith and alleageance unto the kings Majesty his heirs and Lawful Successors as Shall assist and Defend all Jurisdictions Preheminences and Authorities Granted unto his Majesty and annexed unto the Crown as against forrain Princes Persons & Potentates whatsoever be it by Act of Parliament or Otherwise And Generally in all things I Shall Do as a true and faithfull Servant and Subjects Ought to Do to his Majesty So help me God And after the Oath So by him taken the said President Shall Minister the Like Oath to Every One particularly of the said Counsell Leaving out the name of President only

And Finally that after the arrival of the said Ship upon the Coast of Virginia the Counsell[ors?] names published the said Captain Newport Shall with Such Number of Men as Shall be Assigned him by the President and Counsel of the said Colony Spend and Bestow two Months in Discovery of Such ports and Rivers as Can be found in that Country and Shall Give Order for the present Laiding and furnishing of the two Ships abovenamed with all Such principal Comodities and Merchandize as Can there be had and found in Such Sort as he may Return with the said Ships full Laden with Goods and Merchandizes bringing With him full Relation of all that he hath passed in the said Voyage by the end of May next if God Permit.

4. [*Between 20 November and 19 December 1606.*]
   The London Council's 'Instructions given by way of Advice'.[1]

   Instructions given by way of advice by us whom it hath pleased the Kings Ma*jes*tie to appoint of the Counsel for the intended Voyage to Virginia to be Observed by those Captains and Company which are Sent at this *pre*sent to plant there.

As We Doubt not but you will have especial Care to Observe the Ordinances set Down by the Kings Ma*jes*tie and Delivered unto you under the privy Seal So for your better Directions upon your first Landing we have thought Good to recommend unto your Care these Instructions and articles following. When it Shall please God to Send you on the Coast of Virginia you shall Do your best Endeavour to find out a Safe port in the Entrance of Some navigable River making Choise of Such a one as runneth furthest into the Land.[2] and if you happen to Discover Divers portable Rivers and amongst them any one that hath two main branches if the Difference be not Great make Choise of that which bendeth most towards the Northwest for that way shall You soonest find the Other Sea[3] When You have made Choise of the River on which you mean to Settle be not hasty in Landing Your Victual and munitions but

---

[1] Library of Congress, Bland MS, pp. 14–18. First printed by Edward D. Neill in his *History of the Virginia Company of London* (Albany, N.Y., 1869), pp. 8–14, with the same minor alterations noted in Document 3. Reprinted by Edward Arber in his *Capt. John Smith, ... Works* (Birmingham, 1884), pp. xxxiii–xxxvii, from Neill; and by Alexander Brown, in his *Genesis*, I, 79–85, apparently with some reference to the original in the L.C. More recently, it has been reprinted, directly from Arber, in *The original writings & correspondence of the two Richard Hakluyts*, ed. by E. G. R. Taylor (Hakluyt Society, 2nd ser., LXXVI–LXXVII (1935)), II, 492–6.

[2] 'The elder Hakluyt had repeatedly emphasized the importance of settling on a navigable river', Taylor, *Hakluyts*, II, 492, n. 2.

[3] Even as late as 1650, a manuscript map by John Farrer, or Ferrar, attempted to show that the 'Other Sea', the Pacific Ocean, was just beyond the Appalachian Mountains (New York Public Library, inserted in a first edition copy of Edward Williams' *Virgo Triumphans* (London, 1650)). As Professor Taylor has pointed out, there were some supporters of the Virginia venture who thought of the projected colony as primarily a way-station to the Far East (*Hakluyts*, II, 492, n. 3).

first Let Cap*tain* Newport Discover how far that River may be found navigable that you may make Election of the Strongest most Fertile and wholesome place for if you make many Removes besides the Loss of time You Shall greatly Spoil your Victuals and Your cask[s] and with Great pain transport it in Small boats But if you Choose your place so far up as A Bark of fifty tuns will fleet then you may Lay all Your provisions a Shore with Ease and the better Receive the trade of all the Countries about you in the Land and Such A place you may perchance find a hundred miles from the Rivers mouth and the farther up the better for if you sit Down near the Entrance Except it be in Some Island that is Strong by nature An Enemy that may approach you on Even Ground may Easily pull You Out and if he be Driven to Seek You a hundred miles within the Land in boats you shall from both sides of your River where it is Narrowest So beat them with Your muskets as they shall never be Able to prevail Against You. And to the end That You be not Surprised as the French were in Florida by Melindus and the Spaniard in the same place by the french[1] you shall Do Well to make this Double provision first Erect a Little Sconce[2] at the Mouth of the River that may Lodge Some ten men With Whom you Shall Leave a Light boat that when any fleet shall be in Sight they may Come with Speed to Give You Warning. Secondly you must in no Case Suffer any of the natural people of the Country to inhabit between You and the Sea Coast for you Cannot Carry Your Selves so towards them but they will Grow Discontented with Your habitation and be ready to Guide and assist any Nation that Shall Come to invade You and if You neglect this You neglect Your Safety. When You have Discovered as far up the River as you mean to plant Your Selves and Landed your victuals and munitions to the End that Every man may know his Charge you Shall Do well

[1] The story of 'Melindus' (Melendes, properly Don Pedro Menéndez de Avilés) had been made known in Hakluyt's *Principal Navigations*, IX, 1–112.
[2] Misread as 'stoure' by Neill, and so printed by all the others.

THE PRELIMINARIES

to Divide your Six Score men[1] into three parts whereof one forty of them you may appoint to fortifie and build of which your first work must be your Storehouse for Victual 30 Others you may imploy in preparing your Ground and Sowing your Corn and Roots the Other ten of these forty you must Leave as Centinel at the havens mouth The Other forty you may imploy for two Months in Discovery of the River above you and on the Contrary [country?] about you which Charge Captain Newport and Captain Gosnold may undertake of these forty Discoverers when they Do Espie any high Lands or hills Cap*tain* Golnold may take 20 of the Company to Cross Over the Lands and Carrying half a Dozen pickaxes to try if they Can find any mineral. The Other twenty may go on by River and pitch up boughs upon the Banks Side by which the Other boats Shall follow them by the Same turnings You may also take with them a Wherry Such as is used here in the Thames by Which you may Send back to the President for supply of munition or any Other want that you may [be?] not Driven to Return for Every Small Defect.

You must Observe if you Can Whether the River on which you Plant Doth Spring out of Mountains or out of Lakes if it be out of any Lake the passage to the Other Sea will be the more Easy & it is Like Enough that Out of the same Lake you shall find Some Spring which run the Contrary way toward the East India Sea for the Great and famous River of Volga Tan[a]is & Dwina have three heads near joynd and Yet the One falleth into the Caspian Sea the Other into the Euxine Sea and the third into the Polonian Sea.[2] In all Your Passages you must have Great Care not to Offend the naturals if You Can Eschew it and imploy Some few of your Company to trade with them for Corn and all Other lasting Victuals if you [they?] have any and this you must Do before that they

[1] Only 104 or 105 reached Virginia. Perhaps only that number could be recruited.
[2] Polonian was misprinted as Pælonian by Arber, and the mistake copied by Professor Taylor, who rightly points out that 'the analogy with ... Russia was faulty, but it suggests the cosmographer (Hakluyt) behind the notes' (*Hakluyts*, II, 494, n. 1).

perceive you mean to plant among them for not being Sure how your own Seed Corn will prosper the first Year to avoid the Danger of famine use and Endeavour to Store yourselves of the Country Corn. Your Discoverers that passes Over Land with hired Guides must Look well to them that they Slip not from them and for more Assurance let them take a Compass with them and Write Down how far they Go upon Every point of the Compass[1] for that Country having no way nor path if that Your Guides Run from You in the Great Woods or Deserts you Shall hardly Ever find a Passage back. And how Weary Soever your Soldiers be Let them never trust the Country people with the Carriage of their Weapons for if they Run from You with Your Shott which they only fear they will Easily kill them all with their arrows And whensoever any of Yours Shoots before them be sure that they be Chosen out of your best Markesmen for if they See Your Learners miss what they aim at they will think the Weapon not so terrible and thereby will be bould . . . d [? – bould] to Assaillt You. Above all things Do not advertize the killing of any of your men that the Country people may know it if they Perceive they are but Common men and that with the Loss of many of theirs they may Deminish any part of Yours they will make many Adventures upon You if the Country be popalous you Shall Do well also not to Let them See or know of Your Sick men if you have any which may also Encourage them to many Enterprizes. You must take Especial Care that you Choose a Seat for habitation that Shall not be over burthened with Woods near your town for all the men You have Shall not be able to Cleanse twenty acres in a Year besides that it may Serve for a Covert for Your Enimies round about You neither must You plant in a low and moist place because it will prove unhealthful You shall Judge of the Good Air by the People for Some part of that Coast where the Lands are Low have their

---

[1] Professor Taylor comments that 'this is perhaps the first mention of the use of the simple compass traverse in exploration' (*ibid.*, n. 2).

people blear Eyed and with Swollen bellies and Legs but if the naturals be Strong and Clean made it is a true sign of a wholesome Soil. You must take Order to Draw up the Pinnace that is Left with You under your fort and take her Sails and Anchors A Shore all but a Small Kedge[1] to ride by Least Some ill Disposed Persons Slip away with her. You must take Care that your Marriners that Go for wages Do not marr your trade for those that mind not to inhabite for a Little Gain will Debase the Estimation of Exchange and hinder the trade for Ever after and there fore you Shall not admit or Suffer any person whatsoever other then Such as Shall be appointed by the president and Councel there to buy any Merchandizes or Other things whatsoever. It Were Necessary that all Your Carpenters and Other such like Workmen about building Do first build Your Storehouse and those Other Rooms of Publick and necessary Use before any house be Set up for any private person and though the Workman may belong to any private persons yet Let them all Work together first for the Company and then for private men And Seeing order is at the same price with Confusion it shall be adviceably done to Set your houses Even and by a line that You[r] Streets may have a Good breadth & be carried Square about your market place and Every Streets End opening into it that from thence with a few feild peices you may Command Every street throughout which marketplace you may also fortify if you shall think it needful. You Shall do well to Send a perfect relation by Cap*tain* Newport of all that is Done of what height you are Seated how far into the Land what Comodities you find what Soil Woods and their Several Kinds and so of all Other things Else to advertise p*a*rticularly and to Suffer no man to return but by pasport from the president and Councel nor to write any Letter of any

---

[1] Miscopied by the scribe as 'ledge'. The kedge, or kedger, was the smallest anchor 'to use in calme weather in a slow streame...' Captain John Smith, *A Sea Grammar* (London, 1627), 29. See also Sir Henry Manwayring, *The Sea-mans Dictionary* (London, 1644), 3 and 56. A study of the interdependence of these two seamen's handbooks is in preparation by the editor.

thing that may Discourage others. Lastly & Cheifly the way to prosper and to Obtain Good Success is to make yourselves all of one mind for the Good of your Country & your own and to Serve & fear God the Giver of all Goodness for every Plantation which our heavenly father hath not planted shall be rooted out.

A Copy of the Oath for the Kings Councel of Virginia.

You Shall Swear to be a true and faithfull Servant unto the Kings Majesty as One of his Counsel for Virginia You Shall in all things to be moved treated and Debated in that Counsel Concerning Virginia or any the territories of America between the Degrees of 34 and 45. from the Equinoctial Line Northward or the trades thereof faithfully and truely Declare your mind and Opinion according to Your heart and Conscience and Shall keep Secret all matters Committed and revealed to You concerning the Same and that Shall be treated Secretly in that Counsel or this Counsel of Virginia or the more part of them publication shall be made thereof and of all matters of Great importance of [or?] difficulty before You resolve thereupon you Shall make his Majestie[s] Privy Counsel acquainted therewith and follow their Direction therein you shall to the uttermost bear faith & Alleageance to the kings majestie his heirs and Lawfull Successors and Shall assist and Defend all jurisdictions preheminences and Authorities Granted unto his majestie and annext unto the Crown against all forrain Princes Persons prelates or potentates whatsoever be it by act of Parliament or Otherwise and Generally in all things you Shall Do as a faithfull and true Servant and Subject Ought to Do So help You God and the holy Contents of this book –

THE PRELIMINARIES

5. *13 December 1606.*
Examination Concerning Damage to the Susan Constant.[1]

Die sabbato xiij Decembris 1606

Joha*nn*es Coursay de Limehouse nauta vbi *per* decem an*nos* moram fecit annos natus xxviij vel circa Testis in hac *p*arte productus iuratus et examinatus dicit q*uo*d Christoferum Newporte *per* quatuor annos noverit Philippus Barnardo non novit

Philippus Barnardo[2] et navem the Susan Constant et Christoferum Newport respond*ent* (?)

Ad primu*m* articulu*m* allegationis in hac causa date affirmat he knoweth that Mr Dapper M^r wheatley and Robert Colthurst and others theire partners are owners of the ar*ticu*late shipp the Susan Constant of the porte of London and the tacle and apparell thereof and so haue byn ever since the buildinge thereof which ys aboute a yeare past For they builte the same shipp furnished rigged victualed and ma*nn*ed her and sett her to sea on a viadge for Spaine of this ex*ami*nates certaine knowledge from this porte of London

Primus testis Newporte

Ad secundu*m* dicit veru*m* esse that the Susan Constant is of the burthen of one hundreth and twenty tonnes[3] or thereaboutes and was fully laden with victualls and other necessaries for the viadge intended and the ar*ticu*late shipp the Phillipp and Francys is aboute one hundreth tonnes in burthen and had nothinge in her but some *p*arte of her victualls to his knowledge when the dam*m*adge in question hapned and they both then lay in the River of Thames over against Ratcliff

[1] P.R.O., H.C.A. 13/38. Extract, comprising pertinent portions of documents discovered in 1965 by Alison M. Quinn, transcribed by her, and courteously sent to the editor.

[2] Mentioned by Samuel Purchas, *Pilgrimes* (V, 4), as an Italian merchant in London in 1617, who was then interested in the East Indian trade. His ship the *Lion* was encountered by the fleet sent out by the East India Company under Captain Martin Pring (see Chapter I, p. 13), who maintained an interest in Virginia throughout his life.

[3] According to the second part of John Smith's *Map of Virginia* (1612), p. 2, the tonnage was '100 Tonns' (see Document 63, p. 378, below), but the larger figure is evidently correct.

Crosse[1] att an anker of this ex*amin*ates knowledge who was then one of the company of the said shipp the Susan Constant

Ad tertiu*m* quartu*m* et quintu*m* affirmat veru*m* esse that the Susan Constant beinge of greater burthen and deeper laden then the Phillipp and Frances could not be turned or caried aboute by the tide vppon the ebbe so soon as the said shipp the Phillip Frances as also for that the Phillipp Frances was mored to longe and so havinge much cable out was quickly turned aboute vppon the ebbe and came vppon the s*ai*d shipp the Susan Constant before she was turned with the tide and brake of thre of her portes and did her damm*a*dge And as the shippes were borde and bord one vppon the other this ex*ami*nate and company of the Susan Constant spake to them in the Phillipp and Francys and preyed them to vere theire cable or else the one shipp would hurte thother and offered to goe on borde the Phillipp and Francys to helpe to cleare the shippes and save them from hurte Notwithstandinge he sayth that the company then on borde the Phillipp and Francys beinge thre or foure youthes would not vere theire cable but vsed these speeches or the like in effecte viz our barke is as stronge as yo*u*r sides and therofe we will not vere Wherevppon two of this ex*ami*nates company seeinge theire wilfulnes wente on borde the Phillipp and Frances to vere the cable and cleare the shipp and comm*i*nge on borde founde the cables ende at the butts so as there was no more cable to vere out and then they called for a haulster to make fast to the cable so to lengthen yt out and havinge none the company of the Susan Constant would haue brought a haulster to make fast to the cable and they of the Phillipp and Frances would not suffer it to be brought on borde and so by theire owne wilfulnes they receaved such hurte as hapned vnto them for if they had vered the cable or suffered the company of the Susan Constant to doe yt theire had no

---

[1] Ratcliff Cross was that part of Butcher Row between Broad Street and the Thames, now in Limehouse parish. It was about four miles by river from there to Blackwall, from which the Jamestown voyage started.

hurte hapned to the said ships or eyther of them of this examinates knowledge who was then in the Susan Constant and sawe what hapned concerninge the said dammadge

Ad sextum affirmat verum esse that this examinate and company of the Susan Constant seeinge the obstinacy and necgligence of the said company of the Phillipp and Francys did cast and fasten a halster vppon a Carvell that lay thereby at anker so to cleare the shipps and in his iudgement by that meanes had cleared them but that the company of the Carvell cutt the halster which was fastened vnto them vt dicit

Ad septimum affirmat eundem continere in se veritatem for within these two dayes there rode two ships in the same birthes where the said ships the Susan Constant and Phillipp and Francys rode at anker and the one never hurte the other

Ad octavum affirmat eundem continere in se veritatem for this examinate was in the Susan Constant when the said ships were foule one of the other and knoweth the hurte which hapned to the Phillipp and Francys hapned by the faulte negligence and wilfulnes of them that were in the Phillipp and Francys Reddendo rationem vt supra For that this examinate and company did their vttermost endever to cleare the said shipps and could not be suffered by them of the Phillipp and Francys vbi prius dictum est

Ad vltimum dicit predeposita per eum esse vera John Coursey his ✗ marke

Ad Interrogatoria in folio sequente

[The testimony of John Harvie, mariner, and the answer of Iohannes Coursey follow.]

Continuation of examination:
                    Die pre*dicto*

<small>Philippus
Barnardo et
navem the
Susan
Constant</small>

Henricus Ravens[1] de Ratcliff nauta ubi *per* xvj annos moram fecit annos natus quadraginta duos vel circa testis in hac parte p*r*oductus iuratus et examinatus Dicit qu*o*d Philippum Barnardo *per* octo annos Christoferum Newporte per xvj annos et Ro*ber*tum Colthurst ex visu respectiue noverit

Ad primu*m* articulatu*m* libelli affirmat that the ar*ticu*late shipp the Phillipp and Francys is victualled furnished and sett to sea by Phillipp Barnardo and John Francisco Soprani and by them this ex*ami*nate and the mariners are paide theire wages And therefore he thinketh they are owners of the said shipp Ad al*iter* nescit

Ad secundu*m* dicit he knoweth that the Phillipp and Francys lay at anker in the River of Thames within the jurisdiction of the Admiraltie over against Ratcliff betwixte vj and vjj weekes and had ankers cables buoy and all other thinges fitt for such a shipp of his knowledge who is m*aster* of the same shipp

Ad tertiu*m* et quartu*m* affirmat veru*m* esse that the Susan Constant ar*ticu*late came to an anker and cast her ankers so nere vnto the Phillipp and Francys that she could not ride cleare but that the Phillipp and Francys brake downe two of the portes of the said shipp the Susan Constant and therevppon this ex*ami*nate wente to the house of Christopher Newporte beinge Captaine or master of the said shipp the Susan Constant and lefte worde that his shipp was mored to nere to this ex*ami*nates

---

[1] Henry Ravens had sailed with Newport as ship's master early in 1594 (*English Privateering Voyages to the West Indies 1588–1595*, ed. by K. R. Andrews (Hakluyt Society, 2nd ser., CXI (1959)), 298 and 303. In 1609, he sailed for Virginia with Sir Thomas Gates as master's mate. He was put in charge of Gates' long boat, after the admiral had been wrecked on Bermuda reefs, and hopefully sent toward Virginia to inform the colonists that Gates and his company were safe. Apparently he succeeded in reaching the mainland, only to be murdered by the Indians along with his crew of six (Purchas, *Pilgrimes*, XIX, 25 and 43–4).

shipp and that he should take order to more her cleare and warninge was afterwards given by the mariners beinge in the said shippe the Phillipp and Francys of his knowledge

Ad quintum affirmat verum esse that the Phillipp and Francys lay at anker vj or vij weekes in the place aforesaid before the Susan Constant came to anker by her of his knowledge

Ad sextum et scedulam affirmat verum esse that the said shipp the Susan Constant on the xxiijth of November last came vppon the Phillipp and Francys in the night tyme vppon the eb at highe water by the necligence of the company of the said shipp the Susan Constant and brake the beake heade the bowspritt and the sheate anker of the same shipp of this examinates certaine knowledge who came on borde as the said shippes were foule one of the other and sawe that the company of the Susan Constant sate tiplinge and drinkinge and never looked out or endevored to cleare the ships And he knoweth that the said owners haue repayred the said damadge and the timber employed in the mendinge of said said [sic] beake head cost xvij^s viij^d and foure carpenters wrought three dayes in mendinge the same and had ij^s a day for theire worcke which came to xxiiij^s and the paintinge of the said beake heade cost v^s vij^d And he also knoweth that the bowe spritt cost newe makinge xxxiij^s and the sheate anker cost xxxiij^s in repayringe the same which he knoweth to be true for that he disbursed the moneye for the carpenters worcke and the bowespritt and sheate anker mendinge and the owners had a bill for paymente of the rest Whereby he knoweth the premisses to be true

Ad septimum refert se ad registrum huius curie et ad iura

Ad octavum affirmat eundem esse verum Reddendo rationem ut supra

Ad nonum affirmat the owners have susteyned damadge by reason of the said hurtes for that the shipp hath byn stayed from her viadge longer tyme then she would to be repayred and in that tyme the mariners were paid their wages Ac aliter nescit

JAMESTOWN VOYAGES

Ad decimu*m* affirmat eunde*m* esse veru*m* vt ex actis huius curie apparent

Ad ult*imum* dicit predeposita p*er* eu*m* esse vera

[Further questioning follows.]

6. *20 November 1606.*
 Robert Hunt's Will.[1]

In the name of God Amen. This twentieth daye of November in the year of our Lord accordinge to the computac*i*on of the Church of England one thowsand Sixe hundred and Sixe. I Robert Hunt of the parishe of Heathfeilde in the Countye of Sussex Clerke and vicar of the saide parishe beinge whole and sounde ... doe make and ordaine this my last will and Testament//First I committ and bequeathe my soule ... and my bodie to the good will and pleasure of Almightie God. Concerninge my earthlie goodes and landes this is my last will and Testament in manner and forme followinge. First I give vnto Grace Kyne my nowe Servant & to Elizabeth Milles my late Servant to eatch of them Tenn shillinges to be paide within three Monthes after the certaine knowledge of my deathe: Item I give vnto Elizabeth my daughter[2] thirtie poundes of lawfull money of England to be paide to her when she shall come to eighteene yeares of age. Alsoe I give vnto her One Tenement with five acres of lande be it more or less ... Item I give vnto Thomas my Sonne[3] tenn poundes of lawfull money of England to be paide him at the age of one and twenty years[.] Item I give to him one tenement or Coppyhoulde with

---

[1] Extract. P.C.C. 72 Windebank. A portion of this, modernized, appeared in *VMHB*, XXV (1917), 161–2.

[2] 'Elizabeth, daughter of Robert Hunt, Vicar of Heathfield, was baptized on 4 February 1602/3', Charles W. F. Smith, 'Chaplain Robert Hunt and his Parish in Kent', *Historical Magazine of the Protestant Episcopal Church*, XXVI (1957), 20.

[3] Since Robert Hunt was married in Canterbury in 1597, it is evident that his son Thomas could not have been the Thomas Hunt who subscribed an unknown amount to the Virginia Company in 1609 (*ibid.*, p. 19, and Brown, *Genesis*, II, 221).

twelve acres of land be it more or lesse thereto belonging ...
All my other goodes Chattells money annuyties either nowe or
hereafter to be due vnto me I give vnto Elizabeth my wiffe
whome I make my sole executor, and I doe appoint Master
Tristram Siclemore to be the supravisor or overseer of this
my last will and Testament, and I doe given him Tenn shillinges for his labour. Provided alwaies yf Elizabeth my saide
wiffe shall at any time during my life committ the act of
incontinency or shalbe comonlie defamed or vehementlie
suspected for any such acte of incontinency, or if the saide
Elizabeth my wiffe shall during my life or after my deathe
before the provinge of this my will staie and abide in one and
the same house or other place whatsoever (The Churche and
publique assemblies onelie excepted) together with John
Taylor the eldest Sonne of John Taylor of the parishe of
Heathfeild aforesaide. Then my last will and testament is that
she the saide Elizabeth my wiffe shalbe excluded from being
my Executor, and shall loose all other benefitt of this my last
will and testament. And in her place I doe appoint Elizabeth
my daughter to be my sole Executor to whome I doe alsoe
give all my goodes Chattell money and annuyties whatsoever
unbequeathed[.] And I then appoint my brother Steven Hunt
nowe or late of Reculver in the Countie of Kent yeoman to be
the onelie Overseer of trust of this my last will and testament
to the vse and for the benefitt of Elizabeth my daughter and I
doe give vnto him five poundes for his labour, whome also
I doe appoint and intreate (yf my daughter Elizabeth shall hap
to be myne Executor then and not otherwise) to keepe or
cause to be kept hir my saide daughter and my sonne Thomas
in their minority and to putt fourth such money as shalbe due
vnto them soe as may be most for their profitt[.] And I do
further allowe to him all such reasonable charges as he shall
necessarilye expend by being the overseer of this my last will &
testament. In witnes whereof I have written this my last will
and testament with mine owne hande and thereto have sett my

hand and sealle the day and yeare aboue written[.] Ro. Hunt. Sealled and delivered in the presence [of] Thomas Boreman [&] Noe Taylor.

Probatum fuit testamentum... [in London before Master Edmund Pope. 14 July 1608.]

7. *24 November 1606.*
Dispensation for Richard Hakluyt and Robert Hunt.[1]

The King, etc., to our beloved subjects Richard Hakluyt, clerk prebendary both in the collegiate church of Saint Peter, Westminster, and in the cathedral church of the Holy and Undivided Trinity, Bristol, as well as rector of the parish church of Wetheringsett in our county of Suffolk, diocese of Norwich, and one of the perpetual chaplains of our Hospital of le Savoy[2] in our County of Middlesex, and Robert Hunt, clerk, M.A., vicar of the parish church of Heathfield, in our county of Sussex, diocese of Chichester Selsey,[3]

Whereas you, the aforesaid Richard Hakluyt and Robert Hunt, together with our beloved subjects Thomas Gates and George Somers, knights, Edward Maria Wingfield, Thomas Hanham, Ralegh Gilbert, esquires, William Parker, George Popham, and others, by our authority to make habitation and plantation, to lead a colony of a number of our subjects to those parts of America which are commonly called Virginia and other territories of America which either already belong to us or are not actually

[1] Patent Roll, 4 James I, pt. 14. P.R.O., C. 66/1708. Latin. Extract, translated. The editor is indebted to Professor David B. Quinn for obtaining a xerox copy. (*Note:* All names have been spelled in conformity with modern custom. A little more than half of the original has been translated, a large part being verbose, repetitive or pure legal jargon. Nothing significant has been omitted.)

[2] After 1564, parishioners of the demolished church of St Mary-le-Strand were permitted to worship in the chapel of the Savoy manor, so called because it was given by Henry III to Peter II of Savoy, uncle of Queen Eleanor. The chapel came to be called St Mary-le-Savoy on occasion, and the hospital acquired the same name.

[3] The Saxon see of Selsey was transferred to Chichester by William the Conqueror.

already possessed by any Christian prince or people, are licensed to set out shortly for those parts, and

Whereas, since we have learned from accounts worthy of credit that the inhabitants of those parts live in the utmost ignorance of divine worship, and are completely deprived of the knowledge and solace of the word of God, and probably will remain and end their days in such ignorance unless such a great evil is cared for as soon as possible,

Therefore, we ought to that end, out of love for the glory of God, and desiring to work for the good and salvation of souls of those parts, of our special grace and certain knowledge and mere motion . . . give, grant and bestow . . . to you, the aforesaid Richard Hakluyt and Robert Hunt, full and free licence, faculty and power to go to parts of Virginia and America along with the aforementioned Thomas Gates, George Somers, Edward Maria Wingfield, Thomas Hanham, Ralegh Gilbert, William Parker, and George Popham, or with others or another . . . And that you may better and more freely dedicate yourselves to and perform the ministry and preaching of the word of God in those parts, your own selves and each of you may absent yourselves from whatever parish churches, benefices, dignities and ecclesiastical cures, and perpetual hospital chaplaincies already held or attained by you and each of you within our kingdom of England . . . [Specific permission for each of them omitted.]

And also that you and each of you may take and hold all and every tithe, revenue, pension, sum of money, and ancient rights, privilege and ecclesiastical emolument pertaining to or respecting ecclesiastical prebends, dignities, chaplaincies and ecclesiastical benefices, or any of them, . . . as well as any other goods of yours within our kingdom of England we graciously and favorably grant dispensation [from any laws or acts of Parliament to the contrary] to you, Richard Hakluyt and Robert Hunt, and each of you, and your renters, deputies, and assignees and others of yours, to receive, recover, enjoy, profit by, hold and have . . .

And in addition . . . by these presents we grant, concede, and dispense to you the aforesaid Richard Hakluyt and Robert Hunt and each of you that together with the rectorates, vicariates, prebends, dignities, chaplaincies, and ecclesiastical benefices aforesaid which you hold in our kingdom of England, that you be preferred to, acquire and obtain one or more benefices or ecclesiastical dignities, cures or non-cures, whether compatible or not, in the aforesaid parts of Virginia or America, to accept retain, and enjoy . . . Any act, ordinance [etc.,] . . . to the contrary notwithstanding, it is our will also that this our present dispensation, indulgence or licence, during and for the term of five years . . . hold valid . . .

Moreover it is our will and by these presents we grant to you the aforesaid Richard Hakluyt and Robert Hunt that you have and shall have these our letters patent under the great seal of our kingdom of England, properly signed and sealed, without fine or fee, great or small, [levied] against you in our hanaper[1] . . .

In which matter, etc., by the King at Westminster,
the twenty-fourth day of November.

[1] The 'hanaper' was the 'department of Chancery into which fees were paid for the sealing and enrolment of charters and other documents' (*OED*, s.v.).

II

The Original Voyage

NARRATIVE

Before taking up the subject of the first reports from Virginia and the first reactions to them, it is necessary to introduce a foreign observer, who was by temperament and national pride (not to mention religion) antipathetic to the very name of Virginia. This observer was Don Pedro de Zúñiga, Spain's first ledger-ambassador to London for twenty years. Despite his illustrious family name, he was an obscure hidalgo.

Zúñiga arrived early in July 1605, undoubtedly 'briefed' by Philip III's all-powerful *valido* (favourite), Francisco Sandoval y Rojas, Duke of Lerma. But such was the latter's self-seeking improbity that Zúñiga's ability to act seems to have been jeopardized from the start. 'Scarce informed so much as of the common occurrences' in his own kingdom, he was often at great disadvantage in his dealings with King James and the Privy Council.[1] Yet he laboured unremittingly as a spy for his King.

The Gunpowder Plot, which burst on the political scene less than four months after his arrival, aroused popular suspicion against Spaniards in general, and the Ambassador in particular. Nevertheless it was not long before Zúñiga was able to gather a certain amount of far from accurate information about the plans for the Jamestown voyage. As early as 6/16 March 1606,

[1] The phrase descriptive of Lerma expresses the judgment of many Spanish historians, summarized in the biographical sketch of him in the *Enciclopedia Universal Ilustrada* of Espasa-Calpe, LIII (1926), 1280–81: 'De gran ambición y no menor codicia, era, en cambio, hombre de escasas cultura e inteligencia, y carecía en absoluto de escrúpulos. . . .' The quotation in the text is from a letter of 5 February 1606/7, from Lord Salisbury to Sir Charles Cornwallis, James' Ambassador to the Court of Spain, printed in *Memorials of Affairs of State*, compiled by Edmund Sawyer (3 vols., London, 1725), II, 293.

JAMESTOWN VOYAGES

he informed King Philip III that a plan was afoot to send '500 to 600 men ... to people Virginia'.[1] But it was ten or eleven months before he was able to supply any further information. Then at last began the stream of letters from London to the Spanish Court at Valladolid which kept Philip and his Duke as well informed as Zúñiga was able. On the whole, it may be added, he accomplished this with noteworthy success until his recall in May 1610.

The first of Zúñiga's letters of importance for the documentation of the Jamestown voyages bears the date '24th of January, 1607', but is endorsed '24th of December, 1606 – received 6th of February, 1607 [all dates new style].'[2] Since the letter contains no internal evidence which could determine its true date, and since the error is probably to be attributed to the decoder, it is impossible to be certain which date is correct. Mail from London did occasionally reach Valladolid in thirteen days, and no other letter from Zúñiga took longer than a month, but this is not proof that 14/24 January 1607 is the right date.

In any event, the letter only reveals that the ambassador was active, and that his informants were either ill-informed themselves or deliberately inaccurate. Although some of the facts are true, Zúñiga has used so much of his own imagination in putting them together that the picture is distorted. Furthermore, he does not seem to know of the departure of the ships or indeed of their being ready to depart. In fact, neither he nor anyone else seems to have known that the Jamestown fleet pitched and tossed less than a dozen miles from the coast of Kent until the end of January 1607, held in the Downs 'by unprosperous winds'.[3] So far as all England was concerned, seven months of silence followed, while the colonists voyaged to America and sent their first word back.

[1] Archivo General de Simancas, Legajo 2585, 21.
[2] Document no. 8, below.
[3] From the Second Part of *A Map of Virginia* (1612), p. 2 (see Document no. 63 p. 378, below).

Meanwhile, the complaints from Plymouth had taken mild effect. It had apparently already become evident that the council named on 20 November 1606 was too small and too scattered to be able to act promptly on the suggestions or directions of the Privy Council. Furthermore, one of the two ships sent out by the Second Colony (to New England) had been taken by the Spaniards, and word had reached England early in February, if not before. This, and probably other troubles and reverses, forced the issue, and on 9 March 1607 an ordinance was issued, enlarging the Council (Document no. 9, pp. 71–6, below).

At last, on 29 July 1607, Captain Christopher Newport brought the *Susan Constant* and the *Godspeed* back, into Plymouth harbour. There, he promptly dispatched a letter to Sir Robert Cecil, Earl of Salisbury, in which he apologized for not riding in person to London to deliver his news. Lack of a capable ship's master was the reason. Two days later he set sail for the Thames, as is related in a letter from Sir Ferdinando Gorges to Salisbury, dated 7 August. It read in part: 'Master Newport, unto whom these letters were directed, set sail from hence on Friday the last of July. I was not at home when he came first into the harbour, but I understand so much by him since, as I conceive a possibility of great good to be done in the place where they are....'[1]

Assuming that Newport's letter was sent post-haste, it should have reached London not later than 2 August. Ten days later, Zúñiga had heard the news, and sent off a letter to Philip III, dated 12/22 August. In it, he intimated that Newport had not yet sailed up the Thames. On that same day, however, Sir Walter Cope wrote a long and hasty note to Salisbury which proves that Zúñiga was a little slow. Newport had indeed arrived by 12 August and had reported to the Virginia Company.[2]

---
[1] Printed in H.M.C., *Cecil Papers*, XIX, 208.
[2] See the two letters written on the same day; Zúñiga's, in Document no. 11; Cope's, in Document no. 18; below.

With him, Captain Newport brought a number of letters, reports and other documents – the first from the Jamestown Colony. Some of them have apparently been lost, but from those which have survived it is possible to get a vivid picture of the colonists' experiences.

Three of these documents may be called official. They are: 'A relatyon of the discovery of our River, from James Forte into the Maine' (Document 13); 'The Discription of the now discovered River and Country of Virginia' (Document 14); and 'A Breif discription of the People' (Document 15). In addition, there was an official letter from the Virginia council in Jamestown to the council in London, dated 22 June 1607 (Document 12).

Among the personal correspondence which has survived, there is a letter from Robert Tindall to Prince Henry (Document no. 16, pp. 104–6, below), which conveys little information, but makes one wish that the documents mentioned in it might some day be found. Then there is a fragment of a letter from William Brewster, presumably sent to Lord Salisbury although the editor of the Historical Manuscripts Commission's *Calendar of the Cecil Papers*, Vol. XIX, suggests that it may have been sent to Dudley Carleton. Carleton's own letter on Virginia is included below, as Document no. 21.

The two letters of Sir Walter Cope (Documents nos. 18 and 19, pp. 108–11, below) are particularly interesting as substantiating the impractical, giddy characteristics of some elements in the Jamestown colony. These men, lacking the will to work, sought pots of gold at the foot of every rainbow, and fell little short of destroying the settlement through sheer waywardness. Even so hard-headed a business-man as Sir Thomas Smythe appears to have been caught by the Virginian gold fever, as his letter hints (Document no. 20, p. 112, below).

Dudley Carleton's letter to his friend John Chamberlain repeats the stories of Newport and his associates, but is of particular interest as supplying the names of a few of the members

THE ORIGINAL VOYAGE

of influential circles in London who did not interest themselves directly in the venture, at least, not at the beginning.[1]

Once Newport had returned, bringing along with the gold-fantasy the solid news that Jamestown was founded, the entrepreneurs set quickly to work to dispatch further colonists and supplies. Few details have survived (notably the odd item about glass beads and moth-eaten blue cloth, in Document no. 22), but the considerable delay before Newport's departure hints that there was a great deal to do. Nearly two months slipped by before he and Master Nelson got away again, on 8 October. For that period, almost the only surviving source of information is Don Pedro de Zúñiga, always busy, always prying, and usually confused. Nevertheless, his four letters (Documents nos. 23 to 26, pp. 114–22, below) contain much that is of interest. Not least interesting of all is King Philip III's reaction to his Ambassador's recommendations (Document no. 27, pp. 122–3, below). Had Zúñiga had his way, the Virginia colony might well have been wiped out. Had King James been less evasive, the same might have happened. But in the end, Philip III's indolence assured Great Britain that the helpless infant in Virginia, beset by disease and laziness, could hold on.[2] Chapter II tells that story, factually and effectively.

8. [14/] 24 January 1607
   Pedro de Zúñiga to Philip III.[3]

London, the 24th of January, 1607 [new style]
Sir:
After I informed your Majesty that the English were

[1] See Document no. 21, pp. 113–14, below.

[2] It was not until 21 August 1608 that Philip's council of state, influenced by the English Jesuit, Father Creswell, and the English Colonel, Sir William Stanley, urged the King to do something more than talk and write letters (see Irene A. Wright, 'Spanish Policy toward Virginia, 1606–1612', *American Historical Review*, XXV (1920), 450, and Document no. 62, below).

[3] Decoded. Extract, translated. Archivo General de Simancas, Legajo E 2585, 78–9. This and all subsequent Simancas documents have been published, at least in part, in

equipping [*armauan*]¹ some ships to send to Virginia, the matter was held up a great deal, and now I learn that they have made an agreement, in great secrecy, for two ships to go there every month until they land two thousand men, and they will do the same thing from Plymouth [*Plemua*]. Two ships are also ready to leave there, [and] they have agreed with the Rebels [the Dutch] to send what people they can. The justification they advance is that this King [James I] has given them licence and letters patent for planting their religion there [*en aquella parte*], provided they do not plunder anyone, under pain of losing his protection if they do not obey. He gives them permission to occupy any island within a hundred leagues from shore, he commands the second colony (he calls them such, in his letters patent) not to come within 100 leagues of where the other has landed, without mentioning at what distance they must be from your Majesty's subjects; he concedes to one of these colonies all the mainland which lies between 32 and 45 degrees,² and the other from 45 to 55; he commands that each colony have its council, and here [in London] another, Supreme [council] is being chosen, for which there have [so far] been named (and they are ready to take the oath in great secrecy): William Vade [Waad], Lieutenant of the Tower, Anthony Cope, Francis Pofane [Popham], eldest son of the Chief Justice, Dodrig [Doddridge], solicitor of the Court of Wales, and Huaue [Huane? – Romney?],³ a knight. More insolent councillors than these they could not find in the world.

Brown's *Genesis*, in translations often at variance with the editor's. Document no. 8 is the only one of these of which the date is uncertain. Dated 24 January 1607, it is endorsed 'the 24th of December [*a 24 de xbre*] 1606'. At least two other letters were received in twelve or thirteen days, and none took as long as forty-four. Nevertheless, there is no positive evidence that 24 January is the correct date.

¹ Here, and throughout the Zúñiga correspondence, recourse has been had to Sebastián de Covarrubias Orozco's *Tesoro de la Lengua Castellana o Española* (Madrid, 1611; reprinted, Barcelona, 1943).

² Early explorers placed the Bay of Santa Elena at 32° to 32° 30 '. This may have affected Zúñiga's mistake of 32° for 34°.

³ Brown thought *Huane* referred to Sir John (Juan) Trevor, but this seems unlikely to the editor. Sir William Romney seems the least improbable but this is the most that can be said.

They have in mind to obtain from the country above the Cape of Santa Elena[1] the same commodities as from Spain, in the same latitudes, so as to have no need [of Spain]. He [James I] commands that if they reach some river they find its source, to see if in this way they can manage to trade with the Kingdom of China. They want very much for the colony nearest the Cape of Santa Elena to take its route along the coast, and the other to go in a straight line.[2] Your Majesty will see what is most advantageous for your royal service, for all of this is [but] finding a way to encourage your Majesty's rebels, for whom they [the English] feel very sorry on account of their losses on all sides, on the sea as well as on land.

[The remaining two-thirds of the letter relate to other subjects.]

[Endorsed:] London. To His Majesty. [Decoded.]

Don Pedro de Zúñiga, the 24th of December 1606
    Received on the 6th of February [1607]
[Summary of contents.]

9. *9 March 1607.*
Ordinance and Constitution enlarging the Council.[3]

An Ordinance and Constitution enlarging the number of Our Councill for the two severall Colonies and

---

[1] The Cape of Santa Elena was probably modern Hilton Head, on Port Royal Sound. Modern Saint Elena Sound is twenty-odd miles farther north, at 32° 30′.

[2] The meaning of this is far from clear. Since Zúñiga was misinformed as to the proposed southernmost latitude, not to mention his confusion about the location of the northern colony, and had at best a hazy idea of American coastal geography, and since the message was coded in London and decoded in Valladolid (probably by a totally uninformed person), it is useless to try to guess what was meant.

[3] P.R.O., C.O. 5/1354, 49–53, collated with copy in Virginia State Library (referred to as V.S.L.), 'Patents, No. 2, 1643–1651'. Neither copy is very satisfactory, since both are late, that of V.S.L. dating from 1694. The P.R.O. copy is apparently complete, but contains a number of obvious errors. Nevertheless, beyond matters of spelling and punctuation, there is no difference of consequence between the two. First printed by Hening, *Statutes*, I, 76–9, probably from the P.R.O. copy, which was reprinted by Brown, *Genesis*, I, 91–5. V.S.L. copy printed by Bemiss, *Charters*, pp. 23–6, with missing sections supplied from Hening.

Plantations in Virginia and America, between 34. and 45. degrees of Northerly Latitude, and augmenting their Authority, for the better directing and Ordering of such things, as shall concern the said Colonies.
Westm*inste*r 9 March 1607.¹

James by the Grace of God &c*ª*. Whereas Wee by Our Letters Patents under out Great Seal of England, bearing date the tenth day of April last past, haue given Licence to sundry of Our loving Subjects named in the said Letters Patents, and to their Associates to deduce and conduct two severall Collonies or Plantations of sundry of our loving people willing to abide and inhabit in Forreign² parts of Virginia and America, with diuers preheminences, priviledges and Authorities, with other things as in and by the same Letters Patents more particularly it appeareth./

And Whereas Wee according to the effect and true meaning of the said letters Pattents, have by a former instrument signed with Our hands, and Sign Manual, and Sealed with Our Privy Seale of Our Realm of England, Established and ordained, That Our Trusty and wel-beloved Sir W*illia*m Wade Kn*igh*t, Our Lieut*ena*nt of Our Tower of London, Sir Thom*as* Smith Kn*igh*t. Sir Walter Cope Kn*igh*t. Sir George Moor Kn*igh*t. Sir Francis Popham Kn*igh*t. Sir Ferdinando Gorges,³ Kn*igh*t. Sir John Trevor Kn*igh*t. Sir Henry Mountague Kn*igh*t Recorder of Our City of London, Sir W*illia*m Ranmey [Romney] Kn*igh*t. John Dolbridge [Doddridge] Esqu*ire* Our Solicitor Gener*a*ll. Thomas Waire⁴[Warr] Esqu*ire*. John Eldrid [Eldred] of Our City of London Merchant, [Thom*as* James of our Citty of Bristol merch*a*nt;]⁵ and James Bagg of Plymoth in the County of Devon Merchant should be Our Councill for all

---

¹ Omitted in V.S.L. copy.   ² V.S.L., 'certaine'.
³ Written as 'Gee'; under the 'ee' is written 'orges'. V.S.L. copy has 'Georges'.
⁴ The names from Wade to Waire [Warr] are numbered in small figures from 1 to 11, but the person who added the numbers apparently noted the absence of one name (that of Thomas James, supplied from the V.S.L. copy) and did not number either Eldred or Bagg.
⁵ Supplied from the V.S.L. copy.

matters which shall[1] happen in Virginia or in any the Territories of America aforesaid. Or any actions business or Causes for or concerning the same, Which Councill was and[2] is from time to time to be increased altered and changed at the Nomination of Us, Our Heires & Successors, and at Our and their Wills and pleasure./

And whereas Our said Councill haue found by experience their Number being but 14 in all, and most of them dispersed by reason of their seuerall habitations farr remote the one from the other, and many of them in like manner farr remote from Our City of London, where if need require they may receiue directions from Us, & Our Priuy Councill, and from whence directions and Instructions[3] may be by them left, and most[4] readily given for the said Colony,[5] that when very needfull actions[6] requireth, there cannot any competent number of them by any means be drawn together for consultation, for remedy whereof Our loving[7] Subjects of the severall Collonies aforesaid: Haue been Humble Suitors to Us, and haue to that purpose offered to Our Royall consideracion, the names of certaine Sage and discreet persons, and hauing with like humility intreated Us that the said persons or so many of them, as to us shall seem good might be added unto them, and might during Our Pleasure be of Our Councill for Our[8] foresaid Collonies of Our[9] Virginia. Wee therefore for the better Establishing, disposing, Ordering, and directing of the said Severall Collonies within the degrees aforesaid, And of all such Affairs matters and things as shall touch and concern the same Doe by these presents Signed with Our hand and sign Manuall, and Sealed with the Privy Seale of England,[10] Establish and Ordaine That Our Trusty and Well-beloved Sir Thomas

[1] V.S.L., 'should'.
[2] V.S.L. omits 'was and'.
[3] V.S.L., 'Instructions and directions'.
[4] V.S.L., 'more'.
[5] V.S.L., 'colonies'.
[6] V.S.L., 'occasion'.
[7] V.S.L. inserts 'said' before 'loving'.
[8] V.S.L., 'ye'.
[9] V.S.L. omits 'Our'.
[10] V.S.L., 'our Priuy Seale of our Realme of England'.

Chalenor[1] Kn*ight*. S*i*r Henry Nevill Kn*ight*. S*i*r Falke Grenill [Greville] Kn*ight*, S*i*r John Scott Kn*ight*, S*i*r Robert Mantell [Mansell] Kn*ight*, S*i*r Oliuer Cromwell Kn*ight*. S*i*r Maurice Berkeley Kn*ight*. S*i*r Edward Milkbarn [Michelborne] Kn*ight*. S*i*r Thomas Holcroft Kn*ight*. S*i*r Thomas Smith[2] Clarke of Our Pri*u*y Councill S*i*r Robert Killegrew Kn*ight*. S*i*r Herbert Croft Kn*ight*. S*i*r George Coppin Kn*ight*. S*i*r Edward Sanes [Edwin Sandys][3] Kn*ight*. S*i*r Thomas Roe Kn*ight*. S*i*r Anthony Palmer Kn*ight*. Nominated to Us by, and on the behalfe of the said first Colony, S*i*r Edward Hurgerford [Hungerford] Kn*ight*. S*i*r John Mallet Kn*ight*. S*i*r John Gilbert Kn*ight*. S*i*r Thomas Feake [Freake] Kn*ight*. S*i*r Richard Haukins Kn*ight*. S*i*r Barthollomew Mitchell Kn*ight*. Edward Seynior [Seymour] Esqu*ire*. Bernard Greenville Esqu*ire*. Edward Rogers Esqu*ire*, and Mathew Sutcliffe Doctor of Divinity named to Us, by and on behalfe of the said second Colony, Shall together with the persons formerly named, bee *Our* Councill, for all matters which shall or may conduce[4] to the afores*ai*d Plantation,[5] or which shall happen in Virginia, or in[6] any Territories in[7] America, between 34. and 45. degrees of Northerly Latitude, from the Equinoctiall line. And the Islands to the seuerall Collonies limitted and Assigned, that is to say the first Colony from 34. to 41. degrees Northerly latitude.[8] And the second Colony between 38 and 45. degrees of the s*ai*d Latit*u*de.

And Our farther will and pleasure is [and][9] by these presents for Us Our heirs and Successors, [wee][10] do Grant unto the said Councill of Virginia, That they or any twelve of them at the least for the time being, whereof six at the least to be Members of the one of the said Collonies, And six more at least to be members of the said second[11] Colony, Shall haue full power

---

[1] V.S.L. spells this and other names differently.
[2] V.S.L. adds 'Kn*ight*'.
[3] Supplied from V.S.L.
[4] V.S.L., 'conduct'.
[5] V.S.L., 'Plantations'.
[6] V.S.L., omits.
[7] V.S.L., ' of'.
[8] V.S.L., 'degrees of y*e* said latitude'.
[9] Supplied from V.S.L.
[10] Supplied from V.S.L.
[11] V.S.L., 'other'.

and authority to ordaine nominate Elect and chuse any other person or persons at their discretion, to be and to serve as Officer or Officers to all offices & places that shall by them be thought[1] requisit for the business & Affairs of Our said Councill and concerning the Plantation or Plantations aforesaid. And for the Summoning Calling and Assembling of the said Councill, together, when need shall require, or for Summoning or Calling before the said Councill any of the Adventurers or others which shall pass out[2] unto the said seuerall Collonies to inhabit or to Traffique there, or any[3] such like Officer or Officers, which in time shall or may be found of use behoof or Importance unto the Council aforesaid.[4]

And the said Councill or any 12. or more of them as is aforesaid shall in like manner haue full power & Authority from time to time either to continue or to alter or change the said Officers, And to Elect and appoint others in the[ir] rooms & places, And to make & Ordain Acts and Ordinances for the better Ordering, disposing & Marshalling of the said severall Collonies, And the seuerall Adventurer or Adventurers or persons going to Inhabit in the said seuerall Collonys, And of any provision or provisions for the same, Or for the direction of the Officers aforesaid, Or for the making them Subordinate, or under Iurisdiction one of another. And to do and execute euery other Act & things which by any our Grants or Letters Patents heretofore made, they are Warranted or Authoriz'd to do or execute, So as alwaies none of the said Acts & Ordinances, or other things be contrary or repugnant to the true intent & meaning of Our said Letters Patents Granted to the Plantations of the said seuerall Colonies in Virginia, and Territories of America as aforesaid, or contrary to the Laws and Statutes of this Our Realm of England, or in derogacion of Prerogatiue Royall. Witness Our self at Westminster, the ninth

[1] V.S.L. inserts 'fitt and'.
[2] V.S.L., 'on'.
[3] V.S.L. inserts 'other'.
[4] The balance of the P.R.O. text is missing in V.S.L.

day of March, in ye year of Our Raigne of England, France, & Ireland the fourth[1] and of Scotland the Fortieth.[2]

10. *29 July 1607.*
Newport's Letter to Lord Salisbury.[3]

Coppie of a Letter to ye Lord of Salisburie from Captaine Newporte ye 29th of Julie 1607, from Plimouth.

Right Hon*our*able.

My verie good Lord my dutie in most humble wise remembred it maie please your Lordship I arriued here in the sound of Plimouth this daie from the discouery of that parte of Virginia imposed uppon me and the rest of the Colonie for the South parte, in which wee haue performed our duties to the uttermoste of our powers, And haue discouered into the countrie neere two hundred Miles, and a Riuer nauigable for greate shippes one hundred and Fifty miles The Contrie is excellent and verie Riche in gold and Copper,[4] of the gould wee haue brought a Say, and hope to be with your Lordshipp shortlie to shewe it his Majesty and the rest of the Lords, I will not deliver the expectaunce and assurance we haue of greate wealth, but will leaue it to your Lordships Censure when you see the probabilities, I wishe I might haue Come in person to haue brought theis gladd tidings but my inability of body and the not hauing any man to putt in truste[5]

[1] Another hand added the word 'fourth', apparently left blank by the scribe.
[2] Alexander Brown has rightly called attention (*Genesis*, I, 93) to the likelihood of errors in the list of members of the two councils. Sir Thomas Smith, the Clerk, and Sir Anthony Palmer were not members of the first colony, and Greville did not join it until 1617.
[3] Northumberland Papers, Syon House MSS, fo. 268. Calendared in Hist. MSS Comm., Reports, vol. 3, 53–4. Printed, modernized, in Edward D. Neill, *Early Settlement of Virginia and Virginiola*, ... (Minneapolis, 1878); 12; and Brown, *Genesis*, I, 105–6.
[4] The report of gold and copper brought to London by Newport, possibly on Captain Martin's recommendation, led to unnecessary complications.
[5] Master Francis Nelson, later in command of the *Phoenix*, must have been with Newport. One wonders why he was not allowed to bring the ship[s] around to London.

with the shippe and that in her maketh me to defferre my coming till winde and weather be fauourable, And so I moste humblie leaue,

From Plimouth this 29th of Julie 1607
Your L*ordshi*ps moste humbly bounden
Christopher Newporte

11. [*12/*]*22 August 1607.*
Pedro de Zúñiga to Philip III.[1]

22 August, 1607 [n.s.]

Sir:

Of the ships which went to Virginia, one has arrived at Plymouth, and has not yet entered this river, I have learned.[2] They do not come too contented, for in that place there is nothing other than good wood for masts, pine-tree pitch [*pez catran*],[3] and resin, and some earth from which they think they can extract bronze;[4] they say, they think that vineyards can be planted and that these will be very good, because there are many wild grapevines. They have not been able to find the 20 men they left there three years ago now,[5] but they say they found a King who had 150 men in all, whom they left very grateful for a few gifts. I am still trying to learn if they want to keep sending people there, as your Majesty has commanded; since the Lord Chief Justice died, I think this [business] will stop, even though I have heard that, of the ships which went there a year ago, one has returned, [and] they think the voyage easy, as not taking more than a month[6] [*y con auer enten dieb*

---

[1] Decoded. Extract, translated. Archivo General de Simancas. Legajo E 2586, 66. Printed in Brown, *Genesis*, I, 110–11, in translation.

[2] Compare Document 18, pp. 108–10, below.

[3] *Pez* means 'pitch'; *catrán* is from Arabic *qatrân*, 'pitch-like secretion', from the root *qatara*, 'to drip'. The noun *qatrân* is applied particularly to the pitch derived from pine and juniper trees.

[4] Spanish *bronce*; here used undoubtedly for copper.

[5] The reference is obscure. No specific group can be identified with these 20 men.

[6] The whole last sentence is obscure. Obviously, the decoder garbled the message. The meaning, however, seems to be that presented.

(*entendido*) *como delos nauíos que fueron alla* (*hace*, or *ha'*?) *Vnaño seleshatomado* (*se les ha tornado*?) *El Vno, tienen por facil lanauegaçión pornoser demas que un mes*].

[A report on the Dutch 'rebels' follows.]

[Endorsed:] London. To His Majesty. [Decoded.]
    Don Pedro de Zúñiga, the 22nd of August 1607
       Received the 19th of September
[Summary of contents.]

12. *22 June 1607.*
 Letter from the Council in Virginia.[1]

Coppie of a letter from virginia dated 22th of June 1607 the Councell their, to the Councell of virginia here in England.

We acknowledge our selves accomptable for o*ur* time here spent were it but to give you satisfacc*io*n of o*ur* industries and affecc*io*ns to this most hon*ou*rable accion and the better to quicken those good spirritts which haue alreadie bestowed themselves heere and to putt life into such dead vnderstandings or beleefes that muste firste see and feele the wombe of o*ur* labour and this land before they will entertaine any good hope of vs or of the land:

Within lesse then seaven weekes, wee are fortified well against the Indians, we haue sowen good store of wheate. we haue sent yow a taste of Clapboord, wee haue built some houses, wee haue spared some hands to a discouerie and still as god shall enhable vs with strength wee will better and better our proceedinges.

  [1] Northumberland Papers, Syon House MSS, fo. 263. Calendared in Hist. MSS Comm., Reports, vol. 3, 53. Printed in full by Neill in his *Early Settlement of Virginia and Virginiola*, modernized, and copied therefrom by Brown (*Genesis*, I, 106–8). The guess may be hazarded that this official communication was written by Edward Maria Wingfield, then president of the Virginia council in Jamestown.

Our easiest and richest comodity being Sasafrax rootes were gathered vpp by the Sailors with losse and spoile of manie of our tooles and with drawing of our men from our labour to their vses againste our knowledge to our preiudice, wee earnestlie entreate yow (and doe trust) that yow take such order as wee be not in this thus defrauded, since they be all our waged men yett doe wee wishe that they be reasonablie dealt withall so as all the losse neither fall on vs nor them, I beleeue they haue thereof two tonnes at the leaste which if they scatter abroad at their pleasure will pull downe our price for a long time[.][1] this wee leaue to your wisedomes. The land would Flowe with milke and honey if so seconded by your carefull wisedomes and bountifull hands, wee doe not perswade to shoote one Arrowe to seeke another but to finde them both – And wee doubt not but to send them home with goulden heads[.] at leaste our desires, laboures and liues shall to that engage themselues.

wee are sett downe 80. miles within a Riuer,[2] for breadth, sweetnes of water, length navigable vpp into the contry deepe and bold Channell so stored with Sturgion and other sweete Fishe as no mans fortune hath euer possessed the like, And as wee think if more maie be wished in a Riuer it wilbe founde, The soile [is] moste fruictfull, laden with good Oake, Ashe, wallnutt tree, Popler, Pine, sweete woodes, Cedar and others, yett without names that yeald gummes pleasant as Franckumcense, and experienced amongst vs for greate vertewe in healing greene woundes and Aches, wee entreate your succours for our seconds with all expedition leaste that all deuouringe Spaniard lay his rauenous hands uppon theas gold showing

[1] Only five years before, Sir Walter Ralegh had written to Cecil complaining about twenty-two hundredweight of sassafras brought from New England by Gosnold and Gilbert: 'Wheras sarsephraze was worth 10s., 12s., and 20s. a pound before Gilbert returned, his cloying of the market will overthrow all myne, and his owne also' (Edwards, *Ralegh* II, 251). The dumping of nearly twice that amount could indeed pull down the price for a long time.

[2] The correct distance from Jamestown to Cape Henry is fifty-seven miles (see Appendix I).

mountaines, which if we be so enhabled he shall neuer dare to think on:

This noate doth make knowne where our necessities doe moste strike vs, wee beseech your present releiffe accordinglie otherwise to our greatest and laste greifes, wee shall against our willes, not will that which we moste willinglie would:

Captaine Newporte hath seene all and knoweth all, he can fullie satisfie your further expectations, and ease yow of our tedious letters, wee moste humblie praie the heauenly Kings hand to blesse our labours with such counsailes and helpes, as wee may further and stronger proceede in this our Kinges and Contries service

James towne in virginia this 22th of June. An° 1607.

      Your poore Friends

  Edward Maria Wingfeild   Bartholmew Gosnold
  John Smith[1]   John Rattcliffe
  John Martine   George Kendall

13. *21 May – 21 June 1607.*
A relatyon . . . written . . . by a gent. of ye Colony.[2] [Captain Gabriel Archer?]

A relatyon of the Discovery of our River, from James Forte into the Maine: made by Cap*tain* Chr*is*tofer

---

[1] It is noteworthy that Smith's name appears immediately below Wingfield's, even though he had just been released from 'restraint' and sworn a member of the council.

[2] P.R.O., S.P. Colonial, C.O. 1/1, folios 46^r–52^r. Printed along with Documents nos. 14 and 15 by the American Antiquarian Society, in *Archaeologia Americana*, IV (1860), 40–65, generally *ad literam*, but with some errors and several minor alterations. Reprinted therefrom in Arber, *Smith, Works*, pp. xl–lv. Made the subject of a special study in Maurice A. Mook, 'Virginia Ethnology from an Early Relation,' *WMQ*, 2nd ser., XXIII (1943), 101–29. (*Note:* The copy which has been preserved is quite legible, but the scribe has made odd attempts to differentiate between majuscule 'I' and 'J', while leaving 'D' and 'd' virtually indistinguishable. The editor has followed his own judgment in the transcription.)

THE ORIGINAL VOYAGE

Newport:[1] and sincerely written and observed by a gent. of ye Colony.

Thursday the xxjth of May, Cap*tain* Newport (having fitted our shallup with provision and all necessaryes belonging to a discovery) tooke 5 . gentleme*n* . 4 . Maryners . and . 14 . Saylo*urs*, with whome he *p*roceeded with a *p*erfect resolutyon not to returne, but either to finde ye head of this Ryver, the Laake mentyoned by others heretofore, the Sea againe, the Mountaynes Apalatsi, or some issue.[2]

May 21.

The names of the Dysco- verers are thes } Cap*tain* Chr*is*tofer Newport

George Percye esq.
Cap*tain* Gabriell Archer[3]
Cap*tain* Ihon Smyth
M*aster* Ihon Brookes
M*aster* Thom*as* Wotton

Francys Nellson[4]
John Collson[5]
Robert Tyndall[6]
Mathew Fytch
} Maryners

1 Jonas Poole[7]
2 Robert Markham
3 John Crookdeck
4 Olyver Browne
5 Beniamyn White

---

[1] The MS has *xpofer* for Christopher, using the Greek 'chi' and 'rho' ('x' and 'p' in form) as an abbreviation for Christ-, as was common.

[2] 'Some issue' here equals little more than 'something'.

[3] 'Capt: Gabriell Archer' is written in an Italian hand, slightly larger than the other names, while the rest of the document is in secretary hand throughout. This, coupled with characteristics of style and place-naming habits reflected in Archer's previous *Relation* (1602, in Purchas, *Pilgrimes*, XVIII, 302–13), points to him as the author. For brevity's sake, this document is hereafter referred to as *Archer's Relation*.

[4] Nelson was probably already rated 'master', but was not in command of a ship until the following year.

[5] Collson is written Cotson below (p. 97).

[6] Tyndall (better, Tindall) was in the service of Prince Henry (see Document no. 16, below).

[7] 'Corporal' Jonas Poole left several accounts of voyages with Richard Hakluyt, at least some of which were printed in Purchas, *Pilgrimage* (1614 ed.), 742, and *Pilgrimes*, XIII, 11, 195, 265–93; and XIV, 1–24, and 34–47. He was often in the service of the Muscovy Company, and may have been at this time.

JAMESTOWN VOYAGES

6 Rych*ard* Genoway
7 Tho*mas* Turnbrydg
8 Tho*mas* Godword
9 Robert Jackson
10 Charles Clarke
11 Stephen
12 Thomas Skynner
13 Jeremy Deale
14 Danyell[1]

Thus from James Fort we tooke our leaue about noone, and by night we were vp the Ryver . 18 . myle at a lowe meadow point, which I call Wynauk.[2] Here came the people, and entertayned vs with Daunces and much reioycing. This kyngdome Wynauk is full of pearle muskles. the kyng of Paspeiouh[3] and this king is at oddes, as the Paspeians tould me, and Demonstrated by their hurtes: heere we anckored all night.

May 22

Fryday, omitting no tyme, we passed vp some . 16 . myle further, where we founde an Ilet, on which were many Turkeys,[4] and greate store of yonge byrdes like Black birdes, whereof wee tooke Dyvers, which wee brake our fast withall. Now spying . 8 . salvages in a Canoa, we haled them by our worde of kyndnes; Wingapoh,[5] and they came to vs. In conference by signes with them, one seemed to vnderstand our intentyon, and offred with his foote to describe the river to vs: So I gaue him a pen and paper (shewing first ye vse) and he layd out the whole River from the Chesseian[6] bay to the end of it so farr as passadg was for boates: he tolde vs of two

[1] None of the fourteen sailors appear to have remained in, or returned to, Virginia.
[2] See Appendix I. Archer's spelling was influenced by Thomas Hariot's word for sassafras (Quinn, *Roanoke*, I, 329). Sassafras may have been found growing there.
[3] One of the fifty-or-so recorded spellings of the name. See Appendix I.
[4] The turkey was an indigenous wild fowl in North America which had been domesticated only in Mexico (and perhaps Guatemala). It had been known in England for at least fifty years. On Turkey Island, see Appendix I.
[5] See Appendix I.
[6] Chesseian was apparently a mistake for Chesepian, which is written correctly below (p. 85). See Appendix I.

Ilettes in the Ryver we should passe by, meaning that one whereon we were, and then come to an overfall of water, beyond that of two kyngdomes which the Ryver Runes by then a greate Distance of[f], the mountaines Quirank[1] as he named them: beyond which by his relation is that which we expected. This fellow parting from vs promised to procure vs wheate if we would stay a little before, and for that intent went back againe to provide it: but we coming by the place where he was, with many more very Desirous of our Company, stayd not, as being eagre of our good tydinges. He notwithstanding with two wemen and another fellow of his owne consort, followed vs some sixe mile with basketes full of Dryed oysters, and mett vs at a point, where calling to vs, we went ashore and bartred with them for most of their victualls. Here the shoare began to be full of greate Cobble stones, and higher land. The Ryver skantes of his breadth . 2 . mile before we come to the Ilet mentyoned which I call Turkey Ile: yet keepes it a quarter of a mile broade most comonly, and depe water for ⟨fishing⟩[2] shipping. This fellow with the rest overtooke vs agayne vpon the doubling of another point: Now they had gotten mulberyes, little sweete nuttes like Acorns (a verye good fruite) wheate, beanes and mulberyes sodd together and gaue vs. Some of them desired to be sett over the Ryver, which we dyd, and they parted. Now we passed a Reach of . 3 . mile $\frac{1}{2}$. in length, highe stony grownd on Popham syde . 5 . or 6 . fadome . 8 . oares length from the shoare. This daye we went about . 38 . mile and came to an Ankre at a place I call poore Cottage;[3] where we went ashore, and were vsed kyndly by the people, wee sodd our kettle by y^e water syde within nighte, and rested aboorde.

Satterday we passed a few short reaches; and . 5 . mile of poore May 23
Cottage we went a shore. Heer we found our kinde Comrades

[1] The final 'h' of the original manuscript has been corrected to a 'k'. See Appendix I.
[2] Crossed out in the original.
[3] 'Poor Cottage' was possibly the Indian village noted by John Smith opposite the westernmost bit of Farrar's Island. See Appendix I.

againe, who had gyven notice all along as they came of vs: by which we were entertayned with much Courtesye in every place. We found here a Wiroans[1] (for so they call their kynges) who satt vpon a matt of Reedes, with his people about him: He caused one to be layd for Capt*ain* Newport, gaue vs a Deare roasted; which according to their Custome they seethed againe: His people gaue vs mullberyes, sodd wheate and beanes, and he caused his weomen to make Cakes for vs. He gaue our Capt*aine* his Crowne which was of Deares hayre dyed redl [redd]. Certifying him of our intentyon vp the Ryver, he was willing to send guydes with vs. This we found to be a kyng subiect to Pawatah[2] (the Cheife of all the kyng-domes) his name is Arahatec: the Country Arahatecoh.[3] Now as we satt merye banquetting with them, seeing their Daunces, and taking Tobacco, Newes came that the greate kyng Powatah was come: at whose presence they all rose of their mattes (saue the k*yng* Arahatec); sep*ar*ated themselues ap*ar*te in fashion of a Guard, and with a long shout they saluted him. Him wee saluted with silence sitting still on our mattes, our Capt*aine* in the myddest; but presented (as before we dyd to k*yng* Arahatec) gyftes of dyvers sortes, as penny knyves, sheeres, belles, beades, glasse toyes &c. more amply then before. Now this king appointed . 5 . men to guyde vs vp the River, and sent Postes before to provyde vs victuall. I caused now our kynde Consort that described the River to vs, to draw it againe before kyng Arahatec, who in euery thing consented to this draught, and it agreed with his first relatyon. This we found a faythfull fellow, he was one that was appointed guyde for vs. Thus p*ar*ting from Arahatecs ioye, we found the people on either syde the Ryver stand in Clusters all along, still proferring vs victualls, which of some were accepted; as our guydes (that were with vs in the boate) pleased, and gaue them requitall. So

---

[1] Werowance is the usual spelling today. See Appendix I.

[2] This is the earliest mention of Powhatan, See Appendix I and the notes on Document no. 33, below (p. 181).

[3] The usual spelling is Arrohattoc for both. See Appendix I.

THE ORIGINAL VOYAGE

after we had passed some 10 . myle, which (by the pleasure and ioye we tooke of our kinde interteynment, and for the Comfort of our happy & hopefull Discovery) we accompted scarce . 5 . we came to the second Ilet Described in the Ryver; over against which on Popham syde is the habitatyon of the greate kyng Pawatah: which I call Pawatahs Towre;[1] it is scituat vpon a highe Hill by the water syde, a playne betweene it and the water . 12 . score over, wheron he sowes his wheate, beane, peaze, tobacco, pompions, gowrdes, Hempe, flaxe &c. And were any Art vsed to the naturall state of this place, it would be a goodly habitatyon: Heere we were conducted vp the Hill to the kyng, with whome we found our kinde king Arahatec: Thes . 2 . satt by themselues aparte from all the rest (saue one who satt by Powatah, and what he was I could not gesse but they told me he was no Wiroans): Many of his company satt on either syde: and the mattes for vs were layde right over against the kynges. He caused his weomen to bring vs vittailes, mulberyes, strawberryes &c. but our best entertaynment was frendly wellcome. In discoursing with him, we founde that all the kyngdomes from the [word blanked out – Chessipians?] were frendes with him, and (to vse his owne worde) Cheisc.[2] which is all one with him or vnder him. Also wee perceived the Chessipian to be an Enemye generally to all thes kyngdomes: vpon which I tooke occasion to signifye our displeasure with them also: making it knowne y^t we refused to plant in their Country; that we had warres with them also, shewing hurtes scarce whole received by them, for which we vowed revenge, after their maner, pointing to the Sunne: Further we certifyed him that we were frendes with all his people & kyngdomes, neither had any of them offred vs ill, or vsed vs vnkyndly. Herevpon he (very well vnderstanding by the wordes and signes we made; the significatyon of our mean-

[1] While there can be little doubt that Archer's 'ilet' is modern Mayo's Island, the area generally is so built up by now that the archaeological work necessary to fix the spot definitively will prove difficult, if not impossible.
[2] See Appendix I.

ing) moved of his owne accord a leauge of fryndship with vs; which our Capt*ain* kyndly imbraced; and for concluding therof, gaue him his gowne, put it on his back himselfe, and laying his hand on his breast saying Wingapoh Chemuze[1] (the most kynde wordes of salutatyon that may be) he satt downe. Now the Day Drawing on, we made signe to be gone, wherwith he was contented; and sent . 6 . men with vs: we also left a man with him, and dep*ar*ted. But now rowing some 3 . myle in shold water we came to an overfall, impassible for boates any further. Here the water falles Downe through great mayne Rockes, from ledges of Rockes aboue . 2 . fadome highe: in which fall it maketh Divers little Ilettes, on which might be placed 100 . water milnes for any vses. Our mayne Ryver ebbs and flowes . 4 . foote even to ye skert of this Downfall. Shippes of . 200 . or . 300 . toon*n*e may come to within . 5 . myle hereof, and the rest Deepe inoughe for Barges, or small vessells that drawe not aboue . 6 . foote water. Having viewed this place, betweene Content and greefe we left it for this night, determyning the next Day to fitt our selfe for a march by Land. So we road all night betweene Pawatahs Tower and that Ilet I call   wheron is 6 . or . 7 . families. One of our Guydes which we had from Arahatacs Ioy whose name was Nauirans,[2] and now we found to be brother in Lawe to k*ing* Arahatec, desired to sleepe in the boate with vs: we p*er*mitted him, and vsed him with all the kyndnes we coulde: He proved a very trustye frend, as after is Declared. Now we sent for our man to Pawatah, who coming tolde vs of his entertaynm*ent*, how they had prepared mattes for him to lye on, gaue him store of victualls, and made asmuch on him as coulde be./

May 24 Sonday, Whitsonday, our Captayne caused two peeces of porke to be sodd a shore with pease; to which he invyted K*ing* Pawatah: for Arahatec p*er*swading himselfe we would come Downe the Ryver that night, went home before Dynner, for

---

[1] Apparently miscopied, for *chemay* or *chemah*. See Appendix I.
[2] Written as Nauirans and Nauiraus. See Appendix I.

preparatyon against our Coming. But in presence of them both it fell out that we missing two bullet-bagges which had shot and Dyvers trucking toyes in them: we Complayned to theis kynges, who instantly caused them all to be restored, not wanting any thing. Howbeit they had Devyded the shott and toyes to (at least) a dozen seuerall persons; and those also in the Ilet over the water: One also having stollen a knyfe, brought it againe vpon this Comaunde before we supposed it lost, or had made any signe for it: So Captaine Newport gaue thanckes to the Kinges and rewarded the theeves with the same toyes they had stollen, but kept the bulletes: yet he made knowne vnto them the Custome of England to be Death for such offences.

Now Arahatec departed, and it being Dynner tyme, King Pawatah with some of his people satt with vs, brought of his Dyet, & we fedd familiarly, without sitting in his state as before; he eat very freshly of our meate, Dranck of our beere, Aquavite, and Sack. Dynner Done we entred into Discourse of the Ryver how far it might be to the head therof, where they gat their Copper, and their Iron, and how many Dayes Iornye it was to Monanacah, Rahowacah and the Mountaines Quirank:[1] requesting him to haue guydes with vs also in our intended march; for our Captaine Determyned to haue travelled two or . 3 . dayes Iornye a foote vp the Ryver: but without gyving any answer to our Demaundes, he shewde he would meete vs himselfe at the overfall and so we [illegible word crossed out] parted. This Nauirans accompanyed vs still in the boate. According to his promyse he [Pawatah] mett vs; where the fellow whome I haue called our kynde Consort, he that followed vs from Turkey Ile, at the Coming of Pawatah made signe to vs we must make a shoute, which we Dyd. Now sitting vpon the banck by the overfall beholding the same, he began to tell vs of the tedyous travell we should haue if wee

---

[1] The first of these is usually spelled Monacan today, after the Monacan tribe of Indians. The nearest town of the Monacans was the village later known as Mowhemcho, some twelve miles above Mayo's Island. See Appendix I.

proceeded any further, that it was a Daye and a halfe Iorney to Monanacah, and if we Went to Quirank, we should get no vittailes and be tyred, and sought by all meanes to disswade our Captayne from going any further: Also he tolde vs y^t the Monanacah was his Enimye, and that he came Downe at the fall of the leafe and invaded his Countrye. Now What I coniecture of this I haue left to a further experience. But our Captayne out of his Discretyon (though we would faine haue seene further, yea and himselfe as Desirous also) Checkt his intentyon and retorned to his boate; as holding it much better to please the kyng (with whome and all of his Comaund he had made so faire Way) then to prosecute his owne fancye or satisfye our requestes: So vpon one of the little Ilettes at the mouth of the falls he sett vp a Crosse with this inscriptyon Jacobus Rex. 1607. and his owne name belowe: At the erecting hereof we prayed for our kyng and our owne prosperous succes in this his Actyon, and proclaymed him kyng, with a greate showte. The kyng Pawatah was now gone (and as we noted somwhat Distasted with our importunity of proceeding vp further) and all the Salvages likewise saue Nauirans, who seeing vs set vp a Crosse with such a shoute, began to admire; but our Captayne told him that the two Armes of the Crosse signifyed kyng Powatah and himselfe, the fastening of it in the myddest was their vnited Leaug, and the shoute the reverence he dyd to Pawatah. which cheered Nauirans not a litle. Also (which I haue omytted) our Captayne before Pawatah Departed shewed him that if he would, he would gyve the Wiroans of Monanacah into his handes, and make him king of that Country, making signes to bring to his ayde . 500 . men, which pleased the kyng muche, and vpon this (I noted) he told vs the tyme of the yere when his enemyes assaile him.

So farr as we could Discerne the River aboue the overfall, it was full of huge Rockes: About a myle of[f], it makes a pretty bigg Iland;[1] It rvnnes vp betweene highe Hilles which increase

[1] Very likely Belle Isle is meant.

in height one aboue another so farr as wee sawe. Now our kynde Consortes relatyon sayth (which I dare Well beleeve, in that I found not any one report false of the River so farr as we tryed, or that he tolde vs vntruth in any thing ells whatsoeuer) that after a Dayes iorney or more, this River devydes it selfe into two branches, which both come from the mountaynes Quirank. Here he whispered with me that their caquassan[1] was gott in the bites of Rockes and betweene Cliffes in certayne vaynes.

Having ended thus of force our Discovery, our Captayne intended to call of kyng Pawatah, and sending Nauirans vp to him he came downe to the water syde, where he went a shore single vnto him, presented him with a hatchet, and staying but till Nauiraus had tolde (as we trewly perceived) the meaning of our setting vp the Crosse, which we found Dyd exceedingly reioyce him, he came a boorde, with the kyndest farewell that possible might be. Now at our putting of[f] the boate, Nauirans willed vs to make a shout, which we Dyd two seuerall times, at which y*e King* and his Company weaved their skinnes about their heades answering our shout with gladnes in a frendly fashion.

This night (though late) we came to Arahatec Joy, where we found the k*ing* ready to entertayne vs, and had provided some victualls for vs, but he tolde vs he was very sick, & not able to sitt vp long with vs, so we repaired aborde.

Monday he came to the Water syde, and we went a shore to him agayne. He tolde vs that our hott Drynckes he thought caused his greefe, but that he was well agayne, and we were very wellcome. He sent for another Deere which was roasted and after sodd for vs (as before) Our Captayne caused his Dynner to be Dressed a shore also. Thus we satt banquetting all the forenoone. some of his people led vs to their houses, shewed vs the growing of their Corne & the maner of setting it, gave vs Tobacco, wallnutes, mulberyes, strawberryes, and

May 25

---

[1] By implication, the word means 'copper'. See Appendix I.

Respises. One shewed vs the herbe called in their tongue wisacan,[1] which they say heales poysoned woundes, it is like lyverwort or bloudwort. One gaue me a Roote wherewith they poison their Arrowes . they would shew vs any thing we Demaunded, and laboured very much by signes to make vs vnderstand their Languadg.

Nauiraus our guyde and this K*ings* brother made a complaint to Arahatec, that one of his people prest into our boate to[o] vyolently vpon a man of ours; which Capt*aine* Newport (vnderstanding the pronenes of his owne men to such iniuryes) misconstruing the matter, sent for his owne man, bound him to a tree before K*ing* Arahatec, and with a Cudgell soundly beate him. the king p*er*ceiveing the error, stept vp and stayde o*ur* Captaynes hand And sytting still a while, he spyed his owne man that Dyd the iniurye: vpon which he s[i]lently rose, and made towardes the fellow, he seeing him come, rvn*n* away, after ran the king, so swiftly as I assure my selfe he might gyve any of our Company . 6 . score in . 12 . with the king ran also Dyvers others, who all returning brought Cudgells and wandes in their handes all to be tewed, as if they had beaten him extreamly. At Dynner our Captayne gaue the kyng a glasse and some Aquavitæ therin, shewing him the benefytt of the Water, for which he thanckt him kindly: and taking our Leaue of him, he promised to meete vs at a point not farr of: where he hath another house, which he p*er*formed, withall, sending men into the woodes to kill a Dere for vs if they could. This place I call mulbery shade.[2] He caused heere to be prepared for vs pegatewk-Apoan[3] which is bread of their wheat made in Rolles and Cakes; this the weomen make, & are very clenly about it; We had parched meale, excellent good, sodd beanes, which eate as

[1] Variously spelled. See Appendix I.
[2] Probably the Indian village shown on Smith's map just east of Arrohattoc. See Appendix I.
[3] The second element is misprinted *Apyan* in Arber's *Smith, Works* (xlviii). (The infralinear shaft of the 'p' has been swung to the right until it touches the base of the 'o'. The scribe attempted to correct this by putting a diaeresis over the 'o' (ö) but this seems to have been ignored.) See Appendix I.

sweete as filbert kernells in a maner, strawberryes & mulberyes new shaken of the tree dropping on our heades as we satt: He made ready a land turtle which we eate, & shewed that he was hartely reioyced in our Company. He was Desirous to haue a Musket shott of[f], shewing first the maner of their owne skirmishes, which we perceive is violent Cruell and full of Celerity; they vse a tree to Defend them in fight, and having shott an Enemy that he fall, they maull him with a short wodden sworde. Our Captayne caused a gentleman Discharge his peece Souldyer like before him, at which noyse he started, stopt his eares, and exprest much feare, so likewise all about him; some of his people being in our boate leapt over boorde at the wonder hereof: but our course of kyndnes after, & letting him to witt that wee neuer vse this thunder but against our enemyes, yea and that we would assist him with thes to Terrify & kill his Adversaryes, he reioyced the more, and we found it bred a better affectyon in him towardes vs; so that by his signes we vnderstood he would or [ere] long be with vs at our Fort. Captayne Newport bestowed on him a redd wastcote, which highly pleased him, and so Departed, gyving him also . 2 . shoutes as the boate went of. This night we Went some mile, and ankored at a place I Call kynd womans care[1] which is   mile from Mulbery shade. Here we came within night, yet was there ready for vs of bread new made, sodden wheate and beanes, mullberyes, and some fishe vndressed more then all we could eate. Moreover thes people seemed not to craue any thing in requitall, Howbeit our Captain voluntarily distributed guiftes.

Tuesday We parted from kynd womans care, and by Directyon of Nauirans (who still accompanyed in the boate with vs) went a shore at a place I call Queene Apumatecs bowre.[2] He caryed

May 26

---

[1] Since there is a blank in the manuscript where the distance from Mulberry Shade should be entered, it is impossible to locate Kind Woman's Care with any degree of accuracy. See Appendix I.

[2] Queen Appomattoc's Bower has been located fairly accurately at or near the present village of Bermuda Hundred. See Appendix I.

vs along through a plaine Lowe grownd prepared for seede, part wherof had ben lately Cropt: and assending a pretty Hill, we sawe the Queene of this Country comminge in selfe same fashion of state as Pawatah or Arahatec; yea rather with more maiesty: she had an vsher before her who brought her to the matt prepared vnder a faire mulbery tree, where she satt her Downe by her selfe with a stayed Countenance. she would permitt none to stand or sitt neere her: she is a fatt lustie manly woman: she had much Copper about her neck, a Crownet of Copper vpon her hed: she had long black haire, which hanged loose downe her back to her myddle, which only part was Covered with a Deares skyn, & ells all naked. She had her woemen attending on her adorned much like her selfe (saue they Wanted ye Copper). Here we had our accustomed Cates, Tobacco and wellcome. Our Captayne presented her with guyftes liberally, whervpon shee cheered somwhat her Countenance; and requested him to shoote of[f] a peece wherat (wee noted) she shewed not neere the like feare as Arahatec though he be a goodly man. She had much Corne in the grownd: she is subiect to Pawatah as the rest are; yet within herselfe of as greate authority as any of her neighbour Wy[r]oances. Captain Newport stayd here some . 2 . houres & Departed.

Now Leaving her, Nauiraus Dyrected vs to one of kyng Pamaunches howses[1] some . 5 . myle from the Queenes Bower.

Here We were entertayned with greate ioye and gladnes, the people falling to Daunce, the weomen to preparing vitailes, some boyes were sent to Dive for muskles, they gaue vs Tobacco, and very kyndly saluted vs.

This kyng (sitting in maner of the rest) so set his Countenance stryving to be stately, as to our seeming he became foole. Wee gaue him many presentes, and certifyed him of our Iorney to ye falles our League with the greate kyng Pawatah, a most

---

[1] The stated distance makes the identification of this 'house' extremely difficult, unless the route was more circuitous than seems logical today. See p. 94, n. 1.

certayne frendship with Arahatec and kynde entertaynment of the Queene: that we were professed Enemyes to the Chessepians, and would assist King Pawatah against the Monanacans; with this he seemed to be much reioyced; and he would haue had our Captayne staye with him all night, which he refused not, but single with the king walked aboue two flight shott,[1] shewing therby his trew meaning without Distrust or feare. Howbeit, we followed a Loofe of[f],[2] and coming vp to a gallant mulbery tree, we founde Divers preparing vittailes for vs: but the kyng seing our intentyon Was to accompany our Captaine, he alltered his purpose and weaved vs in kyndnes to our boate. This Wyroans Pamaunche I holde to inhabite a Rych land of Copper and pearle. His Country lyes into the land to another Ryver, which by relatyon and Descriptyon of the Salvages comes also comes also from the Mountaynes Quirank, but a shorter Iorney. The Copper he had, as also many of his people, was very flexible, I bowed a peece of the thickness of a shilling rounde about my finger, as if it had ben lead: I found them nice in parting with any; They weare it in their eares, about their neckes in Long lynckes, and in broade plates on their heades: So we made no greate enquyry of it, neither seemed Desirous to haue it. The kyng had a Chaine of pearle about his neck thrice Double, the third parte of them as bygg as pease, which I could not valew lesse worth then . 3 . or . 400 .[11] had the pearle ben taken from the muskle as it ought to be. His kyngdome is full of Deare (so also is moste of all the kyngdomes:) he hath (as the rest likewise) many ryche furres. This place I call Pamaunches pallace, howbeit by Nauviraus his wordes the kyng of Winauk is possessor hereof. The platt of grownd is bare without wood some . 100 . acres, where are set beanes, wheate, peaze, Tobacco, Gourdes, pompions, and other thinges vnknowne to vs in our tongue.

[1] In 1538, John Leland described a flight shot as 'as much as the Tamise is above the bridge' (*OED*), or about three hundred yards.
[2] Note that 'of[f]' strengthened the meaning: 'very far off'.

Now having left this kyng in kyndnes and frendship: We crossed over the Water to a sharpe point which is parte of Winauk on Salisbury syde (this I call careles point)[1] Here some of our men went a shore with Nauiraus, mett . 10 . or . 12 . Salvages, who offering them neither victualls nor Tobacco, they requitted their Courtesy with the like, and left them. This night we came to point Winauk right against which we rested all night. There was an olde man with King Pamaunche (which I omitted in place to specify) who wee vnderstood to be . 110 . yere olde; for Nauirans with being with vs in our boate had learned me so much of the Languadg, & was so excellently ingenious in signing out his meaning, that I could make him vnderstand me, and perceive him also wellny in any thing. But this knowledg our Captaine gatt by taking a bough and singling of the leaues, let one drop after another, saying caische which is . 10[2] . so first Nauirans tooke . 11 . beanes and tolde them to vs, pointing to this olde fellow, then 110 . beanes; by which he awnswered to our demaund for . 10 . yeres a beane, and also euery yere by it selfe. This was a lustye olde man, of a sterne Countenance, tall & straight, had a thinne white beard, his armes overgrowne with white haires, and he went as strongly as any of the rest.

May 27   Wensday we went a shore at point Winauk, where Nauiraus caused them to goe a fisshing for vs, and they brought vs in a shorte space good store: Thes seemed our good frindes but (the cause I knowe not) heere Nauirans tooke some Conceyt, and though he shewed no discontent, yet would he by no meanes goe any further with vs; saying he would but goe vpto kyng Arahatek, and then within some three dayes after he would see vs at our Fort. This greeved out Captayne very Deeply, for the loving kyndnes of this fellow was such as he trusted himselfe with vs out of his owne Country, intended to come to our Forte, and as wee came he would make frendship

[1] Careless Point is hardly mistakeable. It is modern Jordan Point. See Appendix I.
[2] See Appendix I.

for vs, before he would lett vs goe a shore at any place, being (as it seemed) very carefull of our safety. So our Captayne made all haste home, Determyning not to stay in any place as fearing some disastrous happ at our forte. Which fell out as we expected, thus. After our Departure they seeldome frequented our Fort, but by one or two single now and then, practising vpon oportunity, now in our absence, perceiving there secure Caryadg in the fort; and the xxvjth of May being ye Day before our returne, there came aboue . 200 . of them with their kyng and gaue a very furious Assault to our fort, endaungering their overthrowe, had not the Shippes ordinance with their small shott daunted them: They came vp allmost into the Fort, shott through the tentes, appeared in this Skirmishe (which indured hott about an hower) a very valiant people: they hurt vs . 11 . men (wherof one dyed after) and killed a Boy, yet perceived they not this Hurt in vs. We killed Dyvers of them, but one wee sawe them tugg of[f] on ther backes, and how many hurt we knowe not. A little after they made a huge noyse in the woodes, which our men surmised was at ye burying of their slayne men. Foure of the Counsell that stood in front were hurt in mayntayning the Forte, and our president Master Wynckfeild (who shewed himselfe a valiant Gentleman) had one shott cleane through his bearde, yet scaped hurte.

> Thus having ended our Discovery, which we hope may tend to the glory of God, his Maiesties Renowme our Countryes profytt, our owne advauncing, and fame to all posterity: we settled our selues to our owne safety, and began to fortefye; Captayne Newport worthely of his owne accord causing his Sea men to ayde vs in the best parte therof.

Thursday We Laboured, pallozadoing our fort.   May 28
Fryday the Salvages gaue on againe, but with more feare, not   29
daring approche scarce within musket shott: they hurt not any

JAMESTOWN VOYAGES

of vs, but finding one of our dogges they killed him: they shott aboue . 40 . arrowes into, & about the forte.

[May] 30   Satterday, we were quyet.

Sunday they came lurking in the thicketes and long grasse; and a Gent*leman* one Eustace Clovell vnarmed stragling without the Fort, shott . 6 . Arrowes into him, wherwith he came rvninge into the Fort, crying Arme Arme, thes stycking still: He lyved . 8 . Dayes, and Dyed. The Salvages stayed not, but rvn away.

Jvne 1   Monday some . 20 . appeared, shott Dyvers Arrowes at randome which fell short of our Forte, and rann away.

2   Tuesday ⎫ quyet & wrought vpo*n* fortification, Clapboord,
3   Wensday ⎭ & setting of Corne.

4   Thursday by breake of Day . 3 . of them had most adventurously stollen vnder our Bullwark and hidden themselues in the long grasse; spyed a man of ours going out to doe naturall necessity, shott him in the head, and through the Clothes in two places, but missed the skynne.

5   Friday. quyet.

6   Satterday there being among the Gent*lemen* and all the Company a murmur and grudg against certayne p*re*posterous proceedinges, and inconvenyent Courses, put vp a Petytion to the Counsell for reformatyon.

7   Sonday. no accydent.

8   Monday. M*aster* Clovell dyed that was shott with . 6 . Arrowes sticking in him. This afternoone . 2 . salvages presented themselues vnarmed a farr of Crying Wingapoh; there were also three more having bowe and arrowes: those we Coniectured came from some of those kinges with whome We had p*er*fect league: but one of our Gent*lemen* garding in the woodes and having no Comaundem*en*t to the Contrary shott at them: at which (as their Custome is) they fell downe, and after rvn away: yet farther of[f] we heard them crye Wingapoh notwithstanding.

9   Tuesday in cutting downe a greate oke for Clapboord, there

96

issued out of the hart of the tree the quantity of two barricoes of liquor, in taste as good as any vyneger, saue a little smack it tooke of the oke.

Wensday the Counsell scanned the Gentlemans Petityon: wherin Captayne Newport shewing himselfe no lesse Carefull of our Amitye and Combyned frendship, then became him in the deepe Desire he had of our good; vehemently with ardent affectyo*n* wonne our hartes by his fervent p*er*swasyon, to vniformity of Consent, and Callmed that, out of our Loue to him, with ease, which I doubt without better satisfactyon had not contentedly ben caryed. Wee confirmed a faythfull Loue one to another, and in our hartes subscribed an obedyence to our Superyo*ur*s this Day. Captaine Smyth was this Day sworne one of the Counsell, who was elected in England. [Jvne] 10

Thursday, Articles and orders for Gent*lemen* and Soldyers were vpon the Court of Garde, & Content was in the Quarter. 11

Fryday, Cutting downe another tree, the like accident of vineger proceeded. 12

Satterday. 8 . salvages lay close among the weedes and long grasse: and spying one or two of our Maryners M*aste*r Ihon Cotson and M*aste*r Mathew Fitch by themselues, shott Mathew Fytch in the breast somwhat Dangerously, and so rann away this Morning. Our Admiralls men gatt a Sturgeon of. 7. foote long which Captayne Newport gaue vs. 13

Sondaye, two salvages presented themselues vnarmed, to whome our President and Captaine Newport went out. one of these was that fellow I call in my Relatyon of Discovery our kinde Consort, being hee we mett at Turkye Ile. These certifyed vs who were our frendes, and who foes, saying that kyng Pamaunke kyng Arahatec, the kyng of Youghtamong,[1] and the king of Matapoll[2] would either assist vs or make vs peace with Paspeiouk, Tapahanauk,[3] Wynauk, Apamatecoh, 14

[1] This should be spelled Youghtanund. See Appendix I.
[2] The preferred spelling is Mattapanient, although Mattaponi has been perpetuated in the river-name. See Appendix I.
[3] The correct name of this village and tribe was Quiyoughcohannock. See Appendix I.

JAMESTOWN VOYAGES

and Chescaik,¹ our Contracted Enemyes: He counselled vs to Cutt Downe the long weedes rounde about our Forte, and to proceede in our sawing: Thus making signes to be with vs shortly agayne, they parted.

[Jvne] 15 Monday, we wrought vpon Clapborde for England.

16 Tuesday, two salvages without from Salisbury syde being Tapahanauks Country, Captayne Newport went to them in the barge ymagining they had ben our Sonday frendes: but thes were Tapahanauks and cryed (treacherously) Wingapoh, saying their king was on the other syde of a point, where had our Barge gone it was so shold water² as they might haue effected their villanous plott: but our Admirall tolde them Tapahanauk was matah & chirah,³ wherat laughing they went away.

17 Wensdaye.
18 Thursdaye.
19 Frydaye. } no Accydent
20 Satterday.

21 Sondaye, we had a Communyon: Captaine Newport Dyned a shore with our Dyet, and invyted many of vs to Supper as a farewell.

14. *21 May–21 June 1607.*
*Description of the River and Country.*⁴

The Discription of the now discovered River and Country of Virginia; with the Liklyhood of ensuing ritches, by Englands ayd and industry. /

The kings River

This River (we have named o*u*r kinges River) extendes it self

¹ Smith's Kiskiack. See Appendix I.
² The reference undoubtedly is to the shoal water at the mouth of Gray's Creek, opposite Jamestown.
³ See Appendix I.
⁴ P.R.O., S.P. Colonial, C.O. 1/1, folios 53ʳ–55ʳ. Other bibliographical details the same as for Document no. 13. The handwriting, however, is different, and appears less careful At the same time, the style is still that of Gabriel Archer, and there is evidence that he was the author of this document as well.

98

160 myles¹ into the mayne land betwene two fertile and fragrant bankes, two miles, a mile, & where it is least a quarter of a myle broad, navigable for shipping of 300 tunn 150 miles: the rest deep enough for small vessels of six foot draught; it ebbs and flowes 4 foote, even to the skirt of an overfall, where the water falls downe from huge great Rockes: making in the fall five or six severall Ilettes, very fitt for the buylding of water milnes thereon, beyond this not two dayes iourney, it hath two branches which come through a high stoney Country from certaine huge mountaines called Quirank, beyond which needes no relacion (this from the overfall was the report and discription of a faithfull fellow, who I dare well trust vpon good reasons) from these mountaines Quirank come two lesse rivers which runn into this great one,² but whether deep enough for shipps or noe I yet vnderstand not, here be many small Rivers of brookes which vnlade them selues into this mayne river at severall mouthes, which veynes³ devide the salvage kingdomes in many places, and yeeld pleasant seates, in all the Country over by moystening the frutefull mould. The mayne river aboundes with Sturgeon very large and excellent good: having also at the mouth of every brook and in every creek both store and exceeding good fish of divers kindes, and in yᵉ large soundes neere the sea are multitudes of fish, bankes of oysters, and many great crabbs rather better in tast then ours, one able to suffice 4 men: And within sight of land into the sea we expect at tyme of yeare⁴ to have a good fishing for codd: as both at our first entring we might perceive by palpable coniecture seeing the codd follow the shipp yea bite at the as also out of my owne experience not farre of[f]

An overfall

Many small Rivers

Sturgeon

multitudes of fish

Coddfish

---

¹ A reasonably accurate estimate, if Cape Henry is the starting point. By water, the distance from there to Mayo's Island, Richmond, is about 131 statute miles (see Appendix 1).
² The Rivanna joins the James about forty miles west of Richmond by modern road, in the heart of what was then hostile country. An Indian could certainly have made the trip in less than two days, and it was to Powhatan's interest to know how far away the chief village of his non-Algonkian enemy neighbour lay.
³ Obsolete, 'rivulets' (*OED*).   ⁴ Something seems to be left out.

to the northward, the fishing I found in my first voyage to Virginia.[1]

The lands discription Lowland

This land lyeth low at the mouth of the River & is sandy ground, all over besett with fayre pyne trees: but a litle vp the river it is reasonable high; and the further we goe (till we come to the overfall) it still ryseth increasing. It is generally replenisht

full of wood

with wood of all kindes and that the fayrest yea and best that ever any of vs (traveller or workman) ever sawe, being fitt for any vse whatsoeuer, as shipps, howses, plankes, pales boordes mastes, waynscott, Clappboord, for pikes or elswhat.

A frutefull soyle

The soyle is more fertill then canbe wel exprest it is altogether Aromaticall giving a spicy tast to the rootes of all trees plantes and hearbs: of it self a black fatt sandy mould, somewhat slymy in touch and sweet in savour: vnder which about a yard is in most places a redd clay fitt for brick, in other marle, in some, signification of mynnerall, in other gravell stones and rockes, it hath in diverse places fullers earth, and such as comes out of Turky called terra sigillata. It produceth of one corne of that Country wheate sometymes two or three stemmes or

infinit increase

stalkes on which grow eares aboue a spann longe. besett with cornes at the least 300 vpon an eare for the most part 5, 6, & 700. the beanes and peaz of this Country have a great increase also: It yeelds two cropps a yeare. Being tempered and tyme taken I hould it natures nurse to all vegetables, for I assure myself no knowne continent bringes forth any vendible necessaryes which this by planting will not afford: for testemony in part, this we fynd by proof: from the west Indies we brought a certeine delicious fruite called a pina, which the Spanyard by all art possible could never procure to grow in any place, but in his naturall site, this we rudely and carelessly sett in our mould, which fostereth it and keepes it greene, and to what Issue it may come I know not, our west Indy plantes of orenges & Cotten trees thrive well, likewise the potatoes pumpions & mellions: All our garden seedes, that were

[1] Archer was with Gosnold in New England in 1602.

THE ORIGINAL VOYAGE

carefully sowne prosper well, yet we only digged the ground half a   [foot?] deep[,] threw in the seedes at randome carelessly and scarce rakt it. It naturally yeeldes mulbery trees, Cherry trees, vines aboundance, goosberyes, strawberyes, hurtleberryes, Respesses, ground nuttes, scarrettes,[1] the roote called sigilla Christi,[2] certaine sweet thynn shelled nuttes, certaine ground aples, a pleasant fruite any [and?] many other vnknowne. So the thing we crave is some skillfull man to husband sett plant and dresse vynes, suger canes, olives rapes hemp flax, lycoris pruyns, currantes raysons, and all such thinges, as the North Tropick of the world affordes; also saffran woad hoppes and such like.

The Rubish this land naturaly bringeth forth

The liklyhood of profitt by Industry

The Comodityes of this Country, what they are in Esse, is not much to be regarded, the inhabitantes having no comerce with any nation, no respect of profitt, neither is there scarce that we call meum et tuum among them save only the kinges know their owne territoryes, & the people their severall gardens yet this for the present by the consent of all our Seamen, meerly our fishing for Sturgeon cannot be lesse worth then 1000^{li} a yeare, leaving hering and codd as possibilityes.

The Country Comodityes

Sturgeon

Our Clapboord and waynscott (if shipps will but fetch it) we may make as much as England can vent: we can send (if we be frendes with the salvages or be able to force them) 2 3 4 or 5000^{li} a yeare of the earth called terra Sigillata. Saxafrage[3] what store we please. Tobacco after a yeare or two 5000^{li} a yeare. we have (as we suppose) ritch dyes, if they prove vendible, worth more then yet is nominated; we have excellent

Waynscott & Clapbord
Terra Sigillata Saxafrage
Tobacco
Dyes

---

[1] Miscopied, for 'carrots'. See *A true declaration* . . ., p. 31.

[2] *Sigilla Christi* seems to refer to Herb Paris, known as *Sigillum Veneris et Crux Christi*, mentioned in Peter Hotton, *Thesaurus Phytologicus* (Nürnberg, 1738), 509. This work was called to the editor's attention by Mr E. W. Groves, Department of Botany, British Museum (Natural History). Herb Paris was well known in England, though not native to America, but was superficially very similar to a species of Trillium which grows in Virginia. The Virginia plant would be of medicinal value, while Gerarde says that 'Herbe Paris . . . is proued to represse the force of poison' (*OED*, s.v.). The remaining problem is, where did Archer pick up the name *sigilla Christi*?

[3] A not uncommon misnomer for sassafras. Saxifrage was common in Europe; sassafras, native to North America.

JAMESTOWN VOYAGES

<small>Furres
Pitch
Rosen
Turpentine
A maple
gumme
Wisacan or
Virginia bloud
wort which
heales
poysoned
woundes

Iron
Copper
Pearle
muskells</small>

furrs in some places of the Country great store, we can make pitch Rozen and Turpentyne; there is a gumme which bleedeth from a kind of maple (the bark being cutt) not much vnlike a Balsome both in sent and vertue.[1] Apothecary drugges of diverse sortes, some knowne to be of good estimacion, some strange of whose vertue the salvages report wonders – we can by our industry and plantacion of comodious marchandize make oyles wynes soape ashes, wood ashes, extract from minerall earth Iron copper &c: we have a good fishing for muskles, which resemble mother of pearle. & if the pearle we have seene in the kinges eares & about their neckes come from these shells, we know the bankes. To conclude I know not what can be expected from a common wealth that either this land affordes not or may soone yeeld.

15. *21 May–21 June 1607.*
Description of the People.[2]

A Breif discription of the People. /

There is a king in this land called great Pawatah, vnder whose dominions are at least 20^{ty} severall kingdomes, yet each king potent as a prince in his owne territory. these have their Subiectes at so quick Comaund, as a beck bringes obedience, even to the resticucion of stolne goodes which by their naturall inclinac[i]on they are loth to leave. They goe all naked save their privityes, yet in coole weather they weare deare skinns, with the hayre on loose: some have leather stockinges vp to their twistes,[3] & sandalls on their feet, their hayre is black generally, which they weare long on the left side, tyed vp on a knott, about which knott the kinges and best among them have

---

[1] Both the sugar-maple and the red maple were found in Virginia.
[2] P.R.O., S.P. Colonial, C.O. 1/1, folios 55^r–56^v. Other bibliographical details are again the same as for Document no. 13. The handwriting is the same as that of Document no. 14, and the text is continued without further break than a new title. There seems to be no evidence for or against Archer as author of this document.
[3] 'The junction of the thighs' (*OED*).

a kind of Coronett of deares hayre coloured redd, some have chaines of long linckt copper about their neckes, and some chaines of pearle, the comon sort stick long fethers in this knott, I found not a grey eye among them all. their skynn is tawny not so borne, but with dying and paynting them selues, in which they delight greatly. The wemen are like the men, onely this difference; their hayre groweth long al over their heades save clipt somewhat short afore, these do all the labour and the men hunt and goe at their plesure. They live comonly by the water side in litle cottages made of canes and reedes, covered with the barke of trees; they dwell as I guesse by families of kindred & allyance some 40^{tie} or 50^{ti} in a Hatto[1] or small village; which townes are not past a myle or half a myle asunder in most places. They live vpon sodden wheat beanes & peaze for the most part, also they kill deare take fish in their weares, & kill fowle aboundance, they eate often and that liberally; they are proper lusty streight men very strong runn exceeding swiftly, their feight is alway in the wood with bow & arrowes, & a short wodden sword, the celerity they vse in skirmish is admirable. the king directes the batle & is alwayes in front. Their manner of entertainment is vpon mattes on the ground vnder some tree, where they sitt themselues alone in the midest of the matt, & two mattes on each side, on which they[r] people sitt, then right against him (making a square forme) satt we alwayes. when they came to their matt they have an vsher goes before them, & the rest as he sittes downe give a long showt. The people steale any thing comes neare them, yea are so practized in this art that lookeing in our face they would with their foot betwene their toes convey a chizell knife, percer or any indifferent light thing: which having once conveyed they hold it an iniury to take the same from them; They are naturally given to trechery, howbeit we could not

[1] 'Hatto' possibly represents an element cognate with modern Cree *otānow*, 'town', which appears as the second element in the village name Kecoughtan. It may have been pronounced with a glottal stop or other initial throaty sound which the author recorded with an 'h'.

finde it in our travell vp the river, but rather a most kind and loving people. They sacrifice Tobacco to the Sunn fayre picture[1] or a harmefull thing, as a sword or peece also; they strincle some into the water in the morning before they wash. they have many wives, to whome as neare as I could perceive they keep constant. the great king Pawatah had most wives: These they abide not to be toucht before their face. the great diseaze reignes in the men generally, full fraught with noodes botches and pulpable apparances in their forheades, we found aboue a hundred. The wemen are very cleanly in making their bread and prepareing meat. I found they account after death to goe into an other world pointing eastward to the Element, and when they saw vs at prayer they observed vs with great silence and respect especially those to whome I had imparted the meaning of our reverence. To conclude they are a very witty[2] and ingenious people, apt both to vnderstand and speake our language, so that I hope in god as he hath miraculously preserved vs hither from all dangers both of sea and land & their fury so he will make vs authors of his holy will in converting them to our true Christian faith by his owne inspireing grace and knowledge of his deity.

16. *22 June 1607.*
Robert Tindall, Gunner, to Prince Henry.[3]

Mightie Prince:

I thought it no lesse then my duty beinge imployed in this voyage of Verginia, In all humble mannor to make your princelye selfe acquainted with those accidentes which hathe happenned to vs in this our voyage, May it therefore please

---

[1] It may be questioned whether this is correctly copied.
[2] 'Witty' here undoubtedly means 'clever' – not necessarily in a favourable sense. (Fynes Moryson calls Copernicus 'witty' in his *Itinerary* (Glasgow, 1908), IV, 13.)
[3] B.M., Harleian MSS, 7007. Letters to and from Prince Henry, Vol. I. F., fo. 139. Holograph (written in a draughtsman's handwriting). Printed by Edward Arber in Smith, *Works*, and in Brown's *Genesis*.

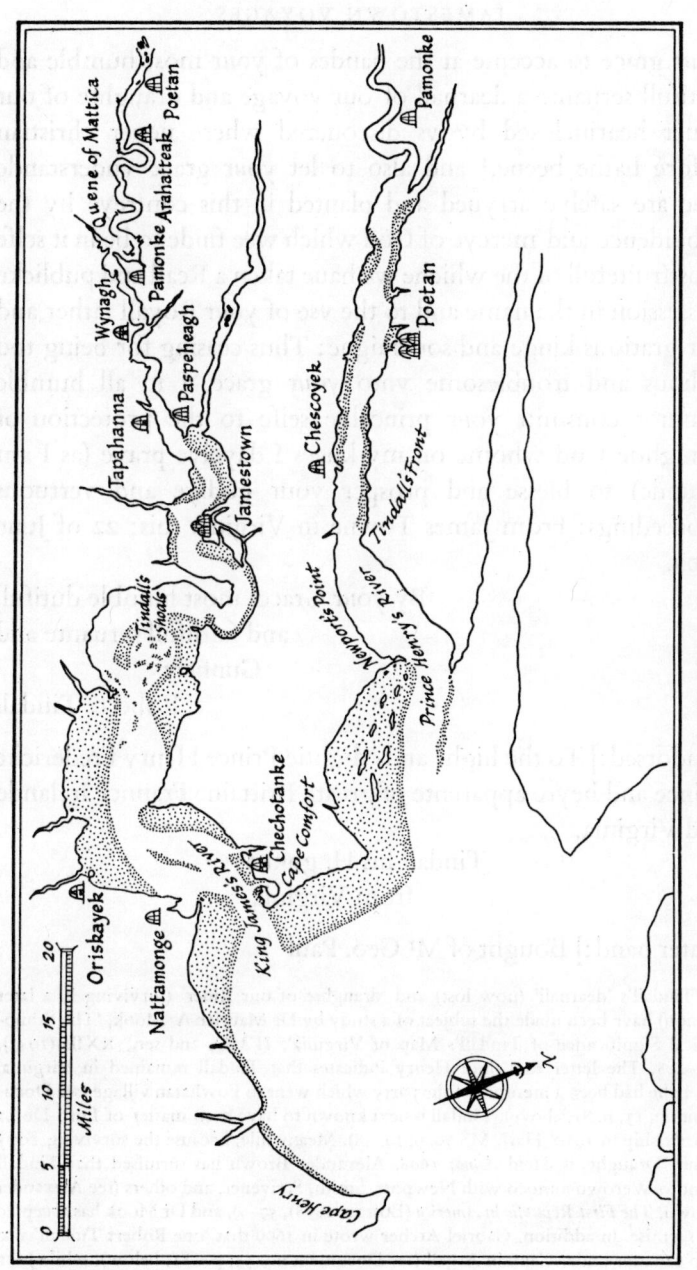

Robert Tindall's 'Draughte of Virginia'

your grace to accepte at the handes of your most humble and dutifull seruante a dearnall of our voyage and draughte of our Riuer hearinclosed by vs discouered where neuer christian before hathe beene,[1] and also to let your grace vnderstande wee are safelye arryued and planted in this contreye by the prouidence and mercye of God which wee finde to be in it selfe mostfruitefull of the whiche we haue taken a Reall and publicke possession in the name and to the vse of your Royall father and our gratious kinge and soueraigne: Thus ceasing for being too tedious and troublesome vnto your grace, I in all humble mannor committ your princelye selfe to the protection of almightie God whome on my knees I dayelye praye (as I am bounde) to blesse and prosper your godlye and vertuous proceedings: From James Towne in Virginia this: 22 of June 1607.

By your Graces most humble dutifull
and faithfull seruante and
Gunner:
Roberte Tindall

[Endorsed:] To the highe and Mightie Prince Henry Fredericke prince and heyre apparente of greate Brittaine Fraunce Irelande and Virginia.
Tindall his H. gunnar
from Virginia

[Later hand:] Bought of Mr Geo. Paul

[1] Tindall's 'dearnall' (now lost) and 'draughte of our Riuer' (surviving in a later version) have been made the subject of a study by Dr Maurice A. Mook, 'The Ethnological Significance of Tindall's Map of Virginia', *WMQ*, 2nd ser., XXIII (1943), 371–408. The letter to Prince Henry indicates that Tindall remained in Virginia, where he had been a member of the party which went to Powhatan village (see Document no. 13, p. 81, above). Tindall is next known to have been master of Lord De La Warr's ship in 1610 (Harl. MS 7009, fo. 58). Meanwhile, because the surviving copy of his 'Draught' is dated *Anno: 1608*, Alexander Brown has surmised that Tindall went to Werowocomoco with Newport, Smith, Scrivener, and others (see Alexander Brown, *The First Republic in America* (Boston, 1898), 57–8), and Dr Mook has accepted his surmise. In addition, Gabriel Archer wrote in 1609 that 'one Robert Tindall' was ship's master under Captain Argall (see Document no. 53, p. 281, below), while John Smith has twice stated that Argall's master was Thomas Sedan [Seddon?] (Arber,

17. *Between 27 May and 22 June, 1607.*
Undated letter from William Brewster.[1]

Sir, it had byne my dvty to have wroot the whoole Iornye vnto you,[2] & so I wovld have done had not this o*u*r evar renowned Captayne, Captayn[e] newport, have cvme him selfe vnto you, whoe will so Ivstly and trvly declare, better then I cann, all this his discoverye, this is all I will saye to you, that svche a Baye, a Ryvar and a land did nevar the eye of mane behovld: and at the head of the Ryvar, which is 160 myles longe, ar Rokes & movntaynes, that prom*m*yseth Infynyt treasver; but o*u*r Forces be yet to[o] weake, to make Fvrther discovery: / nowe is the kinge[s] maies*t*y offered, the moste Statlye, Riche kingedom in the woorld, nevar posseste by anye Christian prynce; be you one meanes amonge manye to Fvrther o*u*r Secondinge, to Conqvar this land, as well as you ware a meanes, to Fvrther the discovery of it: And you, yet maye lyve to see Ingland, moore Riche, & Renowned, then anye kingdon, in all Ewroopa: /
[The rest of the letter has been cut off.][3]

Smith, *Works*, 476, 613). At the same time, Smith has not mentioned Robert Tindall in any of his works (although Sedan *could* be a misprint for Te*n*dall, Thomas would be another man). In view of these uncertainties, it should be repeated that this document and the 1608 draught are the only records of Prince Henry's gunner prior to 1610.

[1] Hatfield House, Cecil Papers, 124/17. Calendared in Hist. MSS Comm., Series 9, Vol. XIX, 202. First printed by Brown, in his *First Republic*, 33-4.

[2] William Brewster was a former servant of Lord Salisbury's, who had been warden of papists between 1598/9 and 1603. Several other communications from him survive at Hatfield House, and Miss Clare Talbot, the Librarian, has confirmed in a personal letter to the editor that all of them are apparently written in the same hand. In his 1603 letters, Brewster continually complains that he is 'ready to starve', and it is to be assumed that Salisbury found a solution to the problem by helping him go to Virginia. Unfortunately, he died there on 10 August 1607, of wounds inflicted by the Indians, and was buried the next day (see Document no. 28, p. 143, below). Since this book was written, a study of William Brewster has appeared: John G. Hunt, 'William Brewster, Gent., of Virginia,' *VMHB*, LXXV (1967), 407-09. This adds a number of pertinent details regarding Brewster's life.

[3] It would be idle to attempt to guess the content of the rest of the letter. The fact that it was deliberately, and neatly, cut off seems to hint that information was sent which it was thought proper to delete. It must be recalled here that George Kendall, a known former agent of Salisbury's whose correspondence curiously turns up in the

[Endorsed:] a part of a letter of william brewester sent from Virginia

18. *12 August 1607.*
Sir Walter Cope to Lord Salisbury.[1]

Right honorable my good Lorde, If we maye beleve ether in wordes or Letters, we are falne vpon a lande, that promises more, then the Lande of promisse: In steed of mylke we fynde pearle. / & golde Inn steede of honye. Thus they saye, thus they wryte / but experyence the wysest Schoolemistress must Leade your Lordships, whose wysedome teaches to be of Slowe beleffe. Vpon thys Tryall I presume yow will byulde, Ther ys but a barrell full of the earth / but ther semes a kingdome full of the oare yow shall not be fedd by handfulls or hattfulls after the Tower measure[2] But the Elsabeth Ionas & the Tryvmphe[3] & all the Shipps of honour maye here haue the bellyes full: for in all ther fortyfycations, after Two Turffes of earth, Thys sparme[4] or oare apearethe on every parte as a sollyde bodye / a Treasure endlesse proportioned by god acordinge to that Sufferaignes harte that Rewardes every one & knowes not how to saye naye. I cowld wyshe your Lordship were at the Tryall / & If yt shall [be] as the proverbe sayes, aureos pollicere

Cecil Papers in the same year as Brewster's, was also among the first colonists, and was one of the seven appointed for the council. Kendall was executed at Jamestown before long, for some misdemeanor (see Philip L. Barbour, 'Captain George Kendall–Mutineer or Intelligencer?' *VMHB*, LXX (1962), 297–313).

[1] Hatfield House, Cecil Papers, 124/18. Calendared in Hist. MSS Comm., series 9, XIX, 417–19. Printed in Brown's *First Republic*, 43–5. This letter is undated, but is attributed to August 1607 in the Hist. MSS Comm. *Calendar*. The date can be known, however, from Cope's second letter to Salisbury, dated 13 August 1607 (see Document no. 19, below).

[2] 'The Tower measure' appears to be a reference to Sir Walter Ralegh, then in the Tower, and his proposal to go to Guiana, in a letter to Salisbury endorsed '1607' (*Calendar*, XIX, 454–5). There is some support for the idea in the fact that Ralegh's letter was written before Newport's return to London.

[3] The *Elizabeth Jonas* and the *Triumph* were respectively commanded by Sir Robert Southwell and Captain (later Sir) Martin Frobisher at the time of the Armada (1588).

[4] 'Sparme' for 'sperm', seed – indicating that the 'gold' was in fine particles.

THE ORIGINAL VOYAGE

montes[,][1] Then that hys Maiestie maye vndertake the honor of yt & proportion our shares as in your wysedomes maye be thought fytt /. If not yet that your worde & presenc[e] maye Comfort the poore Citizen of London who with a lytell helpe would adventure much more In thys most hopefull dyscoverye. & here by the waye gyve me leave to Enforme yow That ther be 50 Cytyzens / who haue allredy Subscribed to adventure 500 li a peece In a present voyage to the east Indyes,[2] I am verely [verily] perswaded that vpon your Lordships mediation, In hys Maiesties name, These adventurs maye Easely be Converted to thys speedye Supply, which might well staye for hys Maiesties Leasure & better meanes, but that In the mowthe of thys Rivere ther ys a place so fortyfyed by nature, That If the Spaniarde who will starte vpon thys alarum, Recover thys place before vs, thys action ys vtterly overthrowne /. & I am credibly Enformed, That one Captaine Hazell who vpon Laniers Enformation was Lately before yow In whytehawle garden, hath gotten awaye Captaine waymoth[3] a man best experyenced In these Coastes & are as Farr as Deale castell outvardes in ther waye towardes spayne / I pray god they maye be stayed Least we repent ther goinge to[o] late

To prove ther ys golde / your Lordships Eyes I hope shall wytnesse To prove ther ys perle ther king of pamont[4] came with a cheyne of perle abowt hys neck, burnt thorow with great hoales & Spoyled, for want of the arte to bore them, & shewed

Sir Thomas Smith ther governor, sayes this ys trewe, and presumes It may be easely Convarted from India to Virginia. a worde of thanks for His Care & dilligenc[e] were well bestowed In yowr Lordships next lettres. They now seek this of themselues

---

[1] The proverb 'to promise golden mountains' was current at the time. See Erasmus, *Collectanea adagiorum* (Paris, 1500), I, ix, 15.

[2] The 'present voyage' was the East India Company's fourth, preparations for which had been commenced in May 1607 (*Register of Letters*, ed. by Sir George Birdwood (London, 1893), 207, n. 1). Sir Thomas Smythe was Governor of the East India Company as well as Treasurer of the Virginia Company.

[3] Captain George Waymouth had been sent to explore the 'Northwest Passage' by the East India Company in 1602. A mutiny forced him to return before he got beyond Greenland. In 1605, he sailed to New England, but was disappointed in his efforts to find employment on his return. During the week of 9–15 August 1607 he was picked up in a Kentish port, suspected of attempting to sail to Spain, to the detriment of the 'Verginian attempt' (see Document no. 21, p. 113, below).

[4] Correctly, Pamunkey.

them shells from whence they were taken[.] pohatan[1] an other of ther kinges came stately Marchinge with a great payre of buckes hornes fastened to hys forehead not knowinge what esteme we make of men so marked, for the Rest I humbly Leave your Lordship to Captaine newport, whose honesty & good desertes I haue knowen many yeares / Remaynyng ever
your Lordships to be
commaunded
Walter Cope

[Postscripts:] The people vsed our men well vntill they found they begann to plant & fortefye, Then they fell to skyrmishing & kylled 3 of our people

we showed thexperyenc[e] made to one beale,[2] an excellent tryer of myneralls / who sayes the tryall was ignorantly made, the earth not halfe tryed / for If yt had yt would haue turned black / & the gold rann together in the bottome. That thys holdes 1200li in the Tonn / That ther ys more in the pott / & he veryly thinkes yt will yealde 2000 at the Least in the Tonn. by Sallisbury shoare, yow must pass to James Towne.

Ther ys Clapborde come fytt as I heare to make wainscott[.] If yowr Lordship praye Captaine Newport to haue the choyse, It will save yow halfe in halfe.

one of ther kinges syck with drinkinge our aquavite, thought him selfe poysoned[.] newport tolde him by signes y^t the nextday he showld be well / & he was so: & tellinge hys cuntry men therof / they came apace olde men & old women vpon Every belliach to him, to know when they showld be well

[Addressed:] To the Right honorable the Earle of Salisbury hys Maiesties Princypall Secretary

[Endorsed:] Sir Water Cope to my Lord. 1607

[1] The younger Powhatan; the Englishmen had not yet met the 'great' Powhatan.
[2] The identity of Beale is not known, unless this is an error for Thomas Bellfield, a member of the Goldsmith's Company who is recorded as having been given a suit of apparel to go to Virginia. (According to Arber, *Smith, Works*, 108 and 412, the Belfield who arrived in Virginia early in 1608 was named Richard.)

19. *13 August 1607.*
Sir Walter Cope to Lord Salisbury.[1]

Sir.

It hath ever bene Incydent to the Secretaryes place, to Receave with the same hande, bothe the good & the badd newes / Thys other daye[2] we sent you newes of golde / And thys daye, we cannot returne yow so much as Copper / Oure newe dyscovery ys more Lyke to prove the Lande of Canaan then the Lande of ophir. Cominge thys daye to Seale vp vnder our Seales, the golden minerall till your Returne / It apeared at sight so suspycyous / That we were not satysfyed vntill we hadd made fowre Tryalls by the best experyenced abowte the cytye/. In the ende all turned to vapore / & Martyne hath cosyned the pore Captaine [Newport],[3] The Kinge & state / & meant as I heare to have cosyned hys owne father / Seeking by thys temptation to have drawen hys father to have made over vnto him somm Supplyes, which otherwyse he dowted never to procure /. yet the wholl Companye metes thys afternowne / abowte the Spedye Supplyes / which will not be now in such measure as formerly I wyshed / . Thus much I thought fytt to advertyze before your Lordship showld mete with hys Maiestie . . .

[The rest of the letter refers to personal matters.]

[Endorsed:] 1606. Sir Wa[l]ter Cope to my Lord, 13 August, at Salisbury.

---

[1] Extract. Hatfield House, Cecil Papers, 117/29. Calendared in Hist. MSS Comm., series 9, Vol. XVIII, 232–3. Printed in Brown's *First Republic*, p. 46. This letter has been misdated in the *Calendar* (12 August, 1606), which was followed by Brown as to day, but not as to year. Miss Clare Talbot, Librarian at Hatfield House, has been kind enough to inform the editor of the correct day (13 August), but was unaware of the mistake in the endorsement. Internal evidence proves that the year was 1607.

[2] 'This other day,' yesterday (*OED*, s.v. *other*, A. 3. b (*b*)).

[3] This must be Captain John Martin, son of Sir Richard Martin, master of the mint, and a member of the council in Virginia. The 'Captaine' undoubtedly was Newport, who brought the 'ore' to London.

20. *17 August 1607.*
Sir Thomas Smythe to Lord Salisbury.[1]

Wheras yt pleased your ho*nour*able Lordshipe to signifie your desire to haue a speedye dispatche of the shippe intended to be sent to virginia, And for asmuch as Captaine Newporte doth fynde his error, in not bringinge of the same ore of which the firste tryall was ther made, he is nowe mynded, to take vpon hym the presente voyadge againe, And resolues neuer to see your Lordshippe before he bringe that with hym which he confidentlie beleeued he had broughte before. And for the better and more speedye effectinge the same we thoughte goode to prouide a nymble pynnace to accompany the other shippe, wherin he may presently returne,[2] And hopes to be heere before the myddle of January next, In which shippe and Pynnace we intende to sende one hundrethe men[3] & victualls with all ncessaries, to releiue them that be ther./ which Course yf yt shall please your Lordshipp to approoue of, shalbe presently effected./ And I humbly rest / –

At the Comaundm*en*te of your
ho*nour*able Lordshippe. /
Tho: Smythe

Auguste 17th. 1607.

[Endorsed:] To the righte ho*nour*able his very good Lorde The'arle of salishburry giue theis.

[1] Hatfield House, Cecil Papers, 122/23. Calendared in Hist. MSS Comm., Series 9, Vol. XIX, 219–20. Printed in Brown's *First Republic*, 47.

[2] The ship was the *John and Francis*, an ex-privateer of unknown tonnage (Andrews, *Elizabethan Privateering*, 181, 217, 267), while the 'nymble pynnace' was the *Phoenix*, under Master Francis Nelson but otherwise not readily identifiable. For details of the voyage, see Document no. 32, pp. 158–62, below.

[3] In the end, 120 colonists are reported to have arrived in Virginia with Newport and Nelson (see Document no. 63, p. 399, below).

21. 18 August 1607.
Dudley Carleton to John Chamberlain.[1]

... you shall vnderstand, that Capt: Newport is come from owr late aduenturers to Virginia hauing left them in an Island in the midst of a great riuer 120 mile into the land. They write much commendations of the aire and the soile and the commodities of it: but siluer and golde haue they none, and they can not yet be at peace with the inhabitants of the cuntrie They haue fortified themselfs and built a small towne which they call Iames-towne, and so they date theyr letters. but the towne me thincks hath no gracefull name, and besides the Spaniards who thinck it no small matter of moment how they stile theyr new populations will tell vs I doubt it comes too neere Villiaco.[2] One Capt: Waiman [Waymouth][3] a speciall fauorit of Sir Walter Copes was taken the last weeke in a port in Kent shipping himself for Spaine, with intent as is thought to haue betraied his frends and shewed the Spaniards a meanes how to defeat this Verginian attempt. The great counsell of that state hath resolued of a dubble supplie to be sent thether with all diligence. . . .[4]

From London this 18th of August. 1607.
Yours most assuredly
Dudley Carleton

... Master [John] Porie tells me of a name giuen by a Duch-

---

[1] Extract. P.R.O., S.P. 14/28. Pertinent extract printed in Arber, *Smith, Works*, lvi; entire letter in Brown, *Genesis*, I, 111–14.

[2] The Italian word *vigliacco* (which influenced Carleton's spelling) was borrowed from Spanish *bellaco* (seventeenth century *vellaco*), 'villain, knave, scoundrel.' Covarrubias (*Tesoro*, p. 997) reports that many 'inquisitive persons' of his day believed the word came from Belial, the Spirit of Evil. (Its true derivation is from Lat. *bellax*, 'warlike, pugnacious.')

[3] See Document no. 18, p. 109, above.

[4] The balance of the body of the letter has to do with the war in the Low Countries, with the detail that John Pory, a friend and pupil of Richard Hakluyt, is visiting him, along with Walter Warner. Pory later became interested in Virginia. Warner, a mathematician, was in the employ of Henry Percy, ninth Earl of Northumberland, and eldest brother of George Percy, then in Virginia.

man[1] who wrote to him in latin from the new towne in Verginia, Iacobopolis, and Master Warner hath a letter from Master George Percie who names theyr towne Iames-fort, which we like best of all the rest because it comes neere to Chemes-ford.[2]

22. 4 September 1607.
Court Minute of the East India Company[3]

Beedes and Cloth sold for iij^{li} 05^s.

At this Courte were sold vnto master Gouernour,[4] for the virginia voyadge Certaine Beedes, & 5 yardes of Blew Cloth remaininge of the first voyadge very much motheaten for the some of iij^{li} v^s[,] viz[.] the Beedes 40^s & the Cloth 25^s.[5]

23. [12/]22 September 1607.
Pedro de Zúñiga to Philip III.[6]

Sir:

I reported to Your Majesty that one of the ships which went to Virginia had arrived at Plymouth, and afterwards Captain Newport arrived in another, which ships are now here [London]. They are hurrying to send these back with some people,

---

[1] The 'Dutchman' still seems to defy identification.
[2] Chemes-ford 'undoubtedly refers to Chelmsford and does represent the old (and to some extent still current) pronunciation' (personal communication to the editor from Mr F. G. Emmison, County Archivist, Chelmsford, Essex, dated 20 April 1966).
[3] India Office Library, London. Court Minute Book, 4 September 1607, fo. 50^v. Abstract printed in Brown's *Genesis*, I, 115.
[4] Sir Thomas Smythe, treasurer in fact if not yet in name of the Virginia Company.
[5] The East India Company's first voyage ended with the return of all ships by mid-September, 1603, and the knighting of the commander, James Lancaster, on 2 October.
[6] Decoded. Translated. Archivo General de Simancas, Legajo E 2586, 65. For some reason, the date of this was misread as December by the copyist for Alexander Brown, although Brown himself was rightly convinced that it should be September. The date when it was received should have eliminated any doubts.

and merchants have invested in the business along with other persons who want to establish themselves there, since that seems the most useful way they have found to play the pirate and make assaults on Your Majesty's fleets. [I hope] Your Majesty will look into the matter. On account of this report, I sent a request for an audience with the King at Salisbury, and it pleased God that since that day I have not been able to rise from my bed, so that I sent further word why I was unable to go on the day appointed for me. [The King] sent to inquire after me most graciously, and the Queen the same, and [i.e., but] more than to be well I want to carry out what Your Majesty has commanded, so as to see just how they regard this business; for I am afraid he [James I] is going to tell me that it is not of his doing, and that he will see that it is remedied while *sub rosa* these [merchants and so on] will push the matter as hard as they can. It would be very advisable for Your Majesty to root out this noxious plant while it is so easy. I hope to God that I will be in condition to talk with the King within a week, because at this time he will be nearer this place,[1] I have found a trustworthy person through whom I can learn everything that goes on in the council (which these people call the Virginia (council)). They are mad about the location, and frightened to death that Your Majesty will throw them out.[2] Their idea is that if they do not carry out [their plan] they will put the King in the position of taking it in his own hands. There are so many here and in other parts of the kingdom who are already arranging to send people there [to Virginia] that it is wise not to regard it lightly, because very soon they will

---

[1] On the day this letter was written, James I was at Theobalds, just west of Waltham Cross, which he had purchased from Salisbury. Because of the illness of the little Princess Mary, it was said that he would return to Hampton Court before long.

[2] This is hardly borne out by the report of the Venetian Ambassador in London, Zorzi Giustinian, which is most optimistic: 'These expeditions and plantations of the English in those parts may very likely go on, for I am told that they are supported by the richest and most powerful gentlemen of the country' (19/29 August, 1607; *Calendar of S.P., Venetian*, XI, 27).

JAMESTOWN VOYAGES

have many people [there], and it will be more difficult to get them out.

[Pious salutation]

[Endorsed:] London. To His Majesty. [Decoded.]
Don Pedro de Zúñiga, the 22nd of September [1607].
Received on the 18th of October.

[Summary of contents.]

24. [25 September/] 5 October 1607.
Pedro de Zúñiga to Philip III.[1]

Sir:

When the King came to Hampton Court, which was on the 22nd of the past month [12/22 September, the day the previous letter was written], I sent to beg audience of him, and he sent to tell me that he would be pleased, [but] to wait until he got back there, because he was leaving the next day to hunt on this other side of London, in some woods and forests which he has near Tibols [Theobalds]. The day before yesterday he got back, and I sent again to ask for an audience. He had a fever that day, and he answered that that, along with the fact that he was waiting for members of his Council to arrive,[2] forced him not to grant it, and that he would let me know when he was in good health. Consequently I have been unable to talk with him regarding the Virginia matter, but I understand that a ship and a patache [pinnace] are leaving for there [Virginia] with up to a hundred and twenty men, and that they take the oath of

[1] Decoded. Translated. Archivo General de Simancas, Legajo E 2586, 64.
[2] Alexander Brown has a footnote (*Genesis*, I, 118) that James I was putting off seeing the ambassador in order to gain time, while the Virginia Company was hurrying Newport off again to Virginia. On the other hand, there was the illness and death of his daughter Mary, and the flight of Hugh O Neill, Earl of Tyrone, from Ireland to Spain, with a small following, not to mention an obscure affair which sent Sir Thomas Shirley the younger to the Tower, which together provide ample reason for Salisbury to have recommended to the King to delay seeing Zúñiga until matters were clearer.

supremacy of all of them.¹ A man who usually tells the truth told me today that these [colonists] are complaining that the King is urging the Scots to go there² and that he favours them more than these. They are very much afraid that Your Majesty is going to order an attack, for their whole move is only to test how Your Majesty takes it. It is thoroughly evident that it is not their desire to people [the land], but rather to practice piracy,³ for they take no women – only men. I have decided not to detain this courier [perhaps 'this mail'] because the King's health may be bad for a few days. I have understood that he is writing to Your Majesty that he wants very much to join you in amity. I believe that some things in the direction of the service of God and Your Majesty are in the making, and a cloud has been lifted from my heart, for I now see that a door is being opened so that we may talk of Religion. May God open it so that His holy service may be completely fulfilled.

[Pious salutation.]

[Endorsed:] London. To His Majesty. [Decoded.] folios 64–7
Don Pedro de Zúñiga, the 5th of October [1607].
Received on the 18th.

25. [28 September/] 8 October 1607.
Pedro de Zúñiga to Philip III.⁴

Sir:

Saturday night [26 September/6 October] I had a message from the chamberlain which informed me that the King

¹ The details are generally correct. The ship was the *John and Francis* and the pinnace the *Phoenix*. The oath of allegiance ('supremacy') was devised by James I to separate loyal Catholics from those who were 'papists' (Pope Paul V had forbidden English Catholics to take it). It was of course anathema to Philip III and the Spaniards.

² Brown has misunderstood this passage (*el Rey da alas a los escoceses para que vayan allá*). The editor does not recall any other reference to this appeal for Scottish emigrants to Virginia.

³ In a sense this may have been Ralegh's notion, but the piratical aspect was by 1607 submerged in the larger plan to colonize for raw material and for trade.

⁴ Decoded. Extract (less than half), translated. Archivo General de Simancas, Legaio E 2586, 68.

would grant me an audience yesterday, Sunday, at two. He received me, as usual, very courteously, and when we were seated I told him how sorry Your Majesties would be to learn of the death of his daughter.¹ He thanked me very much for this. Then I told him that Your Majesty had commanded me to point out how much against good friendship and brotherliness it was for his vassals to dare to want to people Virginia, since it is a part of the Indies belonging to Castile, and that this boldness could have 'inconvenient' results.² He answered that he was not informed as to the details of what was going on, so far as the voyages to Virginia were concerned, and that he had never known that Your Majesty had a right to it [Virginia], for it was a region very far from where the Spaniards had settled; furthermore, it was not stated in the peace treaties with him and with France that his subjects could not go [where they pleased] except to the Indies,³ and since Your Majesty's [subjects] have discovered new regions, so it seemed to him that his also might. I answered that it was a condition of the treaty that they were not under any circumstances to go to the Indies. The King said to me [then] that those who went, went at their own risk, and if they were caught there, there could be no complaint if they were punished. I said to him that it was proper to punish them, but that it would be better if they were restrained here from going – which would bring Your Majesty's vassals and his closer together – and that this scheme of going to settle [people] in Virginia was exposed [by] the shabby deceit with which it is carried out; for the land is very sterile, and consequently there can be no other object in that place than that it seems good for piracy, and that should not be permitted. He repeated to me that he had never known that it belonged to Your Majesty, but since I assured him that it did, and that they could practice piracy from there, he would look

¹ The Lady Mary died on 17 September, aged two and a half.
² 'Inconvenient' and 'inconvenience' were frequent euphemisms for 'unpleasant' or even 'catastrophic' results, such as war.
³ The subject was deliberately omitted.

into the matter, and he would tell his Council to give me satisfaction; and [he said] that he inclined to agree with what I told him, since he had heard that the land was unproductive, and that those who thought to find great riches there were deceived. [He assured me] that he got no benefits from this, and if his subjects went to places where they should not, and were punished for it, neither he nor they could complain. I said again that it was the 'inconveniences' which had to be considered, and that the best remedy was to stop it from here, for it was public news that two ships had sailed for the East Indies from a port in this kingdom,[1] and that two more were being freighted here.[2] The King said to me that they were exasperating people [*terrible gente*], and that he wanted to put the whole thing right. I pointed out to him how well treated his vassals would always be in Your Majesty's kingdoms to which they may go, and with what goodwill Your Majesty has commanded this. He told me that it had become self-evident to him [*hechava (de ver muy bien)* for *se echava?*] how right what I said to him was, for in the last Parliament there had been such an uproar over the two ships which were taken in the Indies. I told him that the rabble[3] always wanted to stir up scandal against us, and that I was not complaining about them, but that I was complaining about some of the council, who had said that Your Majesty had summoned the Earl of Tyrone and those who were with him for the purpose of putting them on the Armada which Your Majesty has, and sending them to Ireland . . .

[Long digression on Irish affairs.]

I thanked him [for the explanation, and then] I said to him again that it was important that a remedy be found for the Virginia affair, for it was necessary to act with some urgency,

[1] The second East India *fleet* was composed of four ships. Zúñiga was confused, or misinformed.

[2] The *John and Francis* and the *Phoenix*, already mentioned.

[3] The epithet (*poblacho*), fortunately for Zúñiga, did not reach the ears of the House of Commons. For the parliamentary discussions of 15–17 June see J. Spedding, *Letters and Life of Francis Bacon*, III (1868), 353–4.

before it got worse; [that] these satisfactions of the council usually take a long time here, and meanwhile these [entrepreneurs] can send more people and fortify themselves there, for I understand that those of Plymouth have established a footing in another region near that one [the first]. I will quickly see what they have to say, and let Your Majesty know, but I think it would be a good idea if the few who are there should be finished outright, because that would cut the root, so that it would not sprout again.

[More on Tyrone, and the usual pious salutation.]

[Endorsed:] London. To His Majesty. [Decoded.]

Don Pedro de Zúñiga, the 8th of October [1607].

Received on the 23rd.

[Summary of contents.]

26. [6/]16 October 1607.
Pedro de Zúñiga to Philip III.[1]

Sir:

I have already written to Your Majesty and sent [a report on] the audience I had regarding the Virginia matter. I sent to Moptoncurt [Hampton Court] to remind the council of the answer which the King had promised me, and the Earl of Salisbury tells me that when he discussed it with the King, [the latter] answered almost the same thing as to me: if the English go where they cannot [i.e., must not] go, they are to be punished, and that now that he has studied [the matter] it appears to him that they cannot go to Virginia, and therefore if something bad happens to them, let it be their fault, for it will not appear to him a thing against friendship and the terms of the Treaty. He says that his not wanting to do what he has been asked (in preventing them from going, and commanding those already there to come back) is because that would seem

[1] Decoded [?]. Extract (about two-thirds), translated. Archivo General de Simancas, Legajo E 2586, 69.

THE ORIGINAL VOYAGE

to him to confirm that Your Majesty is Lord of all the Indies. Those who are urging a settlement in Virginia are hurrying more and more every day to send people, because it has seemed to them that this discussion will rest just where it now stands [*porque les parecia de dormir esta platica con solo lo que se ha tratado della*], and before Christmas five or six ships will sail from here and Plymouth. It will be a service to God and Your Majesty to expel those rogues [*vellacos*] from there, hanging them while so little [effort] is needed to make it possible.

[The rest deals with Tyrone and Ireland.]

[Endorsed:] London. To His Majesty. [Decoded.]
Don Pedro de Zúñiga, the 16th of October 1607.
Received the 28th of the same [month].

[Summary of contents.]
[Note for an answer:]

> On consultation, the Constable of Castile [Don Juan Fernández de Velasco, Spain's representative at the negotiations of the Treaty in 1604] noted that when he discussed peace in England he considered that if he specifically tried to exclude the English from the Indies, and specifically from Virginia, he foresaw the difficulty that they [the English] are in peaceful possession of the latter for more than thirty years; [at the same time] if it was declared that it [Virginia] was not part of the Indies, a gate would be opened leading to ruin. It was decided to obtain their agreement, as was done, that voyages should be made only to those of Your Majesty's kingdoms to which they were commonly made in the old days before the war, so that they [the English] were tacitly excluded from navigating to the Indies,[1] and [the Constable added] that it has always seemed difficult to him to maintain legally that every-

[1] From the English point of view, they were tacitly permitted to keep on doing what they had been doing; namely, sailing to and through the Indies.

thing that is contiguous to the Indies is part thereof, and for that reason it is best to move cautiously [*con tiento*], and that the true [i.e., legally valid] act of possession will be [the act] of throwing out those who are in Virginia before they get further reinforcements, and toward this and other objectives it will be well to command that the Windward Fleet [which in theory patrolled the West Indies from the Virgin Islands to Trinidad], that for so many years had been resolved that it should be done, be made ready promptly and sail to throw out those who are in Virginia, for, since they are few, it will be easy, and that [act] will be enough for them not to return there. And the whole Council was of the same mind.[1] [A brief mention of what was to be done about Ireland.]

27. [*18/*]*28 October 1607.*
Philip III to Don Pedro de Zúñiga.[2]

Your letters of 22 September [and] 3, 5, and 8 of this month have arrived, and this will answer all matters brought up in them; and in the first place I send you very special thanks for the care and diligence you have used in converting the Earl of Salisbury to my service, as can be hoped from what has happened with you and your confidents. . . .
[Mention of various matters, and the kind of rewards to be distributed.]

[1] The endorsement is of importance as reflecting the attitude of Philip III and the Duke of Lerma. As Brown notes (*Genesis*, 125–7), the discussion was recorded in a report dated 10 November 1607, which was endorsed by Philip III: 'Let such measures be taken in this matter as may now and hereafter appear proper.' Nevertheless, when it came to 'implementing' the idea, the Windward Fleet was considered too unready to move quickly, and three illegible signatures attested that the plan could not be relied on. In the end, nothing was done for nearly two years (see Document no. 62, pp. 293–319, below).
[2] Instruction to code. Extract (one fourth), translated. Archivo General de Simancas Legajo E 2571, 215.

THE ORIGINAL VOYAGE

I am quite satisfied with the offices which you performed with that King [James I] on the subject of Virginia, and you are to continue to keep an eye on it in order to provide what is proper. In the meantime, manage to find out what ships leave there for there [England for Virginia], and report to me what you learn.[1]

[Brief paragraph on the Portuguese. No address and no signature.]

[Endorsed:] To Don Pedro de Zúñiga, from Madrid, the 28th of October 1607.

Answer up to the 8th of October.

[1] The disproportionately brief and casual paragraph on Virginia shows how little interest Philip III and his favourite took in England's colonial attempts. This attitude was to continue for many months.

III

In Virginia, from Newport's Departure to the Arrival of the First Supply

NARRATIVE

As Sir Walter Raleigh, the modern man of letters, wrote in his essay on 'The English Voyages of the Sixteenth Century', the English gentleman adventurer was often a cause of trouble on such expeditions as the Jamestown voyages. 'He was full of courage and initiative, but headstrong, giddy, and insubordinate.' As a result, there were quarrels, 'and no one was certain whom to obey, because there were many who took upon them to be masters' (Glasgow edition of Hakluyt's *Principal Navigations*, XII, 55). Nowhere was this more in evidence than during the first few years of life of the Jamestown colony.

Christopher Newport, commander of the fleet and recognized as experienced in American waters, had little known difficulty in maintaining his authority. But that lasted only so long as the colonists were physically at sea. No sooner had they reached land and elected a president (in accordance with their instructions), than they were more at sea mentally – in morale, in behaviour, and even in elementary prudence.

Edward Maria Wingfield, the president thus elected probably because he was the only patentee to accompany the original voyage, was prominent in family background, and not entirely devoid of military experience. At the same time, although at worst in his late forties, Wingfield was rapidly approaching old age, by Elizabethan and Jacobean standards, and was inclined rather to be petulant than dignified, and to give himself airs. His distant cousin Bartholomew Gosnold apparently had both popular backing and ability, but because of his youth (he was about thirty-five) he took second place. Even

125

so, the government of the colony might have been conducted with some measure of firmness had not Wingfield incredibly informed Newport before he left that, while Gosnold could disrupt the colony if he wanted, a former companion of Gosnold's would like to, and was apparently merely biding his time until he could. This self-assertive gentleman was Captain Gabriel Archer, also in his middle thirties, and something of a lawyer by training. The admission was of itself damaging, but that Newport should have told both Gosnold and Archer what the president had said was mischievous to the point of folly. It only required the death of Gosnold for it to be fatal, and this took place on 22 August 1607, nineteen weeks after Newport sailed for England. In three weeks more, Wingfield was deposed. (See Document no. 28, supplemented by Document no. 34, in the next chapter.)

It is likely that in the midst of this contention there was some deliberate attempt at demoralization, under Spanish or Catholic influence, or both. An Irishman named Francis Magnel who appears in a Spanish document (Document no. 31) made a deposition several years later which hints at efforts to undermine the settlement for the benefit of Spain. Yet Spanish archives have not yet revealed any evidence of deliberate plots either inspired by unhappy Catholics or promoted by the Spanish government. Nevertheless, George Kendall, one of the original council in Virginia, was executed for some ill-defined complicity in such an affair, while John Smith was implicated in another so-called mutiny, apparently a Protestant counter-move, the leader of which was an obscure member of the wide-spread and usually affluent family of Calthorp (variously spelled).

Perhaps because such developments were expected, Lord Salisbury seems to have had an agent or two in Virginia, one of whom was surely William Brewster (see Document no. 17), and another very likely the same George Kendall (see Barbour, *Kendall*). That these men had any specific assignment, as it would be called today, is highly doubtful, and certainly unproven. But that one of them was acting loyally for Salisbury and the other possibly indulging in double dealing is strongly hinted by what little evidence survives. A third incident, although not known to be connected with Lord Salisbury, illustrates the intrigue *in posse* at Jamestown. An inconspicuous friend, or 'servant', of one of the notoriously recalcitrant Cornwallis family, Francis Perkin or Perkins by name, sailed with his son on the first relief supply, which was sent from England on 8 October 1607, with Newport in command of the *John and Francis*, and Captain Francis Nelson master of 'a nimble pinnace' which accompanied the ship. Newport arrived at Jamestown on 2 January 1608; Nelson, lost in a fog, only on 20 April. Perkin's letter to his friends in England survived only in a translation which was sent to Philip III of Spain, but it shows that Perkin was observant and accurate.

All this while, up to Newport's return, sickness, death, discontent, jealousy and the Indians wrought havoc with the colony. In that atmosphere, the figure of a young farmer from Lincolnshire began to emerge as Jamestown's real leader: Captain John Smith, more famous in legend than he has been in history. Smith's early life had been little if any more eventful than that of many a young Englishman of those days of English expansion, but his gift of vivid authorship has put it more picturesquely before the reader than modern sober historians would like to have it. This, however, should neither enhance nor detract from Smith's real significance for the Jamestown colony. Smith was considerably younger than Wingfield or even Gosnold (he turned twenty-seven while the original fleet was anchored off the coast of Kent, hoping for more propitious winds). He was not a gentleman by birth but saw no reason why he should not be the equal of those who were, especially after the group reached their Promised Land. He was short, even for a man of 1607, and his stocky, diminutive build was, as is often the case, accompanied by a disproportionately tall and lithe determination. Precisely how he came to be named one of the original council in Virginia is anyone's guess (see Barbour, *Smith*). But as a member of that body, after the death of Gosnold, the deposition of Wingfield, the execution of Kendall, and the infantile gyrations of Captain Ratcliffe, Smith was carried to the top with no competition beyond that provided by Captain John Martin, whose continued ill-health provided many an opportunity for dreams of gold mines where hard work was what was needed.

In any event, it was left to Smith to record the early history of the Jamestown voyages. Newport had brought little of what was needed on his return, and had found much that was wrong with the colony, but did nothing to correct the trouble. His associate, Nelson, arriving ten days after he had sailed back to England, brought food, at least, but had no authority to donate much help. After six weeks, he too was ready to leave. Smith, seeing this, and foreseeing no real relief, dashed off a few concluding paragraphs to a letter he had been preparing for a friend, and entrusted the story to Nelson as the pinnace was about to enter the Atlantic off Cape Henry. It was by far the longest account yet written.

Smith was naturally not alone in telling what was happening. We have already seen the brief communications of Robert Tindall and William Brewster, as well as the official messages taken by Newport the year before. George Percy, youngest brother of the Earl of Northumberland (and just Smith's age), also wrote a lengthy report, already mentioned (Document no. 28), but it is not known just when it was sent to England. And an exceptional 'labourer' named William White either wrote some notes on life among the Indians, or told stories which Smith and Percy both eventually incorporated in their writings (Document no. 30).

But in the end it was Smith's letter which came to be published first. Edited, cut, and possibly altered though it was, in Smith's *Relation* (Document no. 33) the history of the founding

IN VIRGINIA

of the colony finds its first expression. The story is a matter of memoirs rather than history. At times, it seems to contradict what he later wrote, possibly because the editor who published it without his knowledge or consent deleted any passages that could be construed against the Virginia Company or the Jamestown voyages. But however much, or little, the printed *Relation* differs from the original letter, here was the beginning of John Smith's new métier, and the beginning of American history written on the American side of the Atlantic Ocean.

28. *1608? [Before 12 April 1612.]*
George Percy's Discourse.[1]

Observations gathered out of a Discourse of the Plantation of the Southerne Colonie in Virginia by the English, 1606. Written by that Honorable Gentleman Master George Percy.

On Saturday, the twentieth of December in the yeere 1606[2] the fleet fell from London, and the fift of January we anchored in the Downes: but the winds continued contrarie so long, that we were forced to stay there some time, where wee suffered great stormes, but by the skilfulnesse of the Captaine wee suffered no great losse or danger.

The twelfth day of February at night we saw a blazing Starre, and presently a storme. The three and twentieth day we fell with the Iland of Mattanenio[3] in the West Indies. The foure and twentieth day we anchored at Dominico, within fourteene degrees of the Line, a very faire Iland, the Trees full of sweet and good smels inhabited by many Sauage Indians, they were at first very scrupulous to come aboord vs. Wee learned of

The next day Cap. Smith was suspected for a supposed Mutinie, though neuer no such matter. Trade at Dominica

[1] Reproduced from Purchas, *Pilgrimes*, IV, 1685–90 (reprinted, slightly modernized, in Glasgow ed., XVIII, 403–19).
[2] Cf. Smith's *Map* (Document no. 63, p. 378, below): 'on the 19. of December'.
[3] Martinique. The Carib name was Madinina. For a discussion of the voyage, see Barbour, *Smith*, pp. 114–20.

129

them afterwards that the Spaniards had giuen them a great ouerthrow on this Ile, but when they knew what we were, there came many to our ships with their Canoas, bringing vs many kinds of sundry fruites, as Pines, Potatoes, Plantons, Tobacco, and other fruits, and Roane Cloth abundance, which they had gotten out of certaine Spanish ships that were cast away vpon that Iland. We gave them Kniues, Hatchets for exchange which they esteeme much, wee also gaue them Beades, Copper Iewels which they hang through their nosthrils, eares, and lips, very strange to behold, their bodies are all painted red to keepe away the biting of Muscetos, they goe all naked without couering: the haire of their head is a yard long, all of a length pleated in three plats hanging downe to their wastes, they suffer no haire to grow on their faces, they cut their skinnes in diuers workes, they are continually in warres, and will eate their enemies when they kill them, or any stranger if they take them. They will lap vp mans spittle, whilst one

Brutishnesse of the Dominicans spits in their mouthes in a barbarous fashion like Dogges. These people and the rest of the Ilands in the West Indies, and Brasill, are called by the names of Canibals, that will eate mans flesh, these people doe poyson their Arrow heads, which are made of a fishes bone: they worship the Deuill for their God, and haue no other beliefe. Whilest we remayned at this Iland we saw a

Fight betwixt a Whale, the Thresher and Sword-fish Whale chased by a Thresher and a Sword-fish: they fought for the space of two houres, we might see the Thresher with his flayle layon the monstrous blowes which was strange to behold: in the end these two fishes brought the Whale to her end.[1]

Margalanta The sixe and twentieth day, we had sight of Marigalanta, and the next day wee sailed with a slacke saile alongst the Ile of

Guadalupa Bath very hot Guadalupa, where we went ashore, and found a Bath which was so hot, that no man was able to stand long by it, our

---

[1] This passage bears a remarkable similarity to William Strachey's 'Reportory of the wracke' (of Gates's ship off Bermuda, Purchas, *Pilgrimes*, XIX, 21), wherein fights between whales, sword-fish and thrashers are described. If Percy borrowed from Strachey, he cannot have written his 'Discourse' before 1610.

Admirall Captaine Newport caused a piece of Porke to be put in it: which boyled it so in the space of halfe an houre as no fire could mend it. Then we went aboord and sailed by many Ilands, as Mounserot and an Iland called Saint Christopher, both vnhabited about; about two a clocke in the afternoone wee anchored at the Ile of Meuis.[1] There the Captaine landed all his men being well fitted with Muskets and other conuenient Armes, marched a mile into the Woods; being commanded to stand vpon their guard, fearing the treacherie of the Indians, which is an ordinary vse amongst them and all other Sauages on this Ile, we came to a Bath standing in a Valley betwixt two Hils; where wee bathed our selues and found it to be of the nature of the Bathes in England, some places hot and some colder: and men may refresh themselues as they please, finding this place to be so conuenient for our men to auoid diseases, which will breed in so long a Voyage, wee incamped our selues on this Ile sixe dayes, and spent none of our ships victuall, by reason our men some went a hunting, some a fouling, and some a fishing, where we got great store of Conies, sundry kinds of fowles, and great plentie of fish. We kept Centinels and Courts de gard at euery Captaines quarter, fearing wee should be assaulted by the Indians, that were on the other side of the Iland: wee saw none nor were molested by any: but some few we saw as we were a hunting on the Iland. They would not come to vs by any meanes, but ranne swiftly through the Woods to the Mountaine tops; so we lost the sight of them: whereupon we made all the haste wee could to our quarter, thinking there had beene a great ambush of Indians there abouts. We past into the thickest of the Woods where we had almost lost our selues, we had not gone aboue halfe a mile amongst the thicke, but we came into a most pleasant Garden, being a hundred paces square on euery side, hauing many Cotton-trees growing in it with abundance of Cotton-wooll, and many Guiacum trees: wee saw the goodliest tall trees growing so

Meuis

Bath at Meuis

Commodities there

[1] Misprint for Nieves, now Nevis.

thick about the Garden, as though they had beene set by Art which made vs maruell very much to see it.

Aprill

The third day, wee set saile from Meuis: the fourth day we sailed along by Castutia[1] and by Saba: This day we anchored at the Ile of Virgines, in an excellent Bay able to harbour a hundred Ships: if this Bay stood in England, it would be a great profit and commoditie to the Land. On this Iland wee caught great store of Fresh-fish, and abundance of Sea Tortoises, which serued all our Fleet three daies, which were in number eight score persons. We also killed great store of wilde Fowle, wee cut the Barkes of certaine Trees which tasted much like Cinnamon, and very hot in the mouth. This Iland in some places hath very good ground, straight and tall Timber. But the greatest discommoditie that wee haue seene on this Iland is that it hath no Fresh-water, which makes the place void of any Inhabitants.

Tortoises

Vpon the sixt day, we set saile and passed by Becam,[2] and by Saint Iohn deportorico. The seuenth day, we arriued at Mona: where wee watered, which we stood in great need of, seeing that our water did smell so vildly that none of our men was able to indure it. Whilst some of the Saylers were a filling the Caskes with water, the Captaine, and the rest of the Gentlemen, and other Soldiers marched vp in the Ile sixe myles, thinking to find some other prouision to maintaine our victualling; as wee marched we killed two wild Bores, and saw a huge wild Bull, his hornes was an ell betweene the two tops. Wee also killed Guanas, in fashion of a Serpent, and speckled like a Toade vnder the belly. These wayes that wee went, being so troublesome and vilde going vpon the sharpe Rockes, that many of our men fainted in the march, but by good fortune wee lost none but one Edward Brookes Gentleman, whose fat melted within him by the great heate and drought of the Countrey: we were not able to relieue him nor our selues, so he died in that great extreamitie.

Meuis water vnwholsome

Ed. Brookes faint with thirst

[1] Misprint, apparently for St Eustatius.
[2] Vieques, now part of the Commonwealth of Puerto Rico.

IN VIRGINIA

The ninth day in the afternoone, we went off with our Boat to the Ile of Moneta, some three leagues[1] from Mona, where we had a terrible landing, and a troublesome getting vp to the top of the Mountaine or Ile, being a high firme Rocke step, with many terrible sharpe stones: After wee got to the top of the Ile, we found it to bee a fertill and a plaine ground, full of goodly grasse, and abundance of Fowles of all kindes, they flew ouer our heads as thicke as drops of Hale; besides they made such a noise, that wee were not able to heare one another speake. Furthermore, wee were not able to set our feet on the ground, but either on Fowles or Egges which lay so thicke in the grasse: Wee laded two Boats full in the space of three houres, to our great refreshing.

Moneta

Store of fowles

The tenth day we set saile, and disimboged out of the West Indies, and bare our course Northerly. The fourteenth day we passed the Tropicke of Cancer. The one and twentieth day, about fiue a clocke at night there began a vehement tempest, which lasted all the night, with winds, raine, and thunders in a terrible manner. Wee were forced to lie at Hull that night, because we thought wee had beene nearer land then wee were. The next morning, being the two and twentieth day wee sounded; and the three and twentieth and foure and twenteth day, but we could find no ground. The fiue and twentieth day we sounded, and had no ground at an hundred fathom. The six and twentieth day of Aprill, about foure a clocke in the morning, wee descried the Land of Virginia: the same day wee entred into the Bay of Chesupioc[2] directly, without any let or hindrance; there wee landed and discouered a little way, but wee could find nothing worth the speaking of, but faire meddowes and goodly tall Trees, with such Fresh-waters running through the woods, as I was almost rauished at the first sight thereof.

We were driuen to try that night, and by the storme were forced neere the shoare, not knowing where we were

They land in Virginia

At night, when wee were going aboard, there came the

---

[1] Isla del Monito is about three *miles* from Mona.
[2] Borrowed from Hakluyt's *Principal Navigations*.

Sauages creeping vpon all foure, from the Hills like Beares, with their Bowes in their mouthes, charged vs very desperately in the faces, hurt Captaine Gabrill Archer in both his hands, and a sayler in two places of the body very dangerous. After they had spent their Arrowes, and felt the sharpnesse of our shot, they retired into the Woods with a great noise, and so left vs.

The seven and twentieth day we began to build vp our Shallop: the Gentlemen and Souldiers marched eight miles vp into the Land, we could not see a Sauage in all that march, we came to a place where they had made a great fire, and had beene newly a rosting Oysters: when they perceiued our comming, they fled away to the Mountaines, and left many of the Oysters in the fire: we eat some of the Oysters, which were very large and delicate in taste.

The eighteenth day we lanched our Shallop, the Captaine and some Gentlemen went in her, and discouered vp the Bay, we found a Riuer on the Southside running into the Maine; we entered it and found it very shoald water, not for any Boats to swim: Wee went further into the Bay, and saw a plaine plot of ground where we went on Land, and found the place fiue mile in compasse, without either Bush or Tree, we saw nothing there but a Cannow, which was made out of the whole tree, which was fiue and fortie foot long by the Rule. Vpon this plot of ground we got good store of Mussels and Oysters, which lay on the ground as thicke as stones: wee opened some, and found in many of them Pearles. Wee marched some three or foure miles further into the Woods, where we saw great smoakes of fire. Wee marched to those smoakes and found that the Sauages had beene there burning downe the grasse, as wee thought either to make their plantation there, or else to giue signes to bring their forces together, and so to giue vs battell. We past through excellent ground full of Flowers of diuers kinds and colours, and as goodly trees as I haue seene, as Cedar, Cipresse, and other kindes: going a little further we came into a little plat of ground full of fine and beautifull Strawberries, foure times bigger and better than ours in England. All this march we could neither see Sauage nor Towne. When it grew to be towards night we stood backe to our Ships, we sounded and found it shallow water for a great way, which put vs out of all hopes for getting any higher with our Ships, which road at the mouth of the Riuer. Wee rowed ouer to a point of Land, where wee found a channell, and sounded six, eight, ten, or twelue fathom: which put vs in good comfort. Therefore wee named that point of Land, Cape Comfort.[1]

The nine and twentieth day we set vp a Crosse at Chesupioc Bay, and named that place Cape Henry. Thirtieth day, we came with our ships to Cape Comfort; where we saw fiue Sauages running on the shoare; presently the Captaine caused the shallop to be manned, so rowing to the shoare, the Captaine called to them in signe of friendship, but they were at first very timersome, vntil they saw the Captain lay his hand on his heart: vpon that they laid down their Bowes and Arrowes, and came very boldly to vs, making signes to come a shoare to their Towne, which is called by the Sauages Kecoughtan. Wee coasted to their Towne, rowing ouer a Riuer running into the Maine, where these Sauages swam ouer with their Bowes and Arrowes in their mouthes.

When we came ouer to the other side, there was a many of other Sauages which directed vs to their Towne, where we were entertained by them very kindly. When we came first a Land they made a dolefull noise, laying their faces to the ground, scratching the earth with their nailes. We did thinke that they had beene at their Idolatry. When they had ended their Ceremonies, they went into their houses and brought out mats and laid vpon the ground, the chiefest of them sate all in a rank: the meanest sort brought vs such dainties as they had, & of their bread which they make of their Maiz or Gennea wheat, they would not suffer vs to eat vnlesse we sate down, which

Strawberries

Point Comfort

Kecoughtan

[1] The name persists to this day, as do the shallows on the south shore.

we did on a Mat right against them. After we were well
satisfied they gaue vs of their Tabacco, which they tooke in a
pipe made artificially of earthe as ours are, but far bigger, with
the bowle fashioned together with a piece of fine copper. After
they had feasted vs, they shewed vs, in welcome, their manner of
dancing, which was in this fashion: one of the Sauages standing
in the midst singing, beating one hand against another, all the
rest dancing about him, shouting, howling, and stamping against
the ground, with many Anticke tricks and faces, making noise
like so many Wolues or Deuils. One thing of them I obserued;
when they were in their dance they kept stroke with their feet
iust one with another, but with their hands, heads, faces, and
bodies, euery one of them had a seuerall gesture: so they
continued for the space of halfe an houre. When they had
ended their dance, the Captaine gaue them Beades and other
trifling Iewells. They hang through their eares Fowles legs:
they shaue the right side of their heads with a shell, the left side
they weare of an ell long tied vp with an artificiall knot, with a
many of Foules feathers sticking in it. They goe altogether
naked, but their priuities are couered with Beasts skinnes beset
commonly with little bones, or beasts teeth: some paint their
bodies blacke, some red, with artificiall knots of sundry liuely
colours, very beautifull and pleasing to the eye, in a brauer
fashion then they in the West Indies.

The fourth day of May, we came to the King or Werowance
of Paspihe[1]: where they entertained vs with much welcome;
an old Sauage made a long Oration, making a foule noise
vttering his speech with a vehement action, but we knew little
what they meant. Whilst we were in company with the
Paspihes, the Werowance of Rapahanna came from the other
side of the Riuer in his Cannoa: he seemed to take displeasure
of our being with the Paspihes: he would faine haue had vs
come to his Towne, the Captaine was vnwilling; seeing that the
day was so far spent he returned backe to his ships for that night.

[1] For the Indian references here and below, see Appendix I.

IN VIRGINIA

The next day, being the fift of May, the Werowance of Rapahanna sent a Messenger to haue vs come to him. We entertained the said Messenger, and gaue him trifles which pleased him: Wee manned our shallop with Muskets and Targatiers sufficiently: this said Messenger guided vs where our determination was to goe. When wee landed, the Werowance of Rapahanna came downe to the water side with all his traine, as goodly men as any I haue seene of Sauages or Christians: the Werowance comming before them playing on a Flute made of a Reed, with a Crown of Deares haire colloured red, in fashion of a Rose fastened about his knot of haire, and a great Plate of Copper on the other side of his head, with two long Feathers in fashion of a paire of Hornes placed in the midst of his Crowne. His body was painted all with Crimson, with a Chaine of Beads about his necke, his face painted blew, besprinkled with siluer Ore as wee thought,[1] his eares all behung with Braslets of Pearle, and in either eare a Birds Claw through it beset with fine Copper or Gold, he entertained vs in so modest a proud fashion, as though he had beene a Prince of ciuil gouernment, holding his countenance without laughter or any such ill behauiour; he caused his Mat to be spred on the ground, where hee sate downe with a great Maiestie, taking a pipe of Tabacco: the rest of his company standing about him. After he had rested a while he rose, and made signes to vs to come to his Towne: Hee went formost, and all the rest of his people and our selues followed him vp a steepe Hill where his Palace was settled. Wee passed through the Woods in fine paths, hauing most pleasant Springs which issued from the Mountaines: Wee also went through the goodliest Corne fieldes that euer was seene in any Countrey. When wee came to Rapahannos Towne, hee entertained vs in good humanitie.

The eight day of May we discouered vp the Riuer. We landed in the Countrey of Apamatica, at our landing, there came many stout and able Sauages to resist vs with their Bowes

A Flute made of a Reed

[1] Very likely the face was tattooed (Swanton, *Indians of the Southeastern U.S.*, p. 529).

JAMESTOWN VOYAGES

and Arrowes, in a most warlike manner, with the swords at their backes beset with sharpe stones, and pieces of yron able to cleaue a man in sunder. Amongst the rest one of the chiefest standing before them crosse-legged, with his Arrow readie in his Bow in one hand, and taking a Pipe of Tobacco in the other, with a bold vttering of his speech, demanded of vs our being there, willing vs to bee gone. Wee made signes of peace, which they perceiued in the end, and let vs land in quietnesse.[1]

Archers Hope

The twelfth day we went backe to our ships, and discouered a point of Land, called Archers Hope, which was sufficient with a little labour to defend our selues against any Enemy. The soile was good and fruitfull, with excellent good Timber. There are also great store of Vines in bignesse of a mans thigh, running vp to the tops of the Trees in great abundance. We also did see many Squirels, Conies, Black Birds with crimson wings, and diuers other Fowles and Birds of diuers and sundrie collours of crimson, Watchet, Yellow, Greene, Murry, and of diuers other hewes naturally without any art vsing.

We found store of Turkie nests and many Egges, if it had not beene disliked, because the ship could not ride neere the shoare, we had setled there to all the Collonies contentment.[2]

The thirteenth day, we came to our seating place in Paspihas Countrey, some eight miles from the point of Land, which I made mention before: where our shippes doe lie so neere the shoare that they are moored to the Trees in six fathom water.

Their Plantation at Iames Towne

The fourteenth day we landed all our men which were set to worke about the fortification, and others some to watch and ward as it was conuenient. The first night of our landing, about midnight, there came some Sauages sayling close to our quarter: presently there was an alarum giuen; vpon that the sauages ran away, and we not troubled any more by them that night. Not long after there came two Sauages that seemed to be

[1] This ineffectual first step was not mentioned in the official report (Document no. 13, pp. 80–98, above).
[2] Edward Maria Wingfield was opposed to the site (see Smith's *Relation*, Document no. 33, p. 170, below).

Commanders, brauely drest, with Crownes of coloured haire vpon their heads, which came as Messengers from the Werowance of Paspihæ; telling vs that their Werowance was comming and would be merry with vs with a fat Deare.

The eighteenth day, the Werowance of Paspihæ came himselfe to our quarter, with one hundred Sauages armed, which garded him in a very warlike manner with Bowes and Arrowes, thinking at that time to execute their villany. Paspihæ made great signes to vs to lay our Armes away. But we would not trust him so far: he seeing he could not haue conuenient time to worke his will, at length made signes that he would giue vs as much land as we would desire to take. As the Sauages were in a throng in the Fort, one of them stole a Hatchet from one of our company, which spied him doing the deed: whereupon he tooke it from him by force, and also strooke him ouer the arme: presently another Sauage seeing that, came fiercely at our man with a wooden sword, thinking to beat out his braines. The Werowance of Paspiha saw vs take to our Armes, went suddenly away with all his company in great anger. *Land giuen* *These Sauages are naturally great theeues*

The nineteenth day, my selfe and three or foure more walking into the Woods by chance wee espied a path-way like to an Irish pace: wee were desirous to knowe whither it would bring vs; wee traced along some foure miles, all the way as wee went, hauing the pleasantest Suckles, the ground all flowing ouer with faire flowers of sundry colours and kindes, as though it had beene in any Garden or Orchard in England. There be many Strawberries, and other fruits vnknowne: wee saw the Woodes full of Cedar and Cypresse trees, with other trees, which issues out sweet Gummes like to Balsam: wee kept on our way in this Paradise, at length wee came to a Sauage Towne,[1] where wee found but few people, they told vs the rest were gone a hunting with the Werowance of Paspiha: we stayed

---

[1] Probably the unnamed village shown on Smith's map, later occupied by the English as a suburb of Jamestown, with the name 'Pasbyhayes' (Paspahegh). Percy had been in Ireland for two years (1600-2, see Hist. MSS. Comm. *6th Report*, p. 228), and would have heard the word 'pace' there: a pass through woods or between bogs.

there a while, and had of them Strawberries, and other things; in the meane time one of the Sauages came running out of his house with a Bowe and Arrowes and ranne mainly through the Woods: then I beganne to mistrust some villanie, that he went to call some companie, and so betray vs, wee made all the haste away wee could: one of the Sauages brought vs on the way to the Wood side, where there was a Garden of Tobacco, and other fruits and herbes, he gathered Tobacco, and distributed to euery one of vs, so wee departed.

The twentieth day the Werowance of Paspiha sent fortie of his men with a Deere, to our quarter: but they came more in villanie than any loue they bare vs: they faine would haue layne in our Fort all night, but wee would not suffer them for feare of their treachery. One of our Gentlemen hauing a Target which hee trusted in, thinking it would beare out a flight shot, hee set it vp against a tree, willing one of the Sauages to shoot; who tooke from his backe an Arrow of an elle long, drew it strongly in his Bowe, shoots the Target a foote thorow, or better: which was strange, being that a Pistoll could not pierce it. Wee seeing the force of his Bowe, afterwards set him vp a steele Target; he shot again, and burst his arrow all to pieces, he presently pulled out another Arrow, and bit it in his teeth, and seemed to bee in a great rage, so hee went away in great anger. Their Bowes are made of tough Hasell, their strings of Leather, their Arrowes of Canes or Hasell, headed with very sharpe stones, and are made artificially[1] like a broad Arrow: other some of their Arrowes are headed with the ends of Deeres hornes, and are feathered very artificially. Paspiha was as good as his word; for he sent Venison, but the Sawse came within few dayes after.

<small>Their arrowes</small>

<small>Yellow haired Virginian</small>

At Port Cotage in our Voyage vp the Riuer, we saw a Sauage Boy about the age of ten yeeres, which had a head of haire of a perfect yellow and a reasonable white skinne, which is a Miracle amongst all Sauages.

[1] 'Cleverly' – perhaps the most common meaning then.

IN VIRGINIA

This Riuer which wee haue discouered is one of the famousest Riuers that euer was found by any Christian, it ebbes and flowes a hundred and threescore miles where ships of great burthen may harbour in safetie. Wheresoeuer we landed vpon this Riuer, wee saw the goodliest Woods as Beech, Oke, Cedar, Cypresse, Wal-nuts, Sassafras and Vines in great abundance, which hang in great clusters on many Trees, and other Trees vnknowne, and all the grounds bespred with many sweet and delicate flowres of diuers colours and kindes. There are also many fruites as Strawberries, Mulberries, Rasberries and Fruits vnknowne, there are many branches of this Riuer, which runne flowing through the Woods with great plentie of fish of all kindes, as for Sturgeon all the World cannot be compared to it. In this Countrey I haue seene many great and large Medowes* hauing excellent good pasture for any Cattle. There is also great store of Deere both Red and Fallow. There are Beares, Foxes, Otters, Beuers, Muskats, and wild beasts vnknowne.

<small>Riuer of Pohatan</small>

<small>* Low Marshes</small>

The foure and twentieth day wee set vp a Crosse at the head of this Riuer, naming it Kings Riuer, where we proclaimed Iames King of England to haue the most right vnto it. When wee had finished and set vp our Crosse, we shipt our men and made for Iames Fort. By the way wee came to Pohatans Towre where the Captaine went on shore suffering none to goe with him, hee presented the Commander of this place with a Hatchet which hee tooke ioyfully, and was well pleased.

<small>Wee came downe the Riuer</small>

But yet the Sauages murmured at our planting in the Countrie, whereupon this Werowance made answere againe very wisely of a Sauage, Why should you bee offended with them as long as they hurt you not, nor take any thing away by force, they take but a little waste ground, which doth you nor any of vs any good.

I saw Bread made by their women which doe all their drugerie. The men takes their pleasure in hunting and their warres, which they are in continually one Kingdome against

Bread how made

another. The manner of baking of bread is thus, after they pound their wheat into flowre with hote water, they make it into paste, and worke it into round balls and Cakes, then they put it into a pot of seething water, when it is sod throughly, they lay it on a smooth stone, there they harden it as well as in an Ouen.

Distinct habit of Maids and Wiues

There is notice to be taken to know married women from Maids, the Maids you shall alwayes see the fore part of their head and sides shauen close, the hinder part very long, which they tie in a plate hanging downe to their hips. The married women weares their haire all of a length, and is tied of that fashion that the Maids are. The women kinde in this Countrey doth pounce and race their bodies, legges, thighes, armes and faces with a sharpe Iron, which makes a stampe in curious knots, and drawes the proportion of Fowles, Fish, or Beasts, then with paintings of sundry liuely colours, they rub it into the stampe which will neuer be taken away, because it is dried into the flesh where it is sered.

Sauage 160. yeeres old. Bearded.

The Sauages beare their yeeres well, for when wee were at Pamonkies, wee saw a Sauage by their report was aboue eight score yeeres of age. His eyes were sunke into his head, hauing neuer a tooth in his mouth, his haire all gray with a reasonable bigge beard, which was as white as any snow. It is a Miracle to see a Sauage haue any haire on their faces, I neuer saw, read, nor heard, any haue the like before. This Sauage was as lustie and went as fast as any of vs, which was strange to behold.

The fifteenth day of Iune, we had built and finished our Fort which was triangle wise, hauing three Bulwarkes at euery corner like a halfe Moone, and foure or fiue pieces of Artillerie mounted in them, we had made our selues sufficiently strong for these Sauages, we had also sowne most of our Corne on two Mountaines, it sprang a mans height from the ground, this Countrey is a fruitfull soile, bearing many goodly and fruitfull Trees, as Mulberries, Cherries, Walnuts, Ceders, Cypresse, Sassafras, and Vines in great abundance.

Munday the two and twentieth of Iune, in the morning Captaine Newport in the Admirall departed from Iames Port for England.   *Cap. Newports departure*

Captaine Newport being gone for England, leauing vs (one hundred and foure persons) verie bare and scantie of victualls, furthermore in warres and in danger of the Sauages. We hoped after a supply which Captaine Newport promised within twentie weekes. But if the beginners of this action doe carefully further vs, the Country being so fruitfull, it would be as great a profit to the Realme of England, as the Indies to the King of Spaine, if this Riuer which wee haue found had beene discouered in the time of warre with Spaine, it would haue beene a commoditie to our Realme, and a great annoyance to our enemies. The seuen and twentieth of Iuly the King of Rapahanna, demanded a Canoa which was restored, lifted vp his hand to the Sunne, which they worship as their God, besides he laid his hand on his heart, that he would be our speciall friend. It is a generall rule of these people when they swere by their God which is the Sunne, no Christian will keepe their Oath better vpon this promise. These people haue a great reuerence to the Sunne aboue all other things at the rising and setting of the same, they sit downe lifting vp their hands and eyes to the Sunne making a round Circle on the ground with dried Tobacco, then they began to pray making many Deuillish gestures with a Hellish noise foaming at the mouth, staring with their eyes, wagging their heads and hands in such a fashion and deformitie as it was monstrous to behold.   *The Sauages vse to sacrifice to the Sunne*

The sixt of August there died Iohn Asbie of the bloudie Flixe. The ninth day died George Flowre of the swelling. The tenth day died William Bruster Gentleman, of a wound giuen by the Sauages, and was buried the eleuenth day.

The fourteenth day, Ierome Alikock Ancient, died of a wound, the same day Francis Midwinter, Edward Moris Corporall died suddenly.

The fifteenth day, their died Edward Browne and Stephen

Galthrope. The sixteenth day, their died Thomas Gower Gentleman. The seuenteenth day, their died Thomas Mounslic. The eighteenth day, there died Robert Pennington, and Iohn Martine Gentleman, The nineteenth day, died Drue Piggase Gentleman. The two and twentieth day of August, there died Captaine Bartholomew Gosnold one of our Councell, he was honourably buried, hauing all the Ordnance in the Fort shot off with many vollies of small shot.

<small>Death of Cap. Bart. Gosnold</small>

After Captaine Gosnols death, the Councell could hardly agree by the dissention of Captaine Kendall, which afterward was committed about hainous matters which was proued against him.

The foure and twentieth day, died Edward Harington and George Walker, and were buried the same day. The sixe and twentieth day, died Kenelme Throgmortine. The seuen and twentieth day died William Roods. The eight and twentieth day died Thomas Stoodie, Cape Merchant.

The fourth day of September died Thomas Iacob Sergeant. The fift day, there died Beniamin Beast. Our men were destroyed with cruell diseases as Swellings, Flixes, Burning Feuers, and by warres, and some departed suddenly, but for the most part they died of meere famine. There were neuer Englishmen left in a forreigne Countrey in such miserie as wee were in this new discouered Virginia. Wee watched euery three nights lying on the bare cold ground what weather soeuer came warded all the next day, which brought our men to bee most feeble wretches, our food was but a small Can of Barlie sod in water to fiue men a day, our drinke cold water taken out of the Riuer, which was at a floud verie salt, at a low tide full of slime and filth, which was the destruction of many of our men. Thus we liued for the space of fiue moneths in this miserable distresse, not hauing fiue able men to man our Bulwarkes vpon any occasion.[1] If it had not pleased God to haue

<small>Miserable famine</small>

---

[1] Virginia authorities usually discount malaria as the cause of so many deaths, blaming rather some deficiency disease or typhoid, perhaps associated with beri-beri

put a terrour in the Sauages hearts, we had all perished by those vild and cruell Pagans, being in that weake estate as we were; our men night and day groaning in euery corner of the Fort most pittifull to heare, if there were any conscience in men, it would make their harts to bleed to heare the pittiful murmurings & out-cries of our sick men without reliefe euery night and day for the space of sixe weekes, some departing out of the World, many times three or foure in a night, in the morning their bodies trailed out of their Cabines like Dogges to be buried: in this sort did I see the mortalitie of diuers of our people. *Gods goodnesse*

It pleased God, after a while, to send those people which were our mortall enemies to releeue vs with victuals, as Bread, Corne, Fish, and Flesh in great plentie, which was the setting vp of our feeble men, otherwise wee had all perished. Also we were frequented by diuers Kings in the Countrie, bringing vs store of prouision to our great comfort.

The eleuenth day, there was certaine Articles laid against Master Wingfield which was then President, thereupon he was not only displaced out of his President ship, but also from being of the Councell. Afterwards Captaine Iohn Ratcliffe was chosen President.

The eighteenth day, died one Ellis Kinistone which was starued to death with cold. The same day at night, died one Richard Simmons. The nineteenth day, there died one Thomas Mouton.

William White (hauing liued with the Natiues) reported to vs of their customes in the morning by breake of day, before they eate or drinke both men, women and children, that be aboue tenne yeeres of age runnes into the water, there washes themselues a good while till the Sunne riseth, then offer *He was a made man[1]*

(see Wyndham B. Blanton, 'Epidemics, Real and Imaginary,' *Bulletin of the History of Medicine*, XXXI (1957), 454–62, and Gordon W. Jones, 'The First Epidemic in English America,' *VMHB*, LXXI (1963), 3–10).

[1] 'Made man' here probably means 'having his success in life assured' (*OED*, with examples from c. 1590 and 1605).

JAMESTOWN VOYAGES

* The rest is omitted, being more fully set downe in Cap. Smiths Relations

Sacrifice to it, strewing Tobacco on the water or Land, honouring the Sunne as their God, likewise they doe at the setting of the * Sunne[1]

29. 1608? [Before 12 April 1612.]
George Percy, Fragment published in 1614.[2]

* Virg. Voyage, 1606. M.S. Master George Percie

They haue * a certaine herbe called Weysake, like Liuerwort[3] which they chew and spit into poisoned wounds, that are thereby healed in foure and twenty houres. In finding out their medicinable root, (it is the relation of Master George Percy) six of them hold together by the armes, and so go singing, and withall searching: and when they haue found it, sit downe singing, crossing the roote with their hands for a good space, then gather, chew, and spit. He thus describeth their dances; One stands in the middest singing and clapping hands; all the rest dance about him, shouting, hallowing, stamping with antike gesture, like so many Diuels, their feet alwayes (and only) agreeing in one stroke.[4] Landing at Kecoughtan, the Sauages entertained them with a doleful noise, laying their faces to the ground, and scratching the earth with their nailes. The Werowance of Rapahanna, met them, playing on a flute of a reed, with a crowne of Deeres haire coloured red, fashioned like a Rose, with a chaine of Beads about his necke, and Bracelets of Pearle hanging at his eares, in each eare a birds

---

[1] The account ends abruptly here. While it is evident that Purchas cut William White's narrative at this point, it is not clear whether that narrative was part of Percy's *Discourse* or an independent report. Certainly, the opening paragraphs of the *Discourse* seem to have been pruned (no mention of Smith's 'restraint', though noted in the margin, no reference to the new month after the storm, beginning of paragraph two, and so on), and there is evidence that Purchas had more material by Percy (see Document no. 29). In the absence of firm facts, it is best to let the document stand by itself.

[2] Extract. Purchas, *Pilgrimage* (1614), p. 768.

[3] Usually spelled *wighsacan* or *wisacan*. It is compared with liverwort in Document no. 13, p. 90, above.

[4] The balance, except for the sentence describing the women's tattooing, is printed (apparently in full) in the *Discourse* (see Document no. 28, immediately preceding).

claw; of a modest-proud behauiour. The women with an Iron pounce and race their bodies, legs, thighes, and armes, in curious knots and portraitures of fowles, fishes, beasts, and rub a painting into the same, which will neuer out. The Queene of Apametica, was attired with a Coronet beset with many white bones, her eares hanged with copper, a chaine thereof six times compassing her necke. The maids shaue their heads all but the hinder part: the wiues weare it all of a length: the men weare the left locke long, sometimes an ell, which they tie when they please in an artificiall knot, stucke with feathers, the right side shauen, The King of Paspahey was painted all black, with hornes on his head like a Diuell. He testifieth of their hard fare, watching euery third night, lying on the bare cold ground, what wether soeuer came, and warding the next day, a small can of barly sodden in water, being the sustenance for fiue men a day: their drinke brackish and slimie water. This fiue moneths.

30. *1608? [Before 1614.]*
   William White, Fragments published in 1614.[1]

... In some part of the Countrey they haue yearely a sacrifice of children: such a one was performed at Quiyoughcohanock some ten miles from Iames Towne in this manner. Rapahannock ⋆ Werowance[2] made a feast in the woods: the people were so painted, that a Painter with his pensill could not haue done better. Some of them were blacke like Diuels, with hornes and loose haire, some of diuers colours. They continued two dayes

⋆ Will. White

---

[1] Extract. Purchas, *Pilgrimage* (1614), pp. 766–67.
[2] 'Rapahannock' was the mistaken name by which the village (and tribe) of Quiyoughcohannock was first known. Purchas (or White) seems to have attempted a compromise. White was a labourer who arrived with the original settlers, and who lived with the Indians at some uncertain time. He may be the William White who was buried in Elizabeth City on 12 September 1624 (John Camden Hotten, *The Original Lists of Persons of Quality* ... (London, 1874), 257), but his not uncommon name and his lack of prominence make it impossible to trace his career.

dancing in a circle of a quarter of a mile, in two companies, with anticke trickes, foure in a ranke, the Werowance leading the dance; they had rattles in their hands; all in the middest had black hornes on their heads, and greene bowes in their hands: next them were foure or fiue principall men diuersly painted, which with bastinadoes beat forward such as tired in the dance. Thus they made themselues scarce able to go or stand. When they met together they made a hellish noise, and euery one flinging away his bough, ranne (clapping their hands) vp into a tree, and tare it to the ground, and fell into their order againe: thus they did twice. Fourteene well fauoured children, or (if you had rather heare* Captaine Smith) fifteene of the properest yong boyes beteweene ten and fifteene yeares of age they painted white: Hauing brought them forth, the people (saith he) spent the forenoone in dancing and singing about them with Rattles: in the afternoone they put these children to the roote of a tree, all the men standing to guard them, each with a Bastinado of Reeds bound together, in his hand. Then doe they make a Lane betweene them all along, through which there were appointed fiue yong men (White calles them Priests) to fetch these children. Each of these fetcheth a childe, the guard laying on with their bastinadoes, while they with their naked bodies defend the children to their great smart. All this time the women weepe and crie out very passionately, prouiding Mosse, skinnes, Mats, and drie wood, as things fitting the childrens Funerall. When the children are in this manner fetched away, the guard teares downe trees, branches, and boughes, making wreathes for their heads, or bedecking their haire with the leaues. What else was done with the children was not seene, but they were all cast on a heape in a Valley, as dead, where was made a great Feast for all the company.[1]

* Capt. Smith

[1] In Strachey's *Historie* (p. 98), this account is presented almost verbatim, and attributed to George Percy. Virtually the same account appeared in 1612 in Smith's *Map of Virginia* (Document no. 63, pp. 367-8, below), not attributed to anybody. Apparently White was the source for the story, and while Smith printed it first, Percy

IN VIRGINIA

William White relating this sacrifice, saith, That they remoued them from tree to tree three times, and at last carried them into a Valley where the King sate; where they would suffer our men to see, but feasted there two houres. On a sudden all arose with cudgels in their hands, and made a lane as is before said, and the children being laide downe vnder a tree (to their seeming) without life, they all fell into a ring againe and danced about the children a good space, and then sate downe in a circle about the tree. Raphanna, in the middes, caused burthens of wood to be brought to the Altar, made of poles set like a steeple, where they made a great fire to sacrifice their children to the Diuell (whom they call Kewase) who, as they report, suckes their bloud. They were vnwilling to let them stay any longer. They found a woman mourning for yong Paspiha sacrificed at the Towne of Rapahanna.[1]

The Werowance (Captain Smith addeth) being demanded the meaning of this sacrifice, answered, that the children were not all dead, but that the Oke or Diuell did sucke the bloud from their left brest, who chanced to be his by lot, till they were dead, but the rest were kept in the wildernesse by the yong men, till nine Moones were expired, during which time they must not conuerse with any, and of these were made their Priests, and coniurers. This sacrifice they held to be so necessarie, that if they should omit it, their Oke or Diuell, and their other Quiyoughcosughes, or gods, would let them haue no Deere, Turkies, Corne, or Fish; and would besides make a great slaughter amongst them. They thinke that their Werowances and Priests, which they also esteeme Quiyoughcosughes, when

William White

jotted it down and told it to Strachey in Virginia (or Strachey saw it in Smith's work and wanted to favour Percy).

[1] In the 1617 and 1626 edition of the *Pilgrimage* Purchas attempted to clarify the confusion. He added, in both, that 'this Paspiha is now alive, as Mr Rolph hath tince related to me: and the mourning of the women is not for their childrens death, but because they are for diuers moneths detained from them, as we shall after see. Yea, the Virginians themselues, by false reports might delude our Men, and say they were sacrificed when they were not...' (*Pilgrimage* (1617), p. 953; (1626), p. 841). William Strachey found the young werowance of Quiyoughcohannock alive in 1610, and his name was Tatahcoope (*Historie*, pp. 64-5).

they are dead, doe goe beyond the Mountaines towards the setting of the Sunne, and euer remaine there in forme of their Oke, hauing their heads painted with Oyle and Pocones ᵐ finely trimmed with feathers, and shall haue Beads, Hatchets, Copper, and Tobacco, neuer ceasing to dance and sing with their predecessors. The common people, they suppose, shall not liue after death. Some sought to conuert them from these superstitions: the Werowance of Quiyoughcohanock was so farre perswaded, as that he professed to beleeue that our God exceeded theirs, as much as our Gunnes did their Bowes and Arrowes: and many times did send to the President many presents, intreating him to pray to his ⁿ God for raine, for his God would not send him any.¹

William White reporteth these their ceremonies of honoring the Sunne. By breake of day, before they eate or drinke, the men, women, and children aboue ten yeares old, runne into the water, and there wash a good space, till the Sunne arise, and then they offer sacrifice to it, strewing Tobacco on the land or water: the like they doe at Sunneset. He also relateth that one George ᵒ Casson (before mentioned) was sacrificed, as they thought, to the Diuell, being stripped naked, and bound to two stakes, with his backe against a great fire: then did they rippe him and burne his bowels, and dried his flesh to the bones, which they kept aboue ground in a byroome. Many other of our men were cruelly and treacherously executed by them, though perhaps not sacrificed, and none had beene left, if their ambushes and treasons had taken effect. Powhatan thus inuited ᵖ Captaine Ratliffe and thirtie others to trade for corne, and hauing brought them within his ambush, murthered them.

---

¹ This is obviously from Smith. In his day, one 'Pipsco' may have been werowance (Strachey, *ibid.*).
² See *A True declaration of the estate of the colonie in Virginia* (London, 1610), p. 41.

m Pocones is a small Roote, which dried and beat into powder turneth red: they vse it for swellings, aches, and painting

n In that extremitie of miserie which ours since sustained, I haue been told that both the Sauages and fugitiues would obiect our want and their plentie, for theirs, and against our Religion

o The cruell death of George Casson

p Declaration of Virginia²

IN VIRGINIA

31. *1 July 1610.*
Francis Magnel's Relation of the First Voyage and the Beginnings of the Jamestown Colony.[1]

Relation of what Francis Magnel, an Irishman, learned in the land of Virginia during the eight months he was there.

Of the voyage he made and the route the English took at first for the discovery of Virginia.

From England they go to Sancto Domingo [Dominica], from there to Menes [Nevis], from Menes to San Nicolas [St Eustatius?],[2] and from there to Puerto Rico. From Puerto Rico they take the direct route to Virginia, sailing sixteen days north-west until they discover a cape in Virginia which the English call Saint Nicholas [Cape Henry], which is six hundred leagues from Puerto Rico, the relator [Magnel] thinks. And all this sea coast is low land like Florida, and is free from any hazards, and along all of it the water is ten or twelve *brazas*[3] deep, and it is very suitable there for casting anchor.

Throughout this area there is an *arenal* or sand bank [barrier beach] eight leagues out from the shore which is covered with water to a depth of sixteen or eighteen *brazas*. This bank starts in Florida and continues northward until it joins another bank off Newfoundland. One sails between this bank and the mainland some hundred and fifty leagues because the current outside the said bank is very strong. Between the bank and the mainland the tide runs south-south-east and north-north-west. From the point of Saint Nicholas to Cape Comfort is eight leagues.[4] This Cape Comfort is an island which is at the

[1] Translated. Archivo General de Simancas, Legajo E 2587, 98.
[2] It is clear that Magnel did not know where he was at the time, or that he had forgotten.
[3] The Spanish fathom, equal to about five and a half feet.
[4] A Spanish nautical league was about 3·5 English statute miles. But there was a considerably shorter 'land league' which seems to have been used here (see p. 296, n. 1 below). Old Point Comfort is now attached to the mainland by a narrow tongue of land.

entrance of a big river where the English live. This river is at 37° 30′ [north latitude][1]. In order to enter this river it is necessary for the vessels coming in to sail very close to the said island, where they have ten *brazas* of water. And inside of this island half a league up the river there is a great broad bay, the water twelve *brazas* deep, and all the ships England has could find room in it.[2] The English have decided to build a fortress on this island to defend the entrance of the river, but the relator does not know if it is yet finished. From this island or entrance twenty leagues upstream westwards, the English built a walled fort which is on a point that juts out into the river, and the English have decided to cut off the said point so that there will be water all around it. And in the said fort they have installed twenty pieces of artillery, and since then a great deal more artillery has been sent from England. This river is a little more than a league wide for the most part, and at its shallowest it is three *brazas* deep at low tide, and in other places it is ten or twelve *brazas* deep. From this fort, which the English call James-fort, the river extends westwards another twenty leagues, which [distance] the English sailed in pinnaces, taking some of the natives as guides.

Of the commodities which the English find in this region and of its climate.

In this region there are many iron, copper and other mines, [from] which they took [samples] to England, and the English do not want it known what kind of mines they are until after they are well reinforced [*fortificados*] in Virginia. And the relator took a sample from these mines to England which weighed eighty pounds, and found it to contain three *reales*[3] of gold by weight and five of silver, and four pounds of copper. There are many large pearls in that land, and a great quantity

[1] Newport News, on the north shore, is at 37° 0′.
[2] Was he referring to Hampton Roads?
[3] The *real* was a coin valued at six pence at the time. The *pounds* of copper surely refer to weight, not to value.

IN VIRGINIA

of coral,[1] and in the mountains they find stones very much like diamonds, and for the purpose of finding more of these mines and purifying [the ore], the King of England has sent many artisans who understand this business, as well as other workmen trained in all the mechanical arts, to live there./ Many kinds of dyes are found there, some of which they sell in England at forty *reales* the pound. The English make a great deal of soap[2] there, which they take to their country. In the rivers there are a great many salmon, sole and other fish, and as great and good a quantity of cod as in Newfoundland. There is an infinite number of deer in the land, turkeys, swans, and all kinds of fowl. Many wild grapes are natural to the land, from which the English make a wine very similar to that of Alicante, in the opinion of the relator, who has tried one or two.[3] Also there is a great quantity of beans, pease, corn, almonds,[4] walnuts and chestnuts, and above all a lot of flax, which grows wild, without any cultivation. They have a great abundance of skins for very rich furs, especially sable martens, and the [native] King has houses full of them, and they are his wealth. The English take from there [Virginia] many drugs and other necessities for apothecary shops. The land is very pleasant and level, and very fertile, with many big rivers; the air is healthy, and the climate like here in Spain, although a little colder in winter.

Of the Emperor and natives of the land.

The Emperor of Virginia has sixteen Kings under his sway. He and all his vassals deal peacefully with the English, and attend a market which the English hold at their fort daily, and they bring the commodities of their land there to exchange for trinkets the English give them, such as knives, articles made of

---

[1] The reference is surely to shells, not to coral.
[2] Soap ashes were produced, but not in great quantity. Soap was surely a hope, not a product.
[3] That wine was made before Magnel left Virginia is doubtful in the extreme.
[4] Almonds did not exist in Virginia. The reference is undoubtedly to some native nut not identified.

glass, mirrors, little bells, and so on. The natives of the land are robust people and well built, and they usually go clothed in well-dressed deer-skins, which they know how to prepare. Their arms are bows and arrows. The Emperor sends some [of his] men by land every year to West India [*la India occidental*][1] and to Newfoundland and other regions to bring back word of what is going on. And these messengers say that those who are in India treat their natives very badly, and like slaves, and the English tell them that those people are very cruel and wicked, meaning the Spaniards. The English have boys [living] there among those people [the Emperor's] to learn the language, which many of them already know perfectly. The Emperor sent one of his sons to England, where they treated him well, and sent him back to his land. The Emperor, his father, and his people were very happy over what he told them about the good reception and entertainment he found in England.[2] And the English sent the Emperor a crown of polished copper and many copper plates and silk robes[3] for himself, his wives and his children, and the relator returned to England in the ship along with the said son of the Emperor. There they worship the Devil, whom they hold for their God, and they say that he talks to them often, appearing in human shape. The Emperor and his sons promised the English that they would abandon their religion and believe in the God of the English, and it seems easy to convert them because they are so friendly.

> Of the designs and pretensions of the English against His Catholic Majesty, which the said relator learned when he was in Virginia.

In the first place, the natives of Virginia assure the English that they will easily take them to the South Sea by three routes.

---

[1] All of this is grossly exaggerated. By 'West India' Magnel probably meant the 'enemy country' west of the Falls at Richmond.
[2] Magnel was back in England by then.
[3] The robes were of wool, and not the best quality.

IN VIRGINIA

The first route by which they will take them is by land, where it is no more than ten days' journey from the [upper] end of that river where the English have their fort to the South Sea, as the natives affirm. The second route is [this:] a journey of a day and a half from the inland end of that river there is another equally big river which flows into the South Sea. The third route is, twelve leagues from the entrance of that river where the English are, to the north-west, there are four other rivers, which one of those English Captains [John Smith] reached in a pinnace, who says that one of those rivers is of very great importance, and the natives affirm that fourteen leagues beyond the four rivers to the north-west there is another big river which reaches far inland until it joins another big river which comes from [i.e., flows into] the South Sea. The English want nothing more than they want to make themselves lords of the South Sea, so as to have their share of the riches of the Indies, and to be in the way of the traffic of the King of Spain, and to seek other new worlds for themselves. And to the end of making themselves lords of the South Sea they are resolved to build a fortress at the end of each day's journey of the ten days which it takes to go from the head of their river to the South Sea to make the road safe, and two more fortresses on that day-and-a-half journey between the two rivers, [all of] which they hope soon to finish, because they do not intend to make them very strong so long as they serve to defend themselves from those savages.[1]

Also, to the same end, the King of England sent there many of the best carpenters in the kingdom to build ships and boats on those rivers and seas, for which they have great facilities there, since they have a great abundance of the best timber [*maderamiento*] which can be found for ship-building, and the land of itself abounds in pitch, resin, and turpentine, and much hemp grows wild in it, which they plan to use for cables and

---

[1] All of this is highly visionary, but Magnel may have heard some such talk from some of the colonists – hardly the 'serious' ones.

ropes [or cordage] for the ships. And having, as they have, all these facilities for building ships, and along with them, as has been said, so many iron mines for the working of which (as well as of other metals) they have built mills there – it will be very easy for them to build many ships. And according to themselves, the relator heard, as soon as they have twenty or thirty thousand capable Englishmen dwelling there, they can do more harm to the King of Spain than France and England could [together]. The English are much encouraged to make this journey to the South Sea because the natives of Virginia assure them that on the other side of Virginia by the South Sea there is a land where the natives wear long silk robes and red buskins, and that they have a great deal of gold, and that ships often come to the said land which bargain with the natives there and take gold and silk from there, and in proof of this those of Virginia showed the English some knives and other things which they got from those who came in the said ships, and the English judge that the said ships would be Spanish. Item: the English in that land have of themselves declared, and sworn an oath to, the King of England as King of Virginia. And such is the jealousy they have that the secrets of this land be not known that they have issued an order that no one can take letters out of the land, or send any, especially to private persons, unless they are first seen and read by the Governor. And for this same reason they have executed in that James-fort of theirs a Catholic English Captain called Captain Tindol [Kendall],[1] because they knew that he wanted to come to Spain to reveal to His Majesty what goes on in that land, and the many pretensions of the English which he knew, but which the Relator does not know. And to conclude this it must be noted that now that they have discovered that land, they are not following the first route or course which they took past Puerto Rico to discover Virginia, but [now] they take their course from England much farther north, so as not to run

---

[1] For the correct identity of the man executed, see Barbour, *Kendall*.

IN VIRGINIA

across Spanish ships, and also to make the crossing in less time. And the relator himself affirms that he returned from Virginia to England in twenty-one days,[1] because the return voyage is much shorter than the outbound one. And in proof that all that is contained herein is true the said relator promises and commits himself to go personally at His Catholic Majesty's command to bear visible testimony of everything he says, if His Majesty be pleased to employ him in this service.[2]

I, Don Fray Florencio Conry, Archbishop of Tuam, attest that the said relator Francis Magnel, Irishman, has sworn in my presence that everything herein contained he has either seen or heard say and discuss [by and] between the most grave of the English [during the time] when he was in Virginia, and that everything which he said in his language is here faithfully translated into Castilian, and I have signed it as true, in Madrid, the first of July, 1610.

Fray Florencio Conry,
Archbishop of Tuam[3]

[Endorsement:] Relation of Virginia.
To the Council of State.

The substance of this could be conveyed to Don Alonso de Velasco, for him to see if it is true. . . .

[1] Twenty-one days is absurd. It is likely that Magnel confused the length of their passage with the date of their arrival at Blackwall, 21 May 1608 (see Document no. 34).

[2] The meaning apparently is that Magnel would like to show his proof to the King personally, and that he would also like employment, perhaps back in Virginia.

[3] Francis Magnel (or Magner) was examined in London on 16 December 1610. According to his testimony, he had been on a 'Marchauntes voyage for Geanney', but had fallen out with the ship's master and had been discharged at Naples six months before. On his way from Naples to England he met an Irish priest who introduced him to one 'Captayne Ralfe', the pilot who had conveyed Hugh O Neill, Earl of Tyrone, from Ireland to the Continent. Captain Ralfe questioned Magnel on Virginia, and was the immediate cause of Magnel's going to Spain, where he met Sir William Stanley and other disloyal exiles. The examination had rather to do with an Irish plot however, than with the Virginia voyages (see 'The examinacion of Fraunces Magner of RackCliff neer London Saylor', P.R.O., S.P. Dom., S.P. 14/58, fo. 198).

32. *28 March 1608.*
Francis Perkin[s] in Jamestown to a Friend in England.[1]

Illustrious Sir.

After my due commendations to you, with thanks for the many kindnesses you have done me and trouble you have gone to for me, which I am able to repay only with prayers to God (and I want to serve you in any way I can), I am so bold as to beg you once more for a favour at this present moment, although you have just cause to forsake me, since when I left I did not say good-bye to so good a friend as you have always been to me. But the hope I have of your customary kindness will [I trust] excuse me this time, for this fault occurred only because I was afraid that something would interfere with this voyage, which I so much wanted to make. I will not fail to make amends, for if I do not look to you to help me and try to make peace with my Lady and obtain in my absence what I explained to you before I left, all the more since I had time to present the matter in person, [otherwise] the whole affair will result in serious detriment and damage to me.[2] But, completely trusting in your usual kindness, I beg you to be so good as to approach Sir William Waad, Sir Thomas Smythe, Sir Walter Cope, Sir Thomas Chaloner, Sir George More and the others [concerned],[3] to have me appointed one of the council here in Virginia, not only as an honour to me, but also to enable me the better to pay my debts. There are members of the council

---

[1] Translated. Archivo General de Simancas, Legajo E 2586, 111–14. The name of the writer appears as Francis Perkins, labourer, in Arber, *Smith, Works*, p. 108, and as Francis Perkins, gentleman, *ibid.*, p. 411. In Spanish it is spelled Perquin. The division into paragraphs is the editor's, and punctuation has been supplied to help clarify the messy Spanish of the original. Evidently the clerk who translated Perkins' letter was none too literate in either English or Spanish, but the sense is always obvious.

[2] Without further clues, Perkins' troubles must remain obscure. The identity of 'my Lady' (*Madama*) is not known.

[3] These were all appointed to the council in the ordinance of 9 March 1607 (Document no. 9). The council in Virginia at that time consisted in Captain Ratcliffe, president, Captain John Smith, Captain John Martin and Matthew Scrivener (aged 26). Edward Maria Wingfield had been deposed, the others were dead.

IN VIRGINIA

who understand affairs of state no better than I do, and whom I equal in business [affairs]. It would be a pleasure to see so many competent and intelligent [men] come from our country that I should not deserve to appear among them.

With regard to our trip over and my opinion of this country, I will inform you the best I can. We left Gravesend Thursday the eighth of October, 1607. We arrived at Plymouth the following Thursday [15 October], where we stayed until Monday [19 October], and since the wind was not favourable we had to put in at Falmouth, where we rode out a great storm until Friday [23 October], after which we continued our voyage, [and] in five weeks and two days we arrived at the island of Santo Domingo [i.e., Dominica, 29 November], which is in the West Indies, and we spent the whole day there trading with the savages, who came on board naked bringing us potatoes, bananas, pineapples (which are a very delicious fruit), bread they call 'casadra' [cassava] made of certain roots, parrots, cocks and hens, linen, and other things which they gave us in exchange for iron hatchets, saws, knives, rosaries, little bells, and other similar trifles which they esteem very highly and are of great worth to those who take them along on similar voyages. And so skirting the other islands in that region for that whole week [to 5 December] we came near the island of San Juan [Puerto Rico] on the north side, and on Sunday, two weeks later [20 December], we sighted America. The following Thursday [24 December] the ship which accompanied us, called the *Phoenix*, lost us in a dense fog which came up when we were not more than ten or twelve leagues from the entrance to the port, and we have had no further news of it since, That ship brought about forty men who were to stay here with us.

The ship called the *John and Francis*, with Captain Christopher Newport, arrived at Jamestown on the second of January.[1] The river is very fair and wide, but full of shoals and oyster-

[1] The figure looks very much like 20, but it must be 2°, Spanish *segundo*.

banks. The land [is] low-lying and forested right down to the coast. We had warm weather all the time. Afterwards it got so very cold and the frost was so sharp that I and many others suffered frozen feet. A month after this, we went to a region where there was a great deal of frost and snow. The neighbouring region has a great abundance of wild swans, herons and cranes, geese, wild ducks, mallards, and many other birds, as long as winter lasts, with the prettiest parrots there are. The cold was so intense that one night the river at our fort froze almost all the way across, although at that point it is as wide again as the one at London. The ice in the river froze some fish which, when we took them out after the ice was melted, were very good, and so plump that they could be fried in their own fat, without anything added.

After we disembarked, which was on Monday, the following Thursday [7 January][1] there was a fire that spread so that all the houses in the fort were burned down, including the storehouse for munition and supplies, leaving only three [unburned]. Everything my son and I had was burned, except a mattress which had not yet been taken off the ship. Thanks to God, we are at peace with all the inhabitants of the surrounding country, trading for corn and supplies. They value very highly indeed [our] reddish copper.[2] Their great Emperor, or Werowance, which is the name of their kings, has sent some of his people to show us how to plant the native wheat [corn], and to make some gear such as they use to go fishing, and surely for all we can guess it is very probable that the land will prove very fertile and good, and extensive enough to accommodate [*entretener*] a million people. What we are doing most just now is clearing the forests, for the wheat [corn] sprouts in great quantity [of itself].

[1] Wingfield's *Discourse* (Document no. 34, p. 227, below) gives 7 January as the date of the fire, but curiously gives 'the viijth of January' as the date of Smith's return from the Indians and Captain Newport's appearance 'the same eevening'. The editor has not found any sound explanation of the 'viijth' for the 'second'.

[2] Lane had pointed out the greater attraction of English 'redder and harder' copper for the Indians (Quinn, *Roanoke*, I, p. 268).

IN VIRGINIA

I have sent to my Lady your wife a pair of turtle-doves, others [another pair?] to my Lady Catherine, and others to Sir William Cornwallis,[1] hoping that when our [ships] make another trip I will have better things to send you. I am sending an ear of the native wheat [corn], with two pots of our ordinary earth,[2] and two more to my Lady Catherine, and [two] more to Sir William the elder.

There are many little animals here with skins of fine fur. If I come across any I will send them for you and your friends to see. There is an abundance of [fresh] fodder for any kind of live stock, especially pigs and goats, even if there were a million of them. There is also around the fort, where we have cleared away the trees,[3] a very great quantity of strawberries and other tasty herbs, and, sir, considering that this misfortune of the fire has caused a general lack of everything among us, especially to me, who have suffered a great deal these last [few] years – so much a lack that I do not have even paper and ink with which to write our friends. I beg you to see that my Lady Catherine does not get angry with me, but that, with the usual nobility of her heart and the affection in which she has been pleased to hold me in the past, she will find a way, jointly with you and Sir William Cornwallis, to recommend as urgently as possible my petition, especially with Sir William Smith, since he more than anyone else carries weight in matters of this sort [*de este estado*, in error for *de este índole?*]. Begging at the same time my Lady Catherine to be so kind as to get Sir William Cornwallis to send me ten pounds worth of discarded clothing, be it [outer]

---

[1] The 'Lady Catherine' was undoubtedly the wife of Sir William Cornwallis the younger, son of Sir Charles (died 1629). Sir William the elder, mentioned below, was the older brother of Sir Charles. He lived at Highgate, near the residence of Zúñiga. By his first wife, Lucy Nevill (aunt of George Percy of the Jamestown voyages), he had a daughter Elizabeth, who married Sir William Sandys, mentioned later in the letter, undoubtedly a relative of Sir Edwin Sandys of the Virginia Company.

[2] The transcription of this document made for Brown has '*balas*' of earth, but the original seems to read '*vasas*' for '*vasijas*', any kind of pot. The Indian pots were made of clay, or 'ordinary earth'.

[3] This is a further, and important, bit of confirmation that the English did not occupy any recently held Indian site.

apparel, underwear, doublet, breeches, mantle, hose, or whatever he likes, for we need everything because the fire burned all we had, and anything will be of use to us. Beg my Lady Catherine also for me to approach Sir William Sans [Sandys] in like manner, for I swear to repay them the value of anything they send me, with the duty of acknowledging that it is by her kindness and that of those gentlemen [*caballeros*, knights] that I and mine live, and if this [sum] is not enough to supply the needs of many, may my Lady and those gentlemen [*señores*] do me the kindness at least of granting to me and my son, out of their generosity, such of their things as are of little use to them, but of great value to me. I beg you not to be angry with me for this liberty and boldness, but that you remember me, out of your goodness, for I am so far and so separated from my friends, and do me also the favour to grant reasonable kindnesses to my wife if she should have occasion to appeal to you. Begging you to inform my Lady Catherine of the contents of this letter, and if you like to read all of it [to her], and at the same time recommending me most humbly to her and to those gentlemen, in whose kindness and favour all of my trust is placed, I beg our Lord to guard all of you, this 28 of March, 1608.

> Your servant while he lives,
> Francis Perkin. From Jamestown
> in Virginia.

I am sending to my Lady Catherine and to my Lady your wife, to each of them six pounds of sassafras to use in medicines, or between linens. It used to be worth forty *reales* [one pound sterling] the pound not long ago, and is no less efficacious now than then. I shall not fail to send my Lady Catherine, you, and Sir William Cornwallis some trees, fruit, herbs, flowers, and other new things produced by this land, begging you in the meantime to receive what I can now send in the spirit in which I offer it.

IN VIRGINIA

[Endorsed:] Letter from Virginia to send to His Majesty. [Sent with the following letter from Pedro de Zúñiga.]

London. Don Pedro de Zúñiga. [16/]26 June 1608.

Sir:

I have already informed Your Majesty about what is going on in Virginia. Captain Newport returned and brought a few things of little importance, so that it becomes more evident that the main [thing] they find [to do] in that place is fortify themselves and carry on piracy from there. This [business] is in greater straits for money than one can imagine, and in spite of that they have raised some with which to send this Newport back, with two good ships and people, and they will leave here in two months, for they are already making preparations and victualling. He has chosen the most suitable people available here, and since they are called to plunder, they all go very gladly. I have obtained this letter which one of those who are there writes to a friend, and I thought to send it so that Your Majesty may see what progress they make and the way they behave there. This Newport brought a lad who they say is the son of an emperor of those lands and they have coached him that when he sees the King he is not to take off his hat, and other things of this sort, so that I have been amused by the way they honour him, for I hold it for surer that he must be a very ordinary person.[1] May our Lord &c.

[Endorsed:] London. To His Majesty. 1608.
Don Pedro de Zúñiga, the 26th of June [1608].

[1] This must have been Namontack, described by John Smith as Powhatan's 'trusty servant, and one of a shrewd subtill capacity' (Document no. 63, p. 392). The Venetian Ambassador, Zorzi Giustinian, seems to have seen political significance in the visit: 'One of the ships ... has returned. It brings one of the chief inhabitants to treat with the King for some agreement about that navigation' (25May/4 June, 1608; *Calendar of S.P., Venetian*, XI, 137). It would appear that the Virginia Company for publicity purposes palmed him off as a son of the 'Emperor'. The Earl of Northumberland, probably for the sake of his brother George Percy, helped out with three shillings' worth of 'rings and other pieces of copper given to the Virginia Prince' (H.M.C., *Sixth Report* (1877), 229a).

Received the 13th of July.

[*Note:* Neither endorsement indicates that either letter was encoded or decoded.]

IN VIRGINIA

33. *Before 2 June 1608.*
Captain John Smith, A true relation.[1]

A TRVE RE-
lation of such occur-
rences and accidents of noateas
hath hapned in Virginia since the first
planting of that Collony, which is now
resident in the South part thereof, till
the last returne from
thence.

Written by Captaine Smith *one of the said Collony, to a worshipfull* friend of his in England.

LONDON
Printed for *Iohn Tappe,* and are to bee folde at the Grey=
hound in Paules-Church-yard, by *W. W.*
1608

---

[1] The text followed here is that of the British Museum copy, C. 33, c. 5, except that the address 'To the Courteous Reader', lacking therein, has been supplied from the

[¶] To the Courteous Reader.[1]

Courteous, Kind & indifferent Readers, whose willingnesse to reade & heare this following discourse, doth explaine to the world your hearty affection, to the prosecuting and furtherance of so worthy an action: so it is, that like to an vnskilfull actor, who hauing by misconstruction of his right Cue, ouer-slipt himselfe, in beginning of a contrary part, and fearing the hatefull hisse of the captious multitude, with a modest blush retires himself in priuate; as doubting the reprehension of his whole audience in publicke, and yet againe vpon further deliberation, thinking it better to know their censures at the first, and vpon submission to reape pardon, then by seeking to smother it, to incurre the danger of a secret scandall: Imboldening himselfe vpon the curteous kindnesse of the best, and not greatly respecting the worst, comes fourth againe, makes an Apollogie for himselfe, shewes the cause of his error, craues pardon for his rashnes, and in fine, receiues a generall applauditie of the whole assemblie: so I gentle Readers, happening vpon this relation by chance (as I take it, at the second or third hand)

---

copy in the New York Historical Society Library. This copy contains some eight minor corrections of misprints, and is annotated in an early hand (probably before 1630). In addition, the copy contains the second issue of the title, for which the fourth issue has been substituted, from a copy in the New York Public Library. These issues, varying only in the statement of authorship, have been described by Wilberforce Eames in the Sabin/Eames *Dictionary*, XX, 254–8: (1) 'Written by a Gentleman of the said Collony'; (2) 'Written by Th. Watson Gent. one of the said Collony'; (3) (after it was learned that Smith was the author) 'Written by Captaine Smith Coronell of the said Collony', 'Coronell' being altered by hand to 'one' in some copies; and (4) the title page as here given. (See also W. C. Ford's note in *Proceedings of the Massachusetts Historical Society*, LVIII (1924–5), 245–6.)

[1] It is evident that John Smith wrote this account in the form of a letter to a friend, whose identity is still well concealed. It was finished after Francis Nelson had sailed from Jamestown, but was hurried down the river in time to catch up with Nelson, then off Cape Henry, on 2 June 1608. Nelson reached London by 7 July, after a quick voyage, and Smith's letter must have been delivered not long thereafter. It evidently aroused much interest, and before long was recommended for printing. That it was put through the press in haste is shown by the difficulties with the title, and the fact that it was entered for publication on 13 August (see Barbour, *Smith*, 290–2). A few resultant and self-evident misprints have been silently corrected.

induced thereunto by diuers well willers of the action, and none wishing better towards it then my selfe, so farre foorth as my poore abilitie can or may stretch too, I thought good to publish it: but the Author being absent from the presse, it cannot be doubted but that some faults haue escaped in the printing, especially in the names of Countries, Townes, and [¶ᵛ] People, which are somewhat strange vnto vs: but most of all, and which is the chiefe error, (for want of knowledge of the Writer) some of the bookes were printed vnder the name of Thomas Watson, by whose occasion I know not, vnlesse it were the ouer rashnesse, or mistaking of the workemen, but since hauing learned that the saide discourse was written by Captaine Smith, who is one of the Counsell there in Virginia: I thought good to make the like Appollogie, by shewing the true Author so farre as my selfe could learne, not doubting, but that the wise noting it as an error of ignorance, will passe it ouer with patience, and if worthy an applauditie, to reserue it to the Author, whose paines in my iudgement deserueth commendations; som:what more was by him written, which being as I thought (fit to be priuate) I would not aduenture to make it publicke what more may be expected concerning the scituation of the Country, the nature, of the clime, number of our people there resident, the manner of their gouernment, and liuing, the commodities to be produced, & the end & effect it may come too, I can say nothing more then is here written, only what I haue learned and gathered from the generall consent of all (that I haue conuersed withall) as-well marriners as others, which haue had imployment that way; is that the Country is excellent & pleasant, the clime temperate and health full, the ground fertill and good, the commodities to be expected (if well followed) many, for our people, the worst being already past, these former hauing indured the heate of the day, whereby those that shall succeede, may at ease labour for their profit, in the most sweete, coole, and temperate shade: the action most honorable, and the end to the high glory of

God, to the erecting of true religion among Infidells, to the ouerthrow of superstition and idolatrie, to the winning of many thousands of wandring sheepe, vnto Christs fold, who now, and till now, haue strayed in the vnknowne paths of Paganisme, Idolatrie, and superstition: yea, I say the Action being well followed, as by the graue Senators, and worthy aduenturors, it hath beene worthily begunne: will tend to the euerlasting renowne of our Nation, and to the exceeding good and benefit of our Weale publicke in generall: whose Counsells, labours, godly and industrious endeuours, I beseech the mightie Iehouah to blesse, prosper, and further, with his heauenly ayde, and holy assistance.

Farewell.
I. H.[1]

A TRUE RELATION OF SUCH OCCURRENCES AND ACCIDENTS OF NOTE, AS HATH HAPNED IN VIRGINIA, SINCE THE FIRST PLANTING OF THAT COLLONY, WHICH IS NOW RESIDENT IN THE SOUTH PART THEREOF, TILL THE LAST RETURNE.

Kinde Sir, commendations remembred, &c. You shall vnderstand that after many crosses in the downes by tempests, wee arriued safely vppon the Southwest part of the great Canaries: within foure or fiue daies after we set saile for Dominica, the 26.[2] of Aprill: the first land we made, wee fell with Cape

---

[1] W. C. Ford's note (p. 165, n. 1, above) also suggests that I. H. may have been John Healey, the translator. Independently of this informed guess, Mr Giles de la Mare of London, has called the editor's attention to Healey's interest in the New World, as shown in his translation of Bishop Joseph Hall's *Mundus alter et idem* (London, 1609) with mention of 'Wingandecoia,' and to his departure for Virginia and death there (before the end of 1610). These facts, coupled with Healey's friendship for Thomas Thorpe, publisher of Shakespeare's *Sonnets* and contributor of a commendatory couplet for John Smith's Generall Historie (signed with his characteristic *T. T.*), seem to point all but conclusively to Healey as 'I. H.'.

[2] Manuscript marginal note, hereafter referred to as MS n., '16', and '26' deleted from text. This is curious, since George Percy confirms the '26'. It should be noted that there is evidence here of editorial cutting, and misleading punctuation as a result. There should be a full stop after Dominica, and a comma after Aprill.

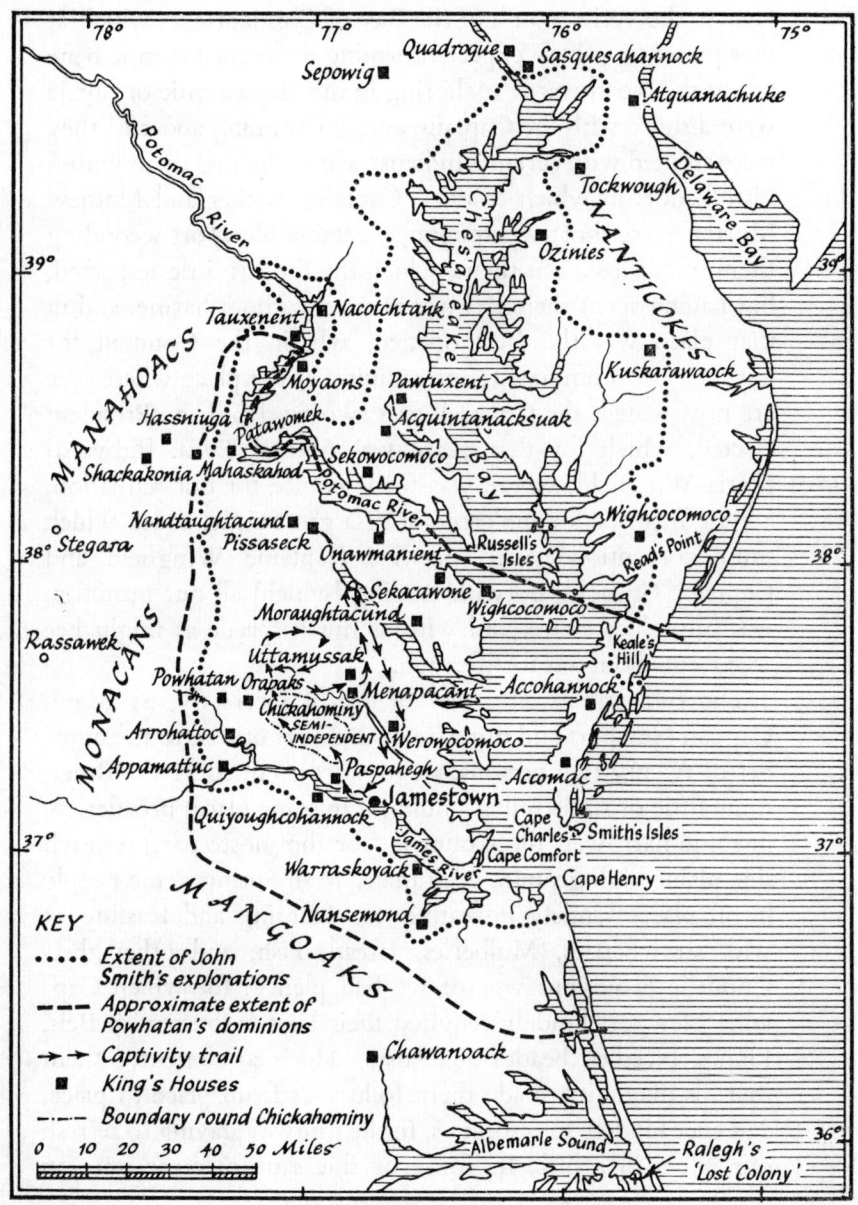

Chesapeake Bay

Henry, the verie mouth of the Bay of Chissiapiacke, which at that present we little expected, hauing by a cruell storme bene put to the Northward: anchoring in this Bay twentie or thirtie went a shore with the Captain, and in comming aboard,[1] they were assalted with certaine Indians, which charged them within Pistoll shot: in which conflict, Captaine Archer and Mathew Morton were shot: whereupon, Captaine Newport seconding them, made a shot at them, which the Indians little respected, but hauing spent their arrowes retyred without harme, and in that place was the Box opened, wherin the Counsell for Virginia was nominated: and arriuing at the place where wee are now seated, the Counsell was sworne, [and] the President elected, which for that yeare was Maister Edm. [Edward] [A3ᵛ] Maria Wingfield, where was made choice for our scituation, a verie fit place for the erecting of a great cittie, about which some contention passed betwixt Captaine Wingfield and Captaine Gosnold, notwithstanding [which] all our prouision was brought a shore, and with as much speede as might bee wee went about our fortification.

The two and twenty day of Aprill [correctly, 21 May], Captain Newport and my selfe with diuers others, to the number of twenty two persons, set forward to discouer the Riuer, some fiftie or sixtie miles, finding it in some places broader, & in some narrower, the Countrie (for the moste part) on each side plaine high ground, with many fresh Springes, the people in all places kindely intreating vs, daunsing and feasting vs with strawberries, Mulberies, Bread, Fish, and other their Countrie prouisions wherof we had plenty: for which Captaine Newport kindely requited their least fauours with Bels, Pinnes, Needles, beades or Glasses, which so contented them that his liberallitie made them follow vs from place to place, and euer kindely to respect vs. In the midway staying to refresh our selues in a little Ile foure or fiue sauages came vnto vs

---

[1] Arber, *Smith, Works*, p. 5, mistakenly explains this as 'on land'; it was 'aboard' ship, after exploring.

which described vnto vs the course of the Riuer, and after in our iourney, they often met vs, trading with vs for such prouision as wee had, and ariuing at Arsatecke,[1] hee whom we supposed to bee the chiefe King of all the rest, moste kindely entertained vs, giuing vs in a guide to go with vs vp the Riuer to Powhatan, of which place their great Emperor taketh his name, where he that they honored for King vsed vs kindely. But to finish this discouerie, we passed on further, where within a mile we were intercepted with great craggy stones in ye midst of the riuer, where the water falleth so rudely, and with such a violence, as not any boat can possibly passe, and so broad disperseth the streame, as there is not past fiue or sixe Foote at a low water, and to the shore scarce passage with a barge, the water floweth foure foote, and the freshes [freshets] by reason of the Rockes haue left markes of the inundation 8 . or 9 . foote: The south side is plaine low ground, and the north side high mountaines, the rockes being of a grauelly [A4] nature, interlaced with many vains of glistring spangles. That night we returned to Powhatan: the next day (being Whitsunday after dinner) we returned to the fals, leauing a mariner in pawn with the Indians for a guide of theirs, hee that they honoured for King followed vs by the riuer. That afternoone we trifled in looking vpon the Rockes and riuer (further he would not goe) so there we erected a crosse, and that night taking our man at Powhatans, Cap. Newport congratulated his kindenes with a Gown and a Hatchet: returning to Arsetecke, and stayed there the next day to obserue the height [latitude] therof, & so with many signes of loue we departed. The next day the Queene of Agamatock[2] kindely intreated vs, her people being no lesse contented then the rest, and from thence we went to another place, (the name wherof I doe not

---

[1] A not uncommon mistake for Arrohattoc, probably from misreading Arohatock (a variant spelling). MS n. changes to 'Arsaticke'. The map sent by Zúñiga to Spain on 31 August/10 September 1608 (see Document no. 41), shows Arsatecke.

[2] Misprint for Apamatock. MS n. has 'Appamettu[ck]', the last letter or two being cut off in binding.

remember) where the people shewed vs the manner of their diuing for Mussels, in which they finde Pearles.

That night passing by Weanock[1] some twentie miles from our Fort, they according to their former churlish condition, seemed little to affect vs, but as wee departed and lodged at the point of Weanocke, the people the next morning seemed kindely to content vs, yet we might perceiue many signes of a more Iealousie in them then before, and also the Hinde [servant, lad] that the King of Arseteck[2] had giuen vs, altered his resolution in going to our Fort, and with many kinde circumstances left vs there. This gaue vs some occasion to doubt some mischiefe at the Fort, yet Capt. Newport intended to haue visited Paspahegh and Tappahanocke,[3] but the instant change of the winde being faire for our return we repaired to the fort withall speed, where the first we heard was that 400 . Indians the day before had assalted the fort, & supprised it, had not God (beyond al their expectations) by meanes of the shippes at whom they shot with their Ordinances & Muskets, caused them to retire, they had entred the fort with our own men, which were then busied in setting Corne, their armes beeing then in driefats [tubs, boxes] & few ready but certain Gentlemen of their own, in which conflict, most of the Counsel was hurt, a boy slaine in the Pinnas, and thirteene or fourteene more hurt[.] With all speede we pallisadoed our Fort: (each other day) for sixe or seauen daies we had alarums by ambuscadoes, and foure or fiue cruelly wounded by being abroad: the Indians losse wee know not, but as they report three were slain and diuers hurt.

Captaine Newport hauing set things in order, set saile for England the 22 of June, leauing prouision for 13 . or 14 weeks. The day before the Ships departure, the King of Pamaunke[4]

[1] MS n., 'Weeanock'; a helpful hint of pronunciation.   [2] MS n., again 'Arsaticke'.
[3] MS n., 'Quiocqahannock'. Smith calls the village and the tribe Quiyoughcohanock in all his later works. William Strachey explains: 'Coiacohhanauke ... we comonly (though corruptly) call Tapahanock' (*Historie*, p. 64).
[4] MS n. (trimmed for binding), '[Pa]wmaunckett' (and below) 'Powhaton: kinge'.

IN VIRGINIA

sent the Indian that had met vs before in our discouerie, to assure vs peace, our fort being then palisadoed round, and all our men in good health and comfort, albeit, that throgh some discontented humors, it did not so long continue, for the President and Captaine Gosnold, with the rest of the Counsell being for the most part discontented with one another, in so much, that things were neither carried [out] with that discretion nor any busines effected in such good sort as wisdome would, nor our owne good and safetie required thereby,[1] and through the hard dealing of our President, the rest of the counsell beeing diuerslie affected through his audacious commaund, and for Captaine Martin, (albeit verie honest) and wishing the best good, yet so sicke and weake, and my selfe so disgrac'd through others mallice, through which disorder God (being angrie with vs) plagued vs with such famin and sicknes,[2] that the liuing were scarce able to bury the dead: our want of sufficient and good victualls, with continuall watching, foure or fiue each night at three Bulwarkes, being the chiefe cause: onely of Sturgion wee had great store, whereon our men would so greedily surfet, as it cost manye their liues: the Sack, Aquauitie, and other preseruatiues for our health, being kept onely in the Presidents hands, for his owne diet, and his few associates: shortly after Captaine Gosnold fell sicke, and within three weekes died, Captaine Ratcliffe being then also verie sicke and weake, and my selfe hauing also tasted of the extremitie therof, but by Gods assistance being well recouered. Kendall about this time, for diuers reasens deposed from being [B1] of the Councell: and shortly after it pleased God (in our extremity) to moue the Indians to bring vs Corne, ere it was halfe ripe, to refresh vs, when we rather expected when[3] they would destroy vs:[4] about the tenth of September there was

[1] The Grenville (B.M.) and other copies have 'wherby', not noted in Eames' study, but followed by Arber.
[2] Eames calls attention to a correction here, from 'inplagued vs with such fain and sicknes'.
[3] Inked out in MS n.
[4] MS n. (trimmed in binding, conjecturally restored): 'Choapock [Pipposco crossed

about 46 . of our men dead, at which time Captaine Wingefield hauing ordred the affaires in such sort that he was generally hated of all, in which respect with one consent he was deposed from his presidencie, and Captaine Ratcliffe according to his course was elected.

Our prouision being now within twentie dayes spent, the Indians brought vs great store both of Corne and bread ready made: and also there came such aboundance of Fowles into the Riuers, as greatly refreshed our weake estates, where vppon many of our weake men were presently able to goe abroad. As yet we had no houses to couer vs, our Tents were rotten, and our Cabbins worse then nought: our best commoditie was Yron which we made into little chissels, the president, and Captaine Martins sicknes, constrayned me to be Cape Marchant, and yet to spare no paines in making houses for the company, who notwithstanding our misery, little ceased their mallice, grudging and muttering. As at this time were most of our chiefest men either sicke or discontented, the rest being in such dispaire, as they would rather starue and rot with idlenes, then be perswaded to do anything for their owne reliefe without constraint: our victualles being now within eighteene dayes spent, and the Indians trade decreasing, I was sent to the mouth of y[e] riuer, to Kegquouhtan an Indian Towne, to trade for Corne, and try the riuer for Fish, but our fishing we could not effect by reason of the stormy weather.[1] The Indians thinking vs neare famished, with carelesse kindnes, offred vs little pieces of bread & small handfulls of beanes or wheat, for a hatchet or a piece of copper: In the like maner I entertained their kindnes, and in like scorne offered them like commodities, but the Children, or any that shewed extra-

out]: weeroance [of?] y[e] Quiocqua[ha]nocks did a[ll]wayes at o[ur] greatest nee[d] supply ws w[ith] victualls of [all?] sortes, which hee [did] notwithstanding y[e] Continuall w[ars?] which wee had [in y[e]?] rest of his Con[try?] and uppon his death bed cha[rged] his people y[t] [they?] should for e[ver] keepe good qu[iet?] with y[e] English[.] Pippisco no[w] weeroance doth not for[get] his predecess[or's?] Testament.' Strachey states that 'Chopoke' was 'one of Pipscoes brothers' (*Historie*, p. 65).

[1] MS n. 'Keequotancke[.] Musquasone. Fort Henry[.] Fort Char[les].'

ordinary kindenes, I liberally contented with free gifte[s], such trifles as wel co*n*tented them: finding this colde comfort, I [B1ᵛ] anchored before the Towne, and the next day returned to trade, but God (the absolute disposer of all heartes) altered their conceits, for now they were no lesse desirous of our commodities then we of their Corne: vnder colour to fetch fresh water, I sent a man to discouer [reconnoitre] the Towne, their Corne, and force, to trie their intent, in that they desired me vp to their houses: which well vnderstanding, with foure shot I visited them, with fish, oysters, bread and deere, they kindly traded with me and my men, beeing no lesse in doubt of my intent, then I of theirs, for well I might with twentie men haue fraighted a Shippe with Corne: The Towne conteineth eighteene houses, pleasantly seated vpon three acres of ground, vppon a plaine, halfe inuironed with a great Bay of the great Riuer, the other parte with a Baye of the other Riuer falling into the great Baye, with a little Ile fit for a Castle in the mouth thereof, the Towne adioyning to the maine by a necke of Land of sixtie yardes. With sixteene bushells of Corne I returned towards our Forte: by the way I encountred with two Canowes of Indians, who came aboord me, being the inhabitants of waroskoyack,[1] a kingdome on the south side of the riuer, which is in breadth 5 . miles and 20 mile or neare from the mouth: with these I traded, who hauing but their hunting prouision, requested me to returne to their Towne, where I should load my boat with corne, & with near thirtie bushells I returned to the fort, the very name wherof gaue great comfort to our desparing company: time thus passing away, & hauing not aboue 14 . daies vituals left, some motio*n*s were made about our presidents & Capt. Archers going for England, to procure a supply, in which meane time we had reasonably fitted vs with houses, and our President & Capt. Martin being able to walk abroad, with much ado it was concluded, that the pinnace and barge should goe towards

[1] '[... sk?]ohiucke', in a partly faded MS n.

Powhatan, to trade for corne: Lotts were cast who should go in her, the chance was mine, & while she was a rigging, I made a voiage to Topohanack, where ariuing, there was but certain women & children who fled from their houses, yet at last I [B2] drew them to draw neere, truck they durst not, corne they had plenty, & to spoile I had no commission: In my returne to Paspahegh, I traded with that churlish & trecherous nation: hauing loaded 10 or 12 bushels of corne, they offred [tried] to take our pieces and swords, yet by stelth, but [we] seeming to dislike it, they were ready to assault vs, yet standing vpon our guard in coasting the shore, diuers out of the woods would meet with vs with corn & trade, but least we should be constrained, either to indure ouermuch wrong or directly fal to reuenge, seeing them dog vs, from place to place, it being night, & our necessitie not fit for warres, we tooke occasion to returne with 10 bushells of corne: Cap. Martin after made 2 iournies to that nation of Paspahegh but eache time returned with 8 . or 10 . bushells [only]. All things being now ready for my iourney to Powhatan, for the performance thereof, I had 8 . men and my selfe for the barge, as well for discouerie, as trading, the Pinnace, 5 . Marriners, & 2 landmen to take in our ladings at conuenient places. The 9[1] of Nouember I set forward for the discouery of the country of Chikhamania,[2] leauing the pinnace the next tide to followe and stay for my comming at Point weanock, 20 miles from our fort: the mouth of this riuer falleth into the great riuer at Paspahegh, 8 miles aboue our fort: that afternoone I stayed the eb, in the bay of Paspahegh with the Indians: towards the euening certaine Indians haled me, one of them being of Chikahamania, offred to conduct me to his country, the Paspahegheans grudged therat: along we went by moonelight, at midnight he brought vs before his

---

[1] It was new moon about 8 November, but Smith says a few lines below that they 'went by moonelight' and got to a village at midnight. Presumably the '9' is an error for '19', since there was a full moon on 23 November. (The type is very crowded on this line, leaving no room for a '1'.)

[2] MS n. (trimmed), 'Chickcahom[a?]niacke./'

IN VIRGINIA

Towne, desiring one of our men to go vp with him, whom he kindely intertained, and returned back to the barge: the next morning I went vp to the towne, and shewed them what copper and hatchets they shold haue for corne, each family seeking to giue me most content: so long they caused me to stay y^t 100 at least was expecting my comming by the riuer with corne, what I liked I bought, and least they should perceiue my too great want I went higher vp the riuer: this place is called Manosquosick[1] a quarter of a mile from the riuer, conteining thirtie or fortie houses, vppon an exceeding high land: at the foote of the hill towards the riuer, is a plaine wood, watered with many springes, which fall twentie yardes right downe into the riuer: right against ye same is a great marsh, of [B2^v] 4 . or 5 . miles circuit, deuided in 2 Ilands, by the parting of the riuer, abounding with fish & foule of all-sorts[:] a mile from thence is a Towne called Oraniocke, I further discouered the Townes of Mansa, Apanaock, Werawahone, & Mamanahu*n*t[,] at eche place kindely vsed, especially at the last, being the hart of the Country, where were assembled 200 . people with such abou*n*dance of corne, as hauing laded our barge, as also I might haue laded a ship: I returned to Paspahhegh, & considering ye want of Corne at our Fort, it being night, with ye ebb, by midnight I ariued at our fort, where I found our Pinnis run aground: the next morning I vnladed seaue*n* hogsheds into our store, the next morning I returned againe: the second day I ariued at Mamanahu*n*t, wher ye people hauing heard of my co*m*ming, were ready with 3 or 400 . baskets litle & great, of which hauing laded my barge, with many signes of great kindnes I returned: at my departure they requested me to hear our pieces, being in the midst of the riuer, which in regard of ye eccho seemed a peale of ordnance, many birds and fowles

---

[1] MS n. (trimmed): 'They mocke[d] him[,] for ye na[me] of it is woo[ze?, za?]niucke.' Apparently there is confusion here. Smith's map has Ozenick (for Oozenick? – the MS n. could have been woozeniucke), but the Zúñiga map has Ozaniocke here, and Smith's text mentions Oraniocke immediately below. Manosquosick in fact seems to be an error.

177

they see vs dayly kil that much feared them, so desirous of trade wer they, y^t they would follow me with their canowes, & for any thing giue it me, rather then returne it back: so I vnladed again 7 or 8 . hogsheads at our fort. Hauing thus by Gods assistance gotten good store of corne, notwithstanding some bad spirrits not content with Gods prouidence, still grew mutinous, in so much, that our president hauing ocasion to chide the smith for his misdemeanor [misconduct], he not only gaue him bad language, but also offred to strike him with some of his tooles, for which rebellious act, the smith was by a Iury condemned to be hanged, but being vppon the ladder continuing verry obstinate, as hoping vpon a rescue: when he saw no other way but death with him, he became penitent, & declared a dangerous conspiracy, for which Captaine Kendall as principal, was by a Iury condemned & shot to death. This conspiracy appeased, I set forward for the discouery of the Riuer of Checka Hamania: this third time I discouered ye Townes of Matapamient, Morinogh, Ascacap, moysenock, Righkahauck, Nechanichock, Mattalunt, Attamuspincke, & diuers others,[1] their plenty of corne I found decreased, yet [B3] lading the barge, I returned to our fort: our store being now indifferently wel prouided with corne, there was much adoe for to haue the pinace goe for England, against which Captain Martin & my selfe, standing chiefly against it, and in fine after many debatings, pro & contra, it was re[s]olued to stay a further resolution: this matter also quieted, I set forward to finish this discouery,[2] which as yet I had neglected in regard of ye necessitie we had to take in prouision whilst it was to be had: 40 . miles I passed vp ye riuer, which for the most part is a quarter of a mile broad, & 3 . fatham & a half deep, exceeding oosey, many great low marshes, & many high lands,

---

[1] MS n.: 'The Naturalls much abused him[,] for there is not such a name for any towne in all ye Country sauing ye first[,] Matappanient.' In fact, these names do not appear elsewhere in Smith's books; but see Appendix II.

[2] According to Edward Maria Wingfield, this was on Thursday, 10 December 1607 (see Document no. 34, p. 226, below).

especially about ye midst at a place called Moysonicke,¹ a Peninsule of 4 . miles ci[r]cuit, betwixt two riuers ioyned to the main, by a neck of 40 . or 50 . yards, and 40 . or 50 yards from the high water marke: on both sides in the very necke of the maine, are high hills and dales, yet much inhabited, the Ile declining in a plaine fertile corne field, the lower end a low marsh, more plentie of swannes, cranes, geese, duckes, and mallards, & diuers sorts of fowles none would desire: more plaine fertile planted ground, in such great proportions as there I had not seene,² of a light blacke sandy mould, the cliffes commonly red, white and yellowe coloured sand, & vnder red & white clay, fish great plenty, & people aboundance, the most of their inhabitants, in view of ye neck of Land, where a better seat for a towne cannot be desired: at the end of forty miles this riuer inuironeth many low Ilands, at each high water drowned for a mile, where it vniteth it selfe, at a place called Apokant the highest Towne inhabited. 10 . miles higher I discouered with the barge[;] in the mid way, a great tree hindred my passage which I cut in two: heere the riuer became narrower, 8 . 9 or 10 . foote at a high water, and 6 . or 7 . at a lowe: the streame exceeding swift, & the bottom hard channell, the ground most part a low plaine, sandy soyle, this occasioned me to suppose it might issue from some lake or some broad ford, for it could not be far to the head, but rather then I would endanger the barge, yet to haue beene able to resolue this doubt, & to discharge the imputation of malicious tungs, that halfe suspected I durst not for so long delaying, some of the company as desirous as my self, we resolued to hier a Canow, [B3ᵛ] and returne with the barge to Apocant, there to leaue the barge secure, and put our selues vppon the aduenture: the country onely a vast and wilde wildernes, and but onely that Towne:

¹ MS n.: 'No such tow[n]'. See Appendix II.
² William R. Gerard's analysis of the meaning of the name Chickahominy points to derivation from *tshik*, 'to sweep', hence 'a clearing' (*American Anthropologist*, new ser., VII (1905), 222–49); cf. modern Cree *chekuhum*, 'he chops it'. See also Theodore Stern, 'Chickahominy: The Changing Culture of a Virginia Indian Community', in *Proceedings of the American Philosophical Society*, XCVI (1952), esp. 159–70.

within three or four mile we hired a Canow, and 2 . Indians to row vs ye next day a fowling: hauing made such prouision for the barge as was needfull, I left her there to ride, with expresse charge not any to go ashore til my returne. Though some wise men may condemn this too bould attempt of too much indiscretion, yet if they well consider the friendship of the Indians, in conducting me, the desolatenes of the country, the propabilitie of some lacke [lake], & the malicious iudges of my actions at home, as also to haue some matters of worth to incourage our aduenturers in england, might well haue caused any honest minde to haue done the like, as wel for his own discharge as for the publike good: hauing 2 Indians for my guide & 2 of our own company, I set forward, leauing 7 in the barge: hauing discouered 20 miles further in this desart, the riuer stil kept his depth and bredth, but much more combred with trees: here we went ashore (being some 12 miles higher then ye barge had bene) to refresh our selues, during the boyling of our vituals: one of the Indians I tooke with me, to see the nature of the soile, & to crosse the boughts [bends] of the riuer, the other Indian I left with *Master* Robbinson and Thomas Emry, with their matches light[ed] and order to discharge a peece, for my retreat at the first sight of any Indian, but within a quarter of an houre I heard a loud cry, and a hollowing of Indians, but no warning peece, supposing them surprised, and that the Indians had betraid vs, presently [immediately] I seazed him & bound his arme fast to my hand in a garter, with my pistoll ready bent to be reuenged on him: he aduised me to fly, and seemed ignorant of what was done, but as we went discoursing, I was struck with an arrow on the right thigh, but without harme: vpon this occasion I espied 2 Indians drawing their bowes, which I preuented in discharging a french pistoll: by [the time] that I had charged againe 3 or 4 more did the like, for the first fell downe and fled: at my discharge they did the like, my hinde I made my barricado who offered not to striue, 20 . or 30 . arrowes were shot at me but short, 3 or 4 times I had discharged my pistoll ere the king of Pamaunck [B4] called Opeckankenough[1] with 200 men, inuironed me, eache drawing their bowe, which done they laid them vpon the ground, yet without shot, my hinde treated betwixt them and me of conditions of peace, he discouered [explained] me to be the Captaine, my request was to retire to ye boate, they demaunded my armes, the rest they saide were slaine, onely me they would reserue: the Indian importuned me not to shoot. In retiring being in the midst of a low quagmire, and minding them more then my steps, I stept fast into the quagmire, and also the Indian in drawing me forth: thus surprised, I resolued to trie their mercies, my armes I caste from me, till which none durst approch me: being ceazed on me, they drew me out and led me to the King, I presented him with a compasse diall describing by my best meanes the vse therof, wherat he so amazedly admired, as he suffered me to proceed in a discourse of the roundnes of the earth, the course of the sunne, moone, starres and plannets,[2] with kinde speeches and bread he requited me, conducting me where the Canow lay and Iohn Robbinson slaine, with 20 or 30 . arrowes in him. Emry I saw not, I perceiued by the aboundance of fires all ouer the woods [that they were deer hunting?], at each place I expected when they would execute me, yet they vsed me with what kindnes they could: approaching their Towne, which was within 6 miles where I was taken, onely made as arbors and couered with mats, which they remoue as occasion requires: all the women and children, being aduertised of this accident, came foorth to meet them, the King well guarded with 20 bowmen, 5 flanck and rear, and each flanck before him a sword & a peece, and after him the like, then a bowman, then I on each

[1] MS n. (trimmed): 'Apachancka[nough] was indeede weeraonce bu[t] not King of Pa[wm]unckett: for [his?] brother Powh[atan] ye Emporor wa[s] kinge of y^t p[lace?; people?]

[2] Thomas Hariot had showed such things as compasses to the Indians twenty years before (Quinn, *Roanoke*, I, 375-6), and Smith may have read about it. The passage was used in Purchas' *Pilgrimage* in 1613, p. 634, although Smith himself omitted it from the 1612 *Map of Virginia*.

JAMESTOWN VOYAGES

hand a boweman, the rest in file in the reare, which reare led foorth amongst the trees in a bishion [Ital. *biscione*, 'great snake'], eache his bowe and a handfull of arrowes, a quiuer at back grimly painted: on eache flanck a sargeant, the one running alwaies towards the front the other towards the reare, each a true pace and in exceeding good order, this being a good time continued, they caste themselues in a ring with a daunce, [B4ᵛ] and so eache man departed to his lodging, the Captain conducting me to his lodging, a quarter of Venison and some ten pound of bread I had for supper, what I left was reserued for me, and sent with me to my lodging: each morning 3 . women presented me three great platters of fine bread, more venison then ten men could deuour I had, my gowne, points and garters, my compas and a tablet they gaue me again, though 8 ordinarily guarded me, I wanted not what they could deuise to content me: and still our longer acquaintance increased our better affection: much they threatned to assault our forte, as they were solicited by the King of Paspahegh,[1] who shewed at our fort great signes of sorrow for this mischance: the King tooke great delight in vnderstanding the manner of our ships, and sayling the seas, the earth & skies and of our God: what he knew of the dominions he spared not to acquaint me with, as of certaine men cloathed at a place called Ocanahonan,[2] cloathed like me, the course of our riuer, and that within 4 or 5 daies iourney of the falles, was a great turning of salt water: I desired he would send a messenger to Paspahegh,[3] with a letter I would write, by which they shold vnderstand, how kindly they vsed me, and that I was well,

[1] MS n. (trimmed): '[W]awinckapunck [King] of Paspaheygh'. Although the name does not appear in any of Smith's writings, it is given in Strachey (*Historie*, 66–7), as Wowinchopunck. He was killed by the English on 9 February 1610.
[2] MS n.: '[Oc]onahawan.' The word occurs again immediately below; and a few paragraphs farther on it appears as Ocamahowan. It is possibly the Ohanoak of Ralph Lane (Quinn, *Roanoke*, I, 259). The whole clause has been corrected in ink to read: 'as of certaine men at a place 6 dayes iorny beyond Ocanahonan'. According to Smith's *General Historie* (1624), p. 110, Ocanahowan was 'fiue daies iourney from vs'.
[3] Note the use of the Indian name for the district, in place of 'Jamestown'.

IN VIRGINIA

least they should reuenge my death: this he granted and sent three men, in such weather, as in reason were vnpossible, by any naked to be indured: their cruell mindes towards the fort I had deuerted, in describing the ordinance & the mines in the fields, as also the reuenge Captain Newport would take of them at his returne, their intent, I incerted[1] the fort, the people of Ocanahonum and the back sea, this report they after found diuers Indians that confirmed: the next day after my letter, came a saluage to my lodging, with his sword to haue slaine me, but being by my guard intercepted, with a bowe and arrow he [once again] offred to haue effected his purpose; the cause I knew not, till the King vnderstanding thereof came and told me of a man a dying, wounded with my pistoll: he tould me also of another I had slayne, yet the most concealed they had any hurte: this was the father of him I had slayne, whose fury to preuent, the King presently conducted me to another Kingdome, vpon the top of the next northerly riuer, [C1] called Youghtanan[d],[2] hauing feasted me, he further led me to another branch of the riuer, called Mattapament,[3] to two other hunting townes they led me, and to each of these Countries, a house of the great Emperour of Pewhakan [Powhatan],[4] whom as yet I supposed to bee at the Fals, to him I tolde him I must goe, and so returne to Paspahegh, after this foure or fiue dayes march, we returned to Rasawrack,[5] the first towne they brought me too, where binding the Mats in bundels, they marched two dayes iourney, and crossed the Riuer[6] of Youghtanan[d], where it was as broad as Thames:[7] so conducting me to a place

---

[1] Undoubtedly a misprint for 'incensed', a Lincolnshire and northern dialectal word meaning 'to inform' (*OED* and Brogden's, *Provincial words . . . in Lincolnshire*). Used in the same sense in Shakespeare's (*et al.*) *Henry VIII*, V, i, 43–45: 'Incensed the Lords . . . that he is . . . A most arch-heretic.'
[2] MS n. (trimmed): 'Yoghtanun[t]', the final 't' being inked in after the word in the text.
[3] MS n. (trimmed): 'Matappam[ent]'.
[4] MS n. inks out the word 'of', and corrects the spelling of Powhatan.
[5] MS n.: 'No such towne.' This is correct, for Smith later states that the Indians folded up their houses and took them away. It was a hunting camp only.
[6] MS n.: 'or Creeke'.   [7] MS n.: 'at London'.

183

called Menapacute¹ in Pamaunke, where yᵉ King inhabited: the next day another King of that nation called Kekataugh, hauing receiued some kindnes of me at the Fort, kindly inuited me to feast at his house, the people from all places flocked to see me, each shewing to content me. By this the great King hath foure or fiue houses, each containing fourescore or an hundred foote in length, pleasantly seated vpon an high sandy hill, from whence you may see westerly a goodly low Country the riuer before the which his crooked course causeth many great Marshes of exceeding good ground. An hundred houses, and many large plaines are here togither inhabited, more abundance of fish & fowle, and a pleasanter seat cannot be imagined: the King with fortie Bowmen to guard me, intreated me to discharge my Pistoll, which they there presented me with a mark at six score to strike therwith but to spoil the practise I broke the cocke, whereat they were much discontented though a chaunce supposed.

From hence this kind King conducted mee to a place called Topahanocke,² a kingdome vpon another Riuer northward: the cause of this was, that the yeare before, a shippe had been in the Riuer of Pamaunke, who hauing beene kindly entertained by Powhatan their Emperour, they returned thence, and discouered the Riuer of Topahanocke, where being receiued with like kindnesse, yet he slue the King, and tooke of his people, and they supposed I were hee, but the people reported him a great man that was Captaine, and vsing mee [C1ᵛ] kindly, the next day we departed.

This Riuer of Topahanock,³ seemeth in breadth not much lesse then that we dwell vpon. At the mouth of the Riuer is a Countrey called Cuttata women[,] vpwards is Marraugh tacum

¹ MS n.: 'no [such] pla[ce]'.
² Both here and where the name is repeated, a few lines below, MS n. has Topahanocke clumsily changed in ink to read Rapahanocke, and in the margin, opposite the lower place, 'Rappahannock[e?]'. See Appendix II.
³ MS n.: 'Rappahannocke', but text remains unaltered. Below: 'Fl:' undoubtedly for 'flumen'.

184

IN VIRGINIA

Tapohanock, Appamatuck, and Nantaugs tacum,[1] at Topmanahocks, the head issuing from many Mountaines, the next night I lodged at a hunting town of Powhatans, and the next day arriued at Waranacomoco [Werowocomoco] vpon the riuer of Pamauncke, where the great king is resident: by the way we passed by the top of another little riuer, which is betwixt the two called Payankatank. The most of this Countrey though Desert [uninhabited], yet exceeding fertil, good timber, most hils and dales, in each valley a cristall spring.

Arriuing at Weramocomoco, their Emperour proudly lying vppon a Bedstead a foote high vpon tenne or twelue Mattes, richly hung with manie Chaynes of great Pearles about his necke, and couered with a great Couering of Rahaughcums:[2] At his heade sat a woman, at his feete another, on each side sitting vppon a Matte vppon the ground were raunged his chiefe men on each side the fire, tenne in a ranke, and behinde them as many yong women, each a great Chaine of white Beades ouer their shoulders: their heades painted in redde and with such a graue and Maiesticall countenance, as draue me into admiration to see such state in a naked Saluage, hee kindly welcomed me with good wordes, and great Platters of sundrie Victuals, assuring mee his friendship, and my libertie within foure dayes, hee much delighted in Opechan Comoughs relation of what I had described to him, and oft examined me vpon the same. Hee asked mee the cause of our comming, I tolde him being in fight with the Spaniards our enemie, beeing ouer powred, neare put to retreat, and by extreame weather put to this shore, where landing at Chesipiack, the people shot vs, but at Kequoughtan they kindly vsed vs, we by signes demaunded fresh water, they described vs vp the Riuer was all fresh water, at Paspahegh, also they kindly vsed vs, our

[1] Nantaugs tacum may be (as Marraugh tacum) merely a misprint for one word. MS n. (trimmed): '[?]ntsattaqunt'. An oblique ink line is drawn through the 'N' at the beginning. The 'correct' spelling should probably be Nantaughtacunt.
[2] MS n. (trimmed): '[M]ade of A beast [call]ed a Raracoone [the?] skinne very well [dress?]ed and arty[fic]ially sowed to[get]hur'. Immediately following, Eames reports a correction of a misprint, where 'his' had been omitted.

[C2] Pinn[a]sse being leak[i]e wee were inforced to stay to mend her, till Captaine Newport my father came to conduct vs away. He demaunded why we went further with our Boate, I tolde him, in that I would haue occasion to talke of the backe Sea, that on the other side the maine, where was salt water, my father had a childe slaine, whiche wee supposed Monocan his enemie had done[1] whose death we intended to reuenge.

After good deliberation, hee began to describe mee the Countreys beyonde the Falles, with many of the rest, confirming what not onely Opechancanoyes, and an Indian which had beene prisoner to Pewhatan had before tolde mee, but some called it fiue dayes, some sixe, some eight, where the sayde water dashed amongest many stones and rockes, each storme which caused oft tymes the heade of the Riuer to bee brackish: Anchanachuck he described to bee the people that had slaine my brother, whose death hee would reuenge. Hee desbribed also vpon the same Sea, a mighty Nation called Pocoughtronack [-taonack], a fierce Nation that did eate men, and warred with the people of Moyaoncer, and Pataromerke [Potomac], Nations vpon the toppe of the heade of the Bay, vnder his territories, where the yeare before they had slain an hundred, he signified their crownes were shauen, long haire in the necke, tied on a knot, Swords like Pollaxes.

Beyond them he described people with short Coates, and Sleeues to the Elbowes, that passed that way in Shippes like ours. Many Kingdomes hee described mee to the heade of the Bay, which seemed to bee a mightie Riuer, issuing from mightie Mountaines betwixt the two Seas, the people cloathed at Ocamahowan. He also confirmed, and the Southerly Countries also, as the rest, that reported vs to be within a day & a halfe of Mangoge, two dayes of Chawwonock, 6 . from Roonock [Roanoke], to the south part of the backe sea: he described a countrie called Anone, where they haue abundance of Brasse, and houses walled as ours. I requited his discourse,

[1] Eames reports another misprint corrected here; 'had done' had been omitted.

IN VIRGINIA

seeing what pride hee had in his great and spacious Dominions, seeing that all hee knewe were vnder his Territories.

In describing to him the territories of Europe, which was [C2ᵛ] subiect to our great King, whose subiect I was, the innumerable multitude of his ships, I gaue him to vnderstand the noyse of Trumpets, and terrible manner of fighting [which] were vnder captain Newport my father, whom I intituled the Meworames [Werowance] which they call King of all the waters, at his greatnesse hee admired, and not a little feared: hee desired mee to forsake Paspahegh, and to liue with him vpon his Riuer, a Countrie called Capa Howasicke: hee promised to giue me Corne, Venison, or what I wanted to feede vs, Hatchets and Copper wee should make him, and none should disturbe vs. This request I promised to performe: and thus hauing with all the kindnes hee could deuise, sought to content me: hee sent me home with 4 . men, one that vsually carried my Gowne and Knapsacke after me, two other loded with bread, and one to accompanie me.

This Riuer of Pamaunke is not past twelue mile from that we dwell on, his course northwest, and westerly, as the other. Weraocomoco, is vpon salt water, in bredth two myles, and so keepeth his course without any tarrying some twenty miles, where at the parting of the fresh water and the salt, it diuideth it selfe into two partes, the one part to Goughland [Youghtanand?] as broad as Thames, and nauigable, with a Boate threescore or fourescore miles, and with a Shippe fiftie, exceeding crooked, and manie low grounds and marishes, but inhabited with aboundance of warlike and tall people. The Countrey of Youghtomam, of no lesse worth, onely it is lower, but all the soyle, a fatte, fertill, sandie ground. Aboue Manapacumter, many high sandie Mountaines. By the Riuer is many Rockes, seeming if not of seuerall Mines: The other branch a little lesse in breadth, yet extendeth not neare so farre, nor so well inhabited, somewhat lower, and a white sandie, and a white clay soyle: here is their best Terra Sigillata: The mouth of the

Riuer, as I see in the discouerie therof with captain Newport, is halfe a mile broad, & within foure miles not aboue a Masket shot: the channell exceeding good and deepe, the Riuer straight to the deuisions. Kiskirk [Chiskiac] the nearest Nation to the entrances.

[C3]   Their religion and Ceremonie I obserued was thus: three or foure dayes after my taking[,] seuen of them in the house where I lay, each with a rattle began at ten a clock in the morning to sing about the fire, which they inuironed with a Circle of meale, and after a foote or two from that, at the end of each song, layde downe two or three graines of wheate, continuing this order till they haue included sixe or seuen hundred in a halfe Circle, and after that two or three more Circles in like maner, a hand bredth from other: that done, at each song, they put betwixt euerie three, two or fiue graines, a little sticke, so counting as an old woman her Pater noster.

One disguised with a great Skinne, his head hung round with little Skinnes of Weasels, and other vermine, with a Crownet of feathers on his head, painted as vgly as the diuell, at the end of each song will make many signes and demonstrations, with strange and vehement actions, great cakes of Deere suet, Deare, and Tobacco he casteth in the fire, till sixe a clocke in the Euening, their howling would continue ere they would depart. Each morning in the coldest frost, the principall to the number of twentie or thirtie, assembled themselues in a round circle, a good distance from the towne, where they told me they there consulted where to hunt the next day: so fat they fed mee, that I much doubted they intended to haue sacrificed mee to the Quiyoughquosicke, which is a superiour power they worship, a more vglier thing cannot be described: one they haue for chief sacrifices, which also they call Quiyoughquosick: to cure the sick, a man with a Rattle, and extreame howling, showting, singing, and such violent gestures, and Anticke actions ouer the patient will sucke out blood and flegme from the patient out of their vnable stomacke, or any diseased place, as no labour will more tire them, Tobacco they offer the water in passing in fowle weather. The death of any they lament with great sorrow and weeping: their Kings they burie betwixt two mattes within their houses, with all his beads, iewels, hatchets, and copper: the other in graues like ours.[1] They acknowledge no resurrection. Powhatan hath three brethren, and two sisters, each of his bretheren succeeded other. [C3ᵛ]

For the Crowne, their heyres inherite not, but the first heyres of the Sisters, and so successiuely the weomens heires: For the Kings haue as many weomen as they will, his Subiects two, and most but one.

From Weramocomoco is but 12. miles, yet the Indians trifled away that day, and would not goe to our Forte by any perswasions: but in certaine olde hunting houses of Paspahegh we lodged all night. The next morning ere Sunne rise, we set forward for our Fort, where we arriued within an houre, where each man with the truest signes of ioy they could expresse welcommed mee, except M. Archer, and some 2. or 3. of his, who was then in my absence, sworne Counsellour, though not with the consent of Captaine Martin: great blame and imputation was laide vpon mee by them, for the losse of our two men which the Indians slew: insomuch that they purposed to depose me, but in the midst of my miseries, it pleased God to send Captaine Nuport, who arriuing there the same night, so tripled our ioy, as for a while these plots against me were deferred, though with much malice against me, which captain Newport in short time did plainly see. Now was maister Scriuener, captaine Martin, and my selfe, called Counsellers.

Within fiue or sixe dayes after the arriuall of the Ship, by a mischaunce our Fort was burned, and the most of our apparell,

---

[1] MS n. (trimmed): 'This Author I fy[nde] in many errors wh*ic*[h] they doe impute to h[is] not well vndersta[n]dinge yᵉ language for they doe Ackno[w]ledge both God [&] yᵉ Deuill and yᵗ af[ter] yᵉⁱ are out of this world they shall r[ise] agayne in anothe[r] world where the[y] shall liue at ea[se] and haue great[e?] store of bread a[nd] venison & other [? ?]'.

lodging and priuate prouision, many of our old men diseased, and of our new for want of lodging perished. The Empereur Powhatan each weeke once or twice sent me many presents of Deare, bread [&] Raugroughcuns [raccoons], halfe always for my father, whom he much desired to see, and halfe for me: and so continually importuned by messengers and presents, that I would come to fetch the corne, and take the Countrie their King had giuen me, as at last Captaine Newport resolued to go see him. Such acquaintance I had amongst the Indians, and such confidence they had in me, as neare the Fort they would not come till I came to them, euery of them calling me by my name, would not sell any thing till I had first receiued [C4] their presents, and what they had that I liked, they deferred to my discretion: but after acquaintance, they vsually came into the Fort at their pleasure: The President, and the rest of the Councell, they knewe not, but Captaine Newports greatnesse I had so described, as they conceyued him the chiefe, the rest his children, Officers, and seruants. We had agreed with ye king of Paspahegh, to conduct two of our men to a place called Panawicke beyond Roonok, where he reported many men to be apparelled. Wee landed him at Warraskoyack, where playing the villaine, and deluding vs for rewards, returned within three or foure dayes after without going further. Captaine Newport, maister Scriuener, and my selfe, found the mouth of Pamauncks riuer, some 25 . or 30. miles northward from Cape Henrie,[1] the chanell good as before expressed.

Arriuing at Weramocomoca, being iealous of the intent of

[1] Eames reports some copies with 'Cape Henricke', which is also in the Grenville copy, B.M. Correctly written as Cape Henry on p. 170, and corrected from Cape Henrick here, it was left as Captaine [!] Hendrick on p. 199 and Cape-hendicke on p. 200. The confusion was apparently due to a Cape mentioned by John White in his 'Narrative of the 1590 voyage' (Quinn, *Roanoke*, II, 617) 'that lyeth Southwardes of Kenricks mounts'. Cape Kenrick appears in the Velasco map of 1611 (Quinn, *Roanoke*, II, 851-2 and illustration) as a sharp point where Wimble Shoals now lie, 25 miles north of Cape Hatteras. This point, then a feature of the coastline, was known to the company before they named Cape Henry, and Smith apparently applied the name in error. (Kenrick was an Indian name, meaning 'long sand'; cf. modern Cree *kin-*, 'long', and *-wukaw*, 'sand'.)

IN VIRGINIA

this politick saluage, to discouer his intent the better, I with 20. shot armed in Iacks [jackets of quilted leather] went a shore, the Bay where he dwelleth hath in it 3. cricks, and a mile and a halfe from the chanel all os [ooze],[1] being conducted to the towne, I found my selfe mistaken in the creeke, for they al[l] there were within lesse then a mile, the Emperors sonne called Naukaquawis, the captaine that tooke me, and diuerse others of his chiefe men conducted me to their kings habitation, but in the mid way I was intercepted by a great creek over which they had made a bridge of grained [forked] stakes & railes, the king of Kiskieck, and Namontack, who all the iourney the king had sent to guide vs, had conducted vs this passage, which caused me to suspect some mischiefe: the barge I had sent to meet me at the right landing, when I found my selfe first deceyued, and knowing by experience the most of their courages to proceede from others feare, though fewe lyked the passage, I intermingled the Kings sonne, our conductors, and his chiefe men amongst ours, and led forward, leauing halfe at the one ende to make a guard for the passage of the Front. The Indians seeing the weakenesse of the Bridge, came with a Canow, and tooke me in of [from] the middest with foure or fiue more, being landed wee made a guard for the rest till all were passed, two in a ranke we marched to the [C4ᵛ] Emperors house. Before his house stood fortie or fiftie great Platters of fine bread, being entred the house, with loude tunes they all made signes of great ioy. This proude saluage, hauing his finest women, and the principall of his chiefe men assembled, sate in rankes as before is expressed, himselfe as vpon a Throne at the vpper ende of the house, with such a Maiestie as I cannot expresse, nor yet haue often seene, either in Pagan or Christian, with a kinde countenance hee bad mee welcome, and caused a place to bee made by himselfe to sit, I presented him a sute of red cloath, a white Greyhound, and a Hatte, as Iewels he esteemed them, and with a great Oration made by

[1] Originally 'oft', corrected to 'of' for 'os' but without the 'e'. See p. 195, n. 2.

three of his Nobles, if there be any amongst Saluages,[1] kindly accepted them, with a publike confirmation of a perpetuall league and friendship.

After that, he commaunded the Queene of Apamatuc, a comely yong Saluage, to giue me water, a Turkie-cocke and breade to eate: being thus feasted, hee began his discourse to this purpose. Your kinde visitation doth much content mee but where is your father whom I much desire to see, is he not with you. I told him he remained aboord, but the next day he would come vnto him, with a merrie cou*n*tenance he asked me for certaine peeces which I promised him, when I went to Paspahegh, I told [him] according to my promise, that I proffered the man that went with me foure Demy Culuerings, in that he so desired a great Gunne, but they refused to take them whereat with a lowde laughter, he desired [me] to giue him some of lesse burthen, as for the other I gaue him them, being sure that none could carrie them: but where are these men you promised to come with you, I told him without, who thervpon gaue order to haue them brought in, two after two, euer maintaining the guard without. And as they presented themselues euer with thankes, he would salute me, and caused each of them to haue foure or fiue pound of bread giuen them. This done, I asked him for the corne and ground he promised me. He told me I should haue it, but he expected to haue all these men lay their armes at his feet, as did his subiects. I tolde

[D1] him that was a ceremonie our enemies desired, but neuer our Friends, as we presented our selues vnto him, yet that he should not doubt of our friendship: the next day my Father would giue him a child of his, in full assurance of our loues, and not only that, but when he should thinke it conuenient, wee would deliuer vnder his subiection the Country of Manacam and Pocoughtaonack his enemies.

This so contented him, as immediatly with attentiue silence, with a lowd oration, he proclaimed me Awerowanes [a

[1] MS n. The clause 'if ... Saluages' has parentheses inked in, in place of the commas.

IN VIRGINIA

Werowance] of Powhaton, and that all his subiects should so esteeme vs, and no man account vs strangers nor Paspaheghans, but Powhatans, and that the Corne, weomen and Country, should be to vs as to his owne people: this proffered kindnes for many reasons we contemned not, but with the best Languages and signes of thankes I could expressse, I tooke my leaue.

The King rising from his seat, conducted me foorth, and caused each of my men to haue as much more bread as hee could beare: giuing me some in a basket, & as much he sent a board for a present to my Father: victuals you must know is all there wealth, and the greatest kindnes they could shew vs: arriuing at the Riuer, the Barge was fallen so low with the ebbe, though I had giuen order and oft sent to preuent the same, yet the messengers deceiued mee, the Skies being very thicke and rainie, the King vnderstanding this mischance, sent his Sonne and Mamontacke, to conduct mee to a great house sufficient to lodge mee, where entring I saw it hung round with bowes and arrowes.

The Indians vsed all diligence to make vs fires, & giue vs content: the kings Orators presently entertained vs with a kinde oration, with expresse charge that not any should steale, or take out[1] bowes or arrowes, or offer any iniury.

Presently after he sent me a quarter of Venizon to stay my stomacke: in the euening hee sent for mee to come onely with [D1ᵛ] two shot with me: the company I gaue order to stand vpon their guard, & to maintaine two sentries at the ports all night. To my supper he set before me meate for twenty men, & seeing I could not eate, hee caused it to be giuen to my men: for this is a general custome, that what they giue, not to take againe, but you must either eate it, giue it away, or carry it with you: two or three houres we spent in our aun[ci]ent discourses, which done, I was with a fire stick lighted to my lodging.

The next day the King conducting mee to the Riuer, shewed

---

[1] Arber improperly altered silently to 'our'. The reference is clearly to the bows and arrows hanging round the house walls as described just above.

me his Canowes, and described vnto me how hee sent them ouer the Baye, for tribute beades: and also what Countries paide him Beads, Copper or Skins. But seeing Captaine Nuport, and Maister Scriuener, comming a shore, the King returned to his house, and I went to meete him, with a trumpet before him, wee marched to the King: who after his old manner kindly receiued him, especially a Boy of thirteen yeares old, called Thomas Saluage, whom he gaue him as his Sonne: he requited this kindnes with each of vs a great basket of Beanes, and entertaining him with the former discourse, we passed away that day, and agreed to bargaine the next day, and so returned to our Pinnis: the next day comming a shore in like order, the King hauing kindly entertained vs with a breakfast, questioned with vs in this manner.

Why we came armed in that sort, seeing hee was our friend, and had neither bowes nor arrowes, what did wee doubt? I told him it was the custome of our Country, not doubting of his kindnes any waies, wherewith though hee seemed satisfied, yet Captaine Nuport caused all our men to retire to the water side, which was some thirtie score from thence: but to preuent the worst, Maister Scriuener or I were either the one or other by the Barge, experience had well taught me to beleeue his friendship, till conuenient opportunity suffred [D2] him to betray vs, but quickly this polititian had perceiued my absence, and cunningly sent for mee; I sent for Maister Scriuener to supply my place, the King would demaund for him, I would againe releeue him, and they sought to satisfie our suspition with kind Language, and not being agreed to trade for corne, hee desired to see all our Hatchets and Copper together, for which he would giue vs corne, with that aunceint tricke the Chickahamaniens had oft acquainted me: his offer I refused, offering first to see what hee would giue for one piece, hee seeming to despise the nature of a Merchant, did scorne to sell, but we freely should giue him, and he liberally would requite us.

IN VIRGINIA

Captaine Nuport would not with lesse then twelue great Coppers try his kindnes, which he liberally requited with as much corne as at Chickahamania, I had for one of lesse proportion: our Hatchets hee would also haue at his owne rate, for which kindnes hee much seemed to affect Captaine Nuport, some few bunches of blew Beades I had, which he much desired, and seeing so few, he offred me a basket of two pecks, and that which I drew to be [raised to] three pecks at the least, and yet seemed contented and desired more: I agreed with him the next day for two bushells, for ye ebbe now constrained vs to returne to our Boate, although he earnestly desired vs to stay [for] dinner which was a prouiding, and being ready he sent aboard after vs, which was bread and venizon, sufficient for fiftie or sixtie persons.

The next day hee sent his Sonne in the morning not to bring a shore with vs any pieces, least his weomen and children should feare. Captain Nuports good beliefe would haue satisfied that request, yet twentie or twentie fiue shot we got a shore: the King importuning mee to leaue my armes a board, much misliking my sword, pistol and target, I told him the men that slew my Brother with the like tearmes had perswaded me, and being vnarmed shot at vs, and so betraide vs.

He oft entreated Captaine Nuport that his men might[1] leaue their armes, which still hee commanded to the water side, this day we spent in trading for blew Beads, and hauing neare straighted [fraighted] our Barge. [D2^v]

Captaine Nuport returned with them that came abord, leauing me and Maister Scruiener a shore, to follow in Canowes; into one I got with sixe of our men, which beeing lanched a stones cast from the shore stuck fast in the Ose:[2] Maister Scriuener seeing this example, with seuen or eight more passed the dreadfull bridge, thinking to haue found deeper

---

[1] MS n. The words 'Virginia Barmudas' are boldly and ornamentally written across the bottom of the page. There is no explanation. (The handwriting is apparently not Strachey's.)

[2] The use of this word four times in a few lines seems to support n. 1, p. 191.

195

water on the other creeke, but they were inforced to stay with such entertainment as a saluage, being forced ashore with wind and raine, hauing in his Canow, as commonly they haue, his house and houshold, instantly set vp a house of mats which succoured them from the storme.

The Indians seeing me pestred in the Ose, called to me, sixe or seuen of the Kings chiefe men threw off their skins, and to the middle in Ose, came to bear me out on their heads, their importunacie caused me better to like the Canow then their curtesie, excusing my deniall for feare to fall into the Ose, desiring them to bring me some wood, fire, and mats, to couer me, and I would content them: each presently gaue his helpe to satisfie my request, which paines a horse would scarce haue indured, yet a couple of bells richly contented them.

The Emperor sent his Seaman Mantiuas in the euening with bread and victuall for me and my men, he no more scripulous then the rest seemed to take a pride in shewing how litle he regarded that miserable cold and durty passage, though a dogge would scarce haue indured it, this kindnes I found, when I litle expected lesse than a mischiefe, but the blacke night parting our companies, ere midnight the flood [tide] serued to carry vs aboard: the next day we came ashore, the King with a solemne discourse causing all to depart, but his principall men, and this was the effect, when as hee perceiued [D3] that we had a desire to inuade Monacum, against whom he was no professed enemy, yet thus farre hee would assist vs in this enterprise: First hee would send his spies, perfectly to vnderstand their strength and ability to fight, with which he would acquaint vs himselfe.

Captaine Nuport would not be seene in it himselfe, being great Werowances, they would stay at home, but I, Maister Scriuener, and two of his Sonnes, and Opechankanough. The King of Pamaunke should haue 100. of his men to goe before as though they were hunting, they giuing vs notise where was

IN VIRGINIA

the aduantage we should kill them, the weomen and young children he wished we should spare, & bring them to him, only 100. or 150. of our men he held sufficient for this exploit: our boats should stay at the falls, where we might hew timber, which we might conuey each man a piece till we were past the stones, and there ioyne them, to passe our men by water, if any were shot, his men should bring them backe to our boats, this faire tale had almost made Captaine Nuport vndertake, by this meanes to discouer the South sea, which will not be without trecherie, if wee ground our intent vpon his constancie.

This day we spent in trading, dancing, and much mirth, the King of Pamaunke sent his messenger, as yet not knowing Captaine Nuport, to come vnto him: who had long expected mee, desiring also my Father to visite him: the messenger stayed to conduct vs, but Powhatan vnderstanding that we had Hatchets lately come from Paspahegh, desired the next day to trade with vs, and not to go further.

This new tricke he cunningly put vpon him, but onely to haue what hee listed, and to try whether we would go or stay. Openchankenoughs messenger returned that wee would not come: the next day his Daughter came to entreat me, shewing her Father had hurt his legge, and much sorrowed he could not see me.

Captaine Nuport being not to bee perswaded to go, in that [D3ᵛ] Powhatan had desired vs to stay: sent her away with the like answer, yet the next day vpon better consideration intreatie preuailed, and wee anchored at Cinquoateck, the first twaine [towne] aboue the parting of the riuer, where dwelled two Kings of Pamaunke, Brothers to Powhatan: the one called Opitchapam,¹ the other Katatough,² to these I went a shore,

---

¹ MS n. (trimmed): '[O]pochoppam'.
² MS n. (trimmed): '[I]toyatene', listed by Strachey as Taughaiten (*Historie*, p. 69). Note, however, that MS n. has confused the names. Opitchapam was called Toyatan (or Itoyatin, etc.), after he succeeded Powhatan as despot of Tidewater Virginia (Arber, *Smith, Works*, p. 591). Katatough (or Kequotaugh, etc.) kept his name – despite the many ways the English spelled it.

who kindly intreated mee and Maister Scriuener, sending some presents aboard to Captaine Nuport, whilst we were trucking with these Kings.

Opechankanough[1] his wife, weomen, and children came to meete me with a naturall kind affection, hee seemed to reioyce to see me.

Captaine Nuport came a shore, with many kind discourses wee passed that forenoone: and after dinner, Captaine Nuport went about with the Pinnis to Menapacant which is twenty miles by water, and not one by land: Opechankanough, conducted me and Maister Scriuener by land, where hauing built a feasting house a purpose to entertaine vs with a kind Oration, after their manner and his best prouision, kindly welcomed vs, that day he would not trucke, but did his best to delight vs with content: Captaine Nuport arriued towards euening, whom the King presented with sixe great platters of fine bread, and Pansarowmana,[2] the next day till noone wee traded: the King feasted all the company, and the afternoone was spent in playing, dauncing, and delight, by no meanes hee would haue vs depart till the next day, he had feasted vs with venizon, for which he had sent, hauing spent his first and second prouision in expecting our comming: the next day he performed his promise, giuing more to vs three, then would haue sufficed 30. and in that we carried not away what we left, hee sent it after vs to the Pinnis, with what words or signes of loue he could expresse, we departed.

[D4] Captaine Nuport in the Pinnis, leauing mee in the Barge, to digge a rocke, where wee supposed a Mine at Cinquaoteck which done, ere midnight I arriued at Weracomoco, where our Pinnis anchored, being 20 . miles from Cinquaotecke, the next day we tooke leaue of Powhatan, who in regard of his kindnes

[1] MS n. (trimmed): '[O]pachanckano'.
[2] MS n.: 'w' deleted and 'ns' added at end in ink. In margin, trimmed: 'Pansaromanans [are] accounted a uery [da]ynty dish amongst [the]m, beeing made of ye [cor]ne when it is green [boi?]led and so mingled [am]o*n*gst beanes and so [kep?]t all ye yeare, which is [wh]en it is boyled[,] very [swe]ete and wholesom [me?]ate./

gaue him an Indian, he well affected to goe with him for England in steed of his [Newport's] Sonne, ye cause I assure me was to know our strength and Countries condition: ye next day we arriued at Kiskiack, the people so scornefully entertained vs, as with what signes of scorne and discontent we could, we departed and returned to our Fort with 250 . bushells of Corne, our president being not wholy recouered of his sicknes, in discharging, his Piece brake and split his hand off, [hand, of?] which he is not yet well recouered.

At Captaine Nuports arriuall, wee were victualled for twelue weekes, and hauing furnished him of what hee thought good, hee set saile for England the tenth of Aprill: Maister Scriuener and my selfe with our shallop, accompanied him to Captaine Hendrick [Cape Henry].[1]

Powhatan hauing for a farrewell, sent him fiue or sixe mens loadings, with Turkeyes for swords, which hee sent him in our return to ye fort: we discouered the riuer of Nausamd [Nansemond], a proud warlike Nation, as well we may testifie, [from what happened?] at our first arriuall at Chesiapiack: but that iniury Captaine Nuport well reuenged at his returne, where some of them intising him to their Ambuscadoes by a daunce, hee perceiuing their intent, with a vally [volley] of musket shot, slew one, and shot one or two more, as themselues confesse, the King at our ariuall sent for me to come vnto him: I sent him word what commodities I had to exchange for wheat, and if he would as had the rest of his Neighbours, conclude a Peace, we were contented, at last he came downe before the Boate which rid at anchor some fortie yards from ye shore, he signified to me to come a shore, and sent a Canow with foure or fiue of his men, two whereof I desired to come aboard & to stay, & I would send two to talke with their King a shore, to this hee agreed: the King wee presented with a piece of Copper, which he kindly excepted [accepted], and sent for victualls to entertaine the messengers.

[1] See p. 190, n. 1.

Maister Scriuener and my selfe also, after that, went a shore: the King kindly feasted vs, requesting vs to stay to trade till the next day, which hauing done, we returned to the Fort, this [Nansemond] riuer is a musket shot broad, each side being should bayes [shoaled bays], a narrow channell, but three fadom, his course for eighteene miles, almost directly South, and by West, where beginneth the first inhabitants, for a mile it turneth directly East, towards the West, a great bay and a white chaukie Iland, conuenient for a Fort: his next course South, where within a quarter of a mile, the riuer diuideth in two, the neck a plaine high Corne field, the wester bought [bend] a high plaine likewise, the Northeast answerable in all respects: in these plaines are planted aboundance of houses and people, they may containe 1000 . Acres of most excellent fertill ground, so sweete, so pleasant, so beautifull, and so strong a prospect, for an inuincible strong Citty, with so many commodities, that I know as yet I haue not scene: This is within one daies iourney of Chawwonocke, the riuer falleth into the Kings riuer, within twelue miles of Cape-hendicke [Cape Henry].

At our Fort, the tooles we had were so ordinarily stolen by the Indians, as necessity inforced vs to correct their brauing theeuerie: for he that stole to day, durst come againe the next day. One amongst the rest, hauing stolen two swords, I got the Counsels consent to set in the bilboes: the next day with three more, he came with their woodden swords in the midst of our men to steale, their custome is to take anything they can ceaze off, onely the people of Pamaunke, wee haue not found stealing: but what others can steale, their King receiueth.

I bad them depart, but flourishing their swords, they seemed to defend what they could catch but out of our hands, his pride vrged me to turne him from amongst vs, whereat he offred to strike me with his sword, which I preuented, striking him first: the rest offring to reuenge the blow, receiued such an incounter, and fled; the better to affright them, I pursued them with fiue or sixe shot, and so chased them out of the Iland: the beginning [beginner] of this broyle, litle expecting by his carriage, we durst haue resisted, hauing euen till that present, not beene contradicted, especially them of Paspahegh:[1] These Indians within one houre, hauing by other Saluages, then in the Fort, vnderstood that I threatned to be reuenged, came presently of themselues, and fell to working vpon our wears, which were then in hand by other Saluages, who seeing their pride so incountred, were so submissiue, and willing to doe any thing as might be, and with trembling feare, desired to be friends within three daies after: From Nawsamond which is 30 . miles from vs, the King sent vs a Hatchet, which they had stollen from vs at our being there: the messenger as is the custome, also wee well rewarded and contented.

The twenty of Aprill, being at worke, in hewing downe Trees, and setting Corne, an alarum caused vs with all speede to take our armes, each expecting a new assault of the Saluages: but vnderstanding it a Boate vnder saile, our doubts were presently satisfied, with the happy sight of Maister Nelson, his many perrills of extreame stormes and tempests [passed]. His ship well, as his company could testifie his care in sparing our prouision, was well: but the prouidence thereof, as also of our stones, Hatchets, and other tooles, onely ours excepted, which of all the rest was most necessary, which might inforce vs, to think either a seditious traitor to our action, or a most vnconscionable deceiuer of our treasures.[2] This happy arriuall of Maister Nelson in the *Phenix*, hauing beene then

[1] MS n. (trimmed): 'The Paspaheghs w[ere] alwayes treacher[ous] villaynes and euer s[hall] bee till y^{ei} are capt[iues?; -iued?].

[2] The sentence 'His ship . . . our treasures' seems badly edited, or misprinted. The sense intended is to be found in Smith's *Generall Historie* (1624), p. 53: 'Landing safely all his men, (so well he had mannaged his ill hap,) causing the Indian Isles [West Indies] to feede his company, that his victuall [added] to that we had gotten . . . before, was neare, after [in accordance with] our allowance, sufficient for halfe a yeare. He had not any thing but he freely imparted it, . . . we would not haue wished more then he did for vs' (cf. Document no. 63, p. 395, below, for the same story as told in 1612).

about three monethes missing, after Captaine Nuports arriuall, being to all our expectations lost: albeit that now at the last, hauing beene long crossed with tempestuous weather, and contrary winds, his so vnexpected comming, did so rauish vs with exceeding ioy, that now we thought our selues as well fitted, as our harts could wish, both with a competent number of men, as also for all other needfull prouisions, till a further supply should come vnto vs: whereupon the first thing that was concluded, was, that my selfe, and Maister Scriuener, should with 70. men goe with the best meanes we could prouide, to discouer beyond the Falls, as in our iudgements conueniently we might: sixe or seauen daies we spent only in trayning our men to march, fight, and scirmish in the woods, these willing minds to this action, so quickned their vnderstanding in this exercise, as in all iudgements wee were better able to fight with Powhatans whole force: in our order of battle amongst the Trees, (for Thicks there is few) then the Fort was to repulse 400. at the first assault, with some tenne or twenty shot, not knowing what to doe, nor how to vse a Piece: our warrant being sealed, Maister Nelson refused to assiste vs with the voluntary Marriners, and himselfe as he promised, vnlesse we would stand bound to pay the hire for shippe, and Marriners, for the time they stayed: and further there was some controuersie, through the diuersitie of Contrary opinions, some alleadging, that how profitable, and to what good purpose soeuer our iouney should portend, yet our commission, commanding no certaine designe, we should be taxed for the most indiscreete men in the world, besides the wrong we should doe to Captaine Nuport, to whom only all discoueries did belong, and to no other: the meanes for guides, beside the vncertaine courses of the riuer, from which we could not erre much, each night would fortifie vs in two houres, better then that they first called the Fort, their Townes vpon the riuer, each within one dayes iourney of other, besides our ordinary prouision, might well be supposed to adde reliefe: for truck &

dealing only, but in loue & peace, as with the rest; if they [E2] assalted vs, their Townes they cannot defend, nor their luggage so conuey that we should not share, but admit the worst, 16. daies prouision we had of Cheese, Oatmeale, and bisket[:] besides our randeuous [referring to their boat], we could and might haue hid in the ground. With sixe men, Captaine Martin, would haue vndertaken it himselfe,[1] leauing the rest to defend the Fort, and plant our Corne: yet no reason could be reason, to proceede forward, though we were going aboard to set saile: These discontents caused so many doubts to some, and discouragement to others, as our iourney ended: yet some of vs procured petitions to set vs forward, only with hope of our owne confusions, our next course was to turne husbandmen to fell Trees and set Corne. Fiftie of our men, we imployed in this seruice, the rest kept the Fort, to doe the command of the president, and Captaine Martin, 30. dayes the ship lay expecting ye triall of certain matters which for some cause I keepe priuate: ye next exploit was an Indian hauing stolen an Axe was so pursued by Maister Scriuener, & them next him, as he threw it downe, and flying drew his bow at any that durst incounter him: within foure or fiue dayes after, Maister Scriuener and I, being a litle from the Fort, among the Corne, two Indians, each with a cudgell, and all newly painted with Terrasigillata, came circling about mee, as though they would haue clubed me like a hare: I knew their faining loue is towards me, not without a deadly hatred, but to preuent the worst, I calling maister Scriuener retired to the Fort: the Indians seeing me suspect them, with good tearmes, asked me for some of their men whom they would beate, and went with me into our Fort, finding one that lay ordinarily with vs, only for a spie: they offered to beat him, I in perswading them to forbeare, they offered to beginne with me, being now foure, for two other arrayed in like manner, came in on the other side the Fort: wherevpon I caused to shut the Ports, and apprehend

---

[1] MS n.: 'Hee that knowes n[othing?] feares nothing.'

[E2ᵛ] them. The president and Counsell, being presently acquainted, remembring at the first assault, they came in like manner, and neuer else but against some villanie, concluded to commit them to prison, and expect the euent, eight more we ceazed at that present, an houre after came three or foure other strangers, extraordinarily fitted with arrows, skinnes, and shooting gloues, their iealousie and feare, bewrayed their bad intent, as also their suspitious departure.

The next day came first an Indian, then another as Embassadors for their men, they desired to speake with me, our discourse was, that what Spades, Shouells, swords, or tooles they had stolne, to bring home (if not the next day, they should hang) [:] the next newes was, they had taken two of our men, ranging in the woods, which mischiefe no punishment will preuent but hanging, and these they would should redeeme their owne 16 . or 18 . thus brauing vs to our doores, we desired the president, and Captaine Martin, that afternoone to sally vpon them, that they might but know, what we durst to doe, and at night man[ne]d our Barge, and burnt their Townes, and spoiled, and destroyed, what we could, but they brought our men, and freely deliuered them: the president released one, the rest we brought well guarded, to Morning and Euening prayers. Our men all in armes, their trembling feare, then caused them to much sorrow, which till then scoffed, and scorned at what we durst doe, the Counsell concluded, that I should terrifie them with some torture, to know if I could know their intent, the next day I bound one in hold [custody], to the maine Mast, and presenting sixe Muskets with match in the cockes, forced him to desire life, to answere my demaunds he could not, but one of his Comouodos [misread for *comorados*, 'comrades'] was of the counsell of Paspahegh, that could satisfie me: I releasing him out of sight, I affrighted the other, first with the rack,[1] then with Muskets, which seeing, he desired me to stay, and hee would confesse to this execution: Maister

---

[1] Eames reports copies with 'first with thereat' for 'first with the rack'.

Scriuener came,[1] his discourse was to this effect, that Paspehegh [E3] the Chickahamaniar [-nias?], Youghtanum, Pamaunka, Mattapanient, & Kiskiack. These Nations were altogether a hunting that tooke me, Paspahegh, & Chicahamanya, had entended to surprise vs at worke, to haue had our tools: Powhatan, & al his would seeme friends, till Captaine Nuports returne, that he had againe his man, which he called Namontack, where with a great feast hee would so enamor Captain Nuport & his men, as they should ceaze on him, and the like traps would be laied for the rest.

This trap for our tooles, we suspected the chiefe occasion[2] was foure daies before Powhatan had sent the boy he had to vs, with many Turkies to Maister Scriuener, and mee, vnderstanding I would go vp into his Countries to destroy them, and he doubted it the more, in that I so oft practised my men, whose shooting he heard to his owne lodging, that much feared his wiues, and children; we sent him word, we entended no such thing, but only to goe to Powhatan, to seeke stones to make Hatchets, except his men shoot at vs, as Paspahegh had told vs they would, which if they did shoote but one arrowe, we would destroy them, and least this mischiefe might happen, sent the boy to acquaint him thus much, and request him to send vs Weanock, one of his subiects for a guide, ye boy he returned backe with his Chest, & apparell, which then we had giuen him, desiring another for him, ye cause was, he was practising with the Chikahamanias, as the boy suspected some villanie, by their extraordinary resort, & secret conference from whence they would send him. The boy we keepe, now we would send him many messengers, & presents, the guide we desired he sent vs, & withall requested vs to returne him, either the boy, or some other, but none he could haue, & that day these Indians were apprehended, his sonne with others y^t had loaded at our Fort, returned, & being out of the Fort, rayled on me,

---

[1] Corrected from 'come', using the Grenville copy.
[2] Eames reports a comma after 'occasion' in some copies.

JAMESTOWN VOYAGES

to diuers of our men, to be enemies to him, & to ye Chikamanias, not long after Weanock y^t had bin with vs for our guide, whom wee kept to haue conducted vs in another [E3ᵛ] iourny, with a false excuse returned, and secretly after him, Amocis the Paspaheyan, who allwaies they kept amongst vs for a spie, whom the better to auoide suspition, presently after they came to beate [beare?] away: these presumptions induced me to take any occasion, not onely to try the honesty of Amocis, the spie, but also the meaning of these cunning trickes of their Emperour of Powhatan; whose true meaning Captaine Martin most confidently pleaded.

The confession of Macanoe, which was the counseller of Paspahegh: first, I, then Maister Scriuener, vpon their seuerall examinations, found by them all confirmed, that Paspahegh, and Chickahammenia did hate vs, and intended some mischiefe and who they were that tooke me, the names of them that stole our tooles, and swords, and that Powhatan receiued them, they all agreed: certaine vollies of shot we caused to be discharged, which caused each other to thinke that their fellowes had beene slaine.

Powhatan vnderstanding we detained certaine Saluages, sent his Daughter,[1] a child of tenne yeares old, which not only for feature, countenance & proportion, much exceedeth any of the rest of his people, but for wit, and spirit, the only Nonpariel of his Country: this hee sent by his most trustie messenger, called Rawhunt, as much exceeding in deformitie of person, but of a subtill wit, and crafty vderstanding, he with a long circumstance, told me, how well Powhatan, loued and respected mee, and in that I should not doubt any way of his kindnesse, he had sent his child, which he most esteemed, to see me, a Deere, and bread, besides for a present: desiring me that the Boy might come againe, which he loued exceedingly, his litle Daughter hee had taught this lesson also:

[1] MS n.: 'Pokahuntas', and somewhat below, 'Mator./' Matoaka was her original name; Pocahontas, a pet-name given her by Powhatan.

not taking notice at all of the Indeans that had beene prisoners three daies, till that morning that she saw their fathers, and friends come quietly, and in good tearmes to entreate their libertie.

Opechankanough, sent also vnto vs, that for his sake, we would release two that were his friends, and for a token sent [E4] me his shooting Gloue, and Bracer, which the day our men was taken vpon, separating himselfe from the rest a long time, intreated to speake with me, where in token of peace, he had preferred me the same: now all of them hauing found their peremptorie conditions, but to increase our malice, which they seeing vs begin to threaten to destroy them, as familiarly as before, without suspition, or feare, came amongst vs, to begge libertie for their men: In the afternoone they being gone, we guarded them as before to the Church, and after prayer, gaue them to Pocahuntas, the Kings Daughter, in regard of her fathers kindnesse in sending her: after hauing well fed them, as all the time of their imprisonment, we gaue them their bowes, arrowes, or what else they had, and with much content, sent them packing: Pocahuntas, also we requited, with such trifles as contented her, to tel that we had vsed ye Paspaheyans very kindly in so releasing them. The next day we had suspition of some other practise for an Ambuscado, but perfectly wee could not discouer it, two daies after a Paspaheyan, came to shew vs a glistering Minerall stone: and with signes demonstrating it to be in great aboundance, like vnto Rockes, with some dozen more, I was sent to seeke to digge some quantitie, and the Indean to conduct me: but suspecting this some tricke to delude vs, for to get some Copper of vs, or with some ambuscado to betray vs, seeing him falter in his tale, being two miles on our way, led him ashore, where abusing vs from place to place, and so seeking either to haue drawne vs with him into the woods, or to haue giuen vs the slippe: I shewed him Copper, which I promised to haue giuen him, if he had performed his promise, but for his scoffing and abusing vs, I gaue him twentie lashes with a Rope, and his bowes and arrowes, bidding him shoote if he durst, and so let him goe.[1]

[E4ᵛ] In all this time, our men being all or the most part well recouered, and we not willing to trifle away more time then necessitie enforced vs vnto, we thought good for the better content of the aduenturers, in some reasonable sort to fraight home Maister Nelson with Cedar wood, about which, our men going with willing minds, was in very good time effected, and the ship sent for England; wee now remaining being in good health, all our men wel contented, free from mutinies, in loue one with another, & as we hope in a continuall peace with the Indians, where we doubt not but by Gods gracious assistance, and the aduenturers willing minds, and speedie furtherance to so honorable an action in after times, to see our Nation to enioy a Country, not onely exceeding pleasant for habitation, but also very profitable for comerce in generall, no doubt pleasing to almightie God, honourable to our gracious Soueraigne, and commodious generally to the whole Kingdome.

FINIS

[1] It seems highly likely that a cut was made here, since the book ends with the signature and little space to spare. Compare the similar passage in Document no. 63, p. 396, below. Other cuts appear to have been made throughout the book, but it is difficult to prove just where.

IV

Events in England, 1608

NARRATIVE

It has been seen that Newport's first reports to the Virginia council in London were generally encouraging, and even tinged with excessive optimism regarding the prospects offered by Virginia's natural resources for making investment in the voyages a profitable venture. When he returned almost a year later, however, with more of what John Smith called 'gilded durt' (Document no. 63, p. 394, below), and with news of famine, death, unfriendly Indians, and boisterous disruption within the colony, the disillusionment in London must have been extreme. No surviving document (for the Company's records for that period are missing) attests this, but a letter about Edward Maria Wingfield's deposition, return with Newport, and prospective trial for malfeasance in office, hints that the conditions in Jamestown were far from a secret. To be sure, the letter-writer, Ralph Lord Eure, wrote that Wingfield was 'not yet tried' (*VMHB*, XXVI (1918), 315), but the elaborate defence Wingfield prepared for himself shows that he was ready for whatever might come (Document no. 34). One thing was certain: to survive, the colony needed a strong hand at the helm; stronger than any that had been or was still there.

Indeed, the leaders of the Virginia Company had already made moves for a stronger hand to take charge even before word came of Wingfield's disgrace, and had appealed to the States General of the Netherlands to release from service another of the patentees of the Company, Sir Thomas Gates. This was granted on 24 April 1608 (Document no. 36). Meanwhile, also before Newport's return, the first news of the

Jamestown colony appeared in a continental gazette, the *Mercure François* (Document no. 35).

Don Pedro de Zúñiga soon heard about Newport's arrival (see the accompanying letter to Document no. 32, above), and he forwarded to his master what he considered factual news. After that, although word of Nelson's return reached the ears of John Chamberlain by 7 July (Document no. 37), Zúñiga either heard little, or delayed writing until he had assembled more valuable information. There appears to be no word from him regarding Virginia until September. It was worth the wait, however, for he then sent a copy of what must have been Smith's draft map of Virginia, along with a brief description of the country (Documents nos. 38–40). The description is humdrum, but the map is of great value to any student of Virginia as it was in 1608, for it reports some details not to be found elsewhere, and is untainted by the prejudices of later years. At the same time, it illustrates the misconceptions that existed, and were to continue to exist much too long.

London, amazingly, had by this time decided that Powhatan should be confirmed in his majesty by a solemn bit of mummery which would, they thought, make him a subject king under the superior lordship of James I. Confusing the Algonkian despot with some such monarch as the Inca in Peru, the officers of the Virginia Company came to the conclusion that, with a tawdry copper crown of English make, Powhatan would feel obligated to King James, and obliged to obey the Company's commands. Nothing they could have done, perhaps, could have had results more contradictory to their purpose. Yet with the crown and a scarlet robe for Powhatan, Newport set sail once again, not long after Nelson's pinnace docked in the Thames.

This time, Newport's stay in Virginia, with the ludicrous 'coronation' of the 'Emperor', led to open rupture with Captain John Smith, and when Newport prepared to sail back to London, Smith had ready for him to take to the council a long and saucy letter, a copy of which (undoubtedly somewhat rewritten) was first printed in Smith's *Generall Historie* in 1624 (Document no. 41). Among other correspondence now forgotten, Newport also carried a letter from Peter Winne, one of the two new councillors appointed for Jamestown. It was his first and last communication from there, for he was dead before the end of the winter, cause and other details unknown.

By this time, Sir Thomas Gates was in England, meetings were unquestionably held the records of which have not survived, and a movement was set on foot to reorganize the company, obtain more capital, augment the supply of colonists and *matériel* on an unprecedented scale, and make of the uncertain bridgehead a true and permanent English colony in Virginia.

It is probably to this period that a document found by Susan Myra Kingsbury among the Tanner manuscripts in the Bodleian Library should be assigned. Entitled 'A Iustification for planting in Virginia', this paper seems to record minutes of a meeting of shareholders of the Virginia Company, where the subject of defending England's right to settle in Virginia once again came up. What prompted the discussion is not clear, but it is evident that some of those present were in favour of informing the public through 'some forme of writing' of the legality and 'Iustice' of the Virginia 'action'.

It was claimed that this would encourage those adventurers who had already invested in the enterprise, and attract new support. At the same time, it would serve to intimate to the Spaniards that 'the state would neyther feare nor be ashamed to proceed in ye persecution ther of, if any Course should be held agaynst y^t [by them]'.

While other, minor arguments were advanced in favour of publishing such a justification, the bulk of the document is composed of arguments against it. These point out that the adventurers need no further persuasion, and that the Spaniards might use such a declaration to their own advantage. Several of the ways in which this could be done are pointed out, and it is to be concluded that the matter was either tabled and forgotten, or baldly dropped (see Kingsbury, *Records*, III, 1-3).

John Chamberlain reported on Newport's return in a letter of 23 January 1609 (Document no. 43), and three weeks later wrote that there was no further news except that John Donne 'sought' to be secretary of the colony – a post that did not exist under the first charter. Yet on 17 February, five of the leading promoters of the Jamestown voyages (Waad, Smythe, Sandys, Roe and Romney) wrote to the Corporation of Plymouth proposing the uniting of the dormant second colony with the active first one, at Jamestown, and asking them to 'ioyne freelie togeather and with one com*m*on and patient purse mayneteyne and perfecte ou*r* foundations' (Manuscript, Plymouth City Archives). This letter also mentions 'our Patent', which surely refers to the new one, the second charter, which would not be signed by the King for more than three months.

The whole movement as seen from London at the time is succinctly, and remarkably correctly, summed up in a letter from the new Venetian Ambassador, Marc'Antonio Correr, to the Doge and Senate, dated on the same 17/27 February 1609 as the Virginia Council's letter. The pertinent passage is as follows:

> Here they are busy with the despatch of a ship to the [West] Indies. She is to sail in a month's time. She will have eight hundred persons on board, many oxen and ponies and other things needful for developing a district near Florida, which was discovered by the English under Queen Elizabeth. They found it uninhabited and determined to occupy it and the Queen gave it the name of Virginia. A few years ago in the reign of the present King another ship with a like number of people and cattle was sent out. The Spanish Ambassador has complained to the King more than once; his Majesty pleads that the undertaking is a private one, and that he cannot interfere. All the same I hear that not only are many great personages in the scheme – Lord Salisbury sending a number of stallions and other animals on his own account – but the Prince [Henry] has put some money in it, so that he may, some day, when he comes to the crown, have a claim over the Colony. They are fortifying themselves against possible attacks from the

Spanish or their dependents who inhabit territory not more than ten days' journey away. The King has charged some of the great gentlemen to superintend all that may be necessary to assist the enterprise. (*Calendar of S.P., Venetian*, XI, 237.) [382]

34. 1608. [Finished after 21 May.]
Edward Maria Wingfield, Discourse.[1]

Right wor*ship*full: and more worthy[2]

My due respect to your selves, my allegiance (if I may so terme it) to the Virginean action, my good heede to my poore reputacion[,] thrust a penne into my handes, so iealous am I to bee missing to any of them; if it wandereth in extravagantes, yet shall they not bee idle to those Phisitions, whose loves have vndertaken the saftie and advancement of Virginia.

It is no small comfort that I speake before such gravitie,[3] whose iudgement no forrunner can forestall with any opprobrious vntruths[,] whose wisedomes can easily disroabe malice out of her painted garments from the ever reverenced truth.

I did so faithfully betroth my best indeavors to this noble enterprize as my carriage might endure no suspition: I never turned my face from daunger, or hidd my handes from labour, so watchfull a Sentinel stood my self to my self.

I know wel a troope of errors continually beseege mens

---

[1] Lambeth Palace Library, MSS, 250, folios 382–96. Apparently 'found' by the Rev. James S. M. Anderson while preparing a history of the Church of England in the colonies, this manuscript first appeared in print in 1845, and was published in the United States in an approximately *literatim* copy by the American Antiquarian Society in 1860 (see Documents nos. 13–15). Printed again, after the MS, in Arber's *Smith, Works*, pp. lxxiv–xci, it is only 'discussed' by Brown (*Genesis*, I, 170–2), although the introductory address is printed, with slight modification, in full.

[2] This introduction is in a very neat Italian hand, obviously intended to be signed.

[3] The 'gravitie' must refer to the court of the Virginia Company, in London. According to Wingfield himself (end of the main body of this Document), he 'arryued at Blackwall on Sunday the xxjth of Maye 1608'. The 21st of May was a Saturday, however, and this seems to be the correct date ('on Sunday' was interpolated in the text). He seems to have been summoned by the Company soon afterwards, but Ralph Lord Eure wrote to Sir Robert Harley one week later that he was 'not yet tried' (Barbour, Smith, p. 464). It may seriously be questioned whether any court action was ever taken.

actions, some of them ceased on by malice, some by ignorance: I doo not hoodwinck my carriage in my self love, but freely and humblie submit it to your grave censures.

I do freely and truely Anatomize the governement and governours that your experience may applie medicines accordinglie, and vpon the truth of this iournall do pledge my faith, and life, and so do rest.

         yours to commaund in all service

[Space for signature]

[383] Here followeth what happined in James Towne in Virginia after Captayne Newports departure for England /[1]

Captayne Newport haueing allwayes his eyes and eares open to the proceedinges of the Collonye, 3 . or 4 . dayes before his departure, asked the president how he thought himself setled in the gouernment, whose answere was that no disturbaunce could indaunger him of the Collonye, but it must be wrought eyther by Captayne Gosnold, or M*aste*r Archer; for the one was strong with freinds and followers, and could if he would; and the other was troubled with an ambitious spirit, and would if he could: The Captayne gaue them both knowledg of this the Presidentes opinion, and mooued them with many intreatyes to be myndefull of their dutyes to his M*aie*stie and the Collonye /

June 1607   The 22th Captayne Newport retorned for England, for whose good passadge, and safe retorne wee made many prayers to our allmighty god /

Iune the 25th an Indian Came to vs from the great Poughwaton with the worde of peace, that he desired greatly our freindshipp that the wyroaunces, Paspaheigh, and Tapahanagh

---

[1] This sign almost invariably marks the end of a paragraph in this document. The 'full point' (/.) and 'double full point' (./.) are occasionally used, but they have not been reproduced.

should be our freindes, that wee should sowe and reape in peace, or els he would make warrs vpon them with vs; This message fell out true, for both those wyroaunces haue euer since remayned in peace, and trade with vs: Wee rewarded the messinger, with many tryfles, which were great wonders to him /

This Powatan dwelleth 10 myles from vs vpon the River Pamaonche, which lyeth North from vs; the Powatan in the former iornall mencioned (a dwellar by Cap*tay*n Newports faulls) ys a wyroaunce, and vnder this great Powaton, which before wee knew not /

The 3 of Iuly 7 or 8 Indians presented the President a Dear [383ᵛ] from Pamaonke, a wyroaunce desiring our freindshipp, they Iuly enquired after our shipping, which the President said was gon to Croatoon; they feare much our shipps; and therefore he would not haue them thinck it farr from vs; their wyrounce had a Hatchet sent hym, they wear well Contented with trifles: A litle after this Came a Dear to the President from the great Powatan: he and his messingers were pleased with the like trifles: The President likewise bought diuers tymes Dear of the Indyans, beavars and other flesh, which he always caused to be equally deuided amongst the Collonye /

About this tyme diuers of our men fell sick, wee myssed aboue Forty before September did see vs,[1] amongst whom was the Worthy and Religious gent Cap*tay*n Bartholmew Gosnold, vpon whose lief stood a great part of the good succes, and fortune of our gouernment and Collony: In his sicknes tyme the president did easily foretell his owne deposing from his Comaund, so much differed the p*r*esident and the other Councellors on mannaging the government of the Collonye /

The 7th of Iuly Tapahanah a wyroaunce dweller on Salisbery Iuly side hayled vs with the word of peace, the President with a

[1] John Smith reported 'about the tenth of September there was about 46 . of our men dead' (Document no. 33, pp. 173–4). Gosnold was one of the first to be taken sick (about 1 August), and died 22 August. George Percy listed the names of over a score who died before the epidemic was spent.

Shallopp well manned went to him, he found him sytting on the ground Crossed legged as is their Custome, with one attending on him, which did often saie this is the wyroance Tapahanah, which he did likewise confirme with stroaking his brest, he was well enough knowne for the President had sene him diuerse tymes before, his Countynance was nothing cherefull, for wee had not seene him since he was in the feild against vs, but the President would take no knowledg thereof, and vsed him kindely, giving him a red Wascoat, which he did

[384] desire; Tapahanah did enquire after our shipping; he receyued answer as before, he said his ould store was spent, that his new was not at full groath by a foote; That as sone as any was ripe he would bring it, which promise he truly performed

The   of   Master Kendall was put of[f] from beeing of the Counsell, and committed to prison, for that it did manyfestly appeere he did practize to sowe discord betwene the President and Councell /

Sicknes had not now left vs vj able men in our Towne, gods onely mercy did now watch and Warde for vs, but the President hidd this our weakenes carefully from the salvages, neuer suffring them in all his tyme to come into our Towne /

Septem: The vjth of September Paspaheigh sent vs a boy that was run from vs, this was the first assurance of his peace with vs, besides wee found them no Canyballs: The boye obserued the men & women to spend the most part of the night in singing, or howling, and that euery morning the Women Carryed all the litle Childrenn to the Rivers sides, but what they did there he did not knowe /

The rest of the wyroances doe likewise send our men runnagates to vs home againe, vsing them well during their beeing with them; so as now they being well rewarded at home at their retorne, they take litle ioye to trauell abroad without Pasportes /

The Councell demaunded some larger allowaunce for them

selues, and for some sick their fauorites, which the President would not yield vnto without their Warrantes /

This matter was before propounded by Captayn Martyn, but so nakedly as that he neyther knew the quantity of the stoare to be but for xiij weekes and a half vnder the Cap[e] Merchauntes hand, he prayed them further to Consider the long tyme before wee expected Captayn Newportes retorne, the incertainty of his retorne, if god did not fauour his voyage, the long tyme before our haruest would be ripe, and the doubtfull peace that wee had with the Indyans, which they would keepe no longer then opertunity served to doe vs mischeif / [384ᵛ]

It was then therefore ordered, that euery meale of fish or fleshe should excuse the allowance for poridg, both against the sick and hole /

The Counsell therefore sitting againe vpon this proposition instructed in the former reasons and order, did not thinke it fit to breake the former order by enlarging their allowance, as will appeere by the most voyces reddy to be shewed vnder their handes /

Now was the Comon store of oyle, vinigar, sack, & Aquavite all spent saueing twoe Gallons of each; the sack reserued for the Comunion table, the rest for such extreamityes as might fall vpon vs, which the President had onely made know[n]e to Captayn Gosnold, of which course he liked well, the vessells wear therefore boonged vpp: When Master Gosnold was dead the President did acquaint the rest of the Councell with the said Remnant: but lord how they then longed for to supp vp that litle remnant for they had now emptied all their owne bottles, and all other that they could smell out /

A litle wile after this the Councell did againe fall vpon the President for some better allowance for themselues and some few [of] the sick their privates: The President protested he would not be partiall, but if one had any thing of him, euery man should haue his portion according to their places, Nevertheles that vpon their Warrantes he would deliuer what pleased them to demaund. Yf the President had at that tyme enlarged the proportion according to their request, without doubt in very short tyme he had starued the whole Company, he would not ioyne with them therefore in such an ignorant murder without their owne Warrant /

The President well seeing to what end their ympacience would growe, desired them earnestly & often tymes to bestowe the Presidentshipp amonge themselues, that he could obey, a private man, as well as they could Comaund, but they refused to discharge him of the place, sayeing they mought not doe it, for that hee did his Maiestie good service in yt /

In this meane tyme the Indians did daily relieue vs with Corne and fleshe, that in three weekes the Presidant had reared vpp xx men able to worke, for as his stoare increased he mended the Comon pott; hee had laid vp besides prouision for 3 . weekes, wheate beforehand /

By this tyme the Councell had fully plotted to depose Wingfeild the then President, and had drawne certeyne Artycles in Wrighting amongst them selues and toke their oathes vpon the Evangelistes to obserue them, th'effect whereof was first /

To depose the then President

To make Master Ratcliff the next President

Not to depose the one th'other

Not to take the deposed President into [the] Councell againe

Not to take Master Archer into the Councell or any other without the Consent of euery one of them; To theis they had subscribed, as out of their owne mouthes, at seuerall tymes it was easily gathered /

Thus had they forsaken his Maiesties government sett vs downe in the instruccions, & made it a Triumvirat /

It seemeth Master Archer was nothing acquainted with theis artycles, though all the rest crept out of his noates and Comentaryes that were preferred against the President[;] yet it pleased god to Cast him into the same disgrace and pitt that he prepared for an other, as will appeere hereafter[/]

The 10 of September, M*aste*r Ratcliff, M*aste*r Smyth, and M*aste*r Martynn Came to the Presidentes Tennt with a Warrant subscribed vnder their handes to depose the President, sayeing they thought him very vnworthy to be eyther P*res*ident or of the Councell, and therefore discharged him of bothe: Hee answered them that they had eased him of a great deale of Care, and trouble; that long since hee had diuers tymes profered them the place at an easier rate, and further that the President ought to be remoued (as appeereth in his M*aies*ties instrucc*ions* for our government) by the greater number of xiij voyces Councellors, that they were but three, and therefore wished them to proceede advisedly, but they told him if they did him wrong, they must answere it;[1] Then said the deposed President I ame at yo*ur* pleasure, dispose of me as you will without further Garboile /

Septem:

I will now wright what followeth in my owne name and giue the new President his title, I shalbe the briefer being thus discharged, I was Comytted to a Serieant, and sent to the Pynnasse: [I protested] but I was answered with [,] if they did me wronge, they must answere it /

The 11th of September I was sent for to Come before the President, and Councell vpon their Court daie, they had now made M*aste*r Archer Recorder of Virginia; The President made a speeche to the Collony that he thought it fitt to acquaint them whie I was deposed. I ame now forced to stuff my Paper with frivilous trifles, that our graue and worthy Councell may the better strike those vaynes where the Corrupt blould [blood] lyeth, and that they may see in what manner of governm*ent* the hope of the Collony now travayleth /

[386]

First Master President said that I had denyed him a penny whitle, a Chickyn, a spoonfull of beere, and served him with

---

[1] Roughly here, and in several places below, there is a sign in the margin (three dots, one above, two below, over an elongated 'S') which seems intended to call attention to the passage (='therefore see'?).

foule Corne, and with that pulled some graine out of a bagg shewing it to the Company /

Then start vp Master Smyth, and said that I had tould him playnly how he lied, and that I said though wee were equall heere, yet if he were in England he would thinck scorne his man should be my Companyon[1] /

Master Martyn followed with, he reporteth that I doe slack the service in the Collonye, and doe nothing but tend my pott, spitt, and oven, but he hath starued my sonne, and denyed him a spoonefull of beere; I haue freindes in England shalbe revenged on him, if euer he Come in London /

I asked master President if I should answere theis Complaintes, and whether he had ought els to charge me with all; with that he pulled out a paper booke, loaded full with Artycles against me, and gaue them Master Archar to reade: I tould Master President and the Councell; that by the instruccions for our government, our proceedinges ought to be verball, and I was there ready to answere: but they said they would proceede in that order;[2] I desired a Coppie of the Articles, and tyme giuen me to answere them likewise by wrighting, but that would not be graunted; I badd them then please themselues; [386ᵛ] Master Archer then redd some of the Artycles, when on the suddaine Master President said: staie, staie, wee knowe not whether he will abide our Iudgment, or whether he will appeale to the King, sayeing to me: how saie you, will you appeale to the King or no:[3] I apprehended presently [immediately] that gods mercy had opened me a Waie through their ignorance, to escape their malice, for I never knewe howe I might demaunde an appeale, besides I had secret knowledg how they had foreiudged me to paie fiue fould for anything

---

[1] As it is written, the charge makes little sense. With 'his man' emended to 'this man', however, the passage would read that Smith accused Wingfield of saying, 'Though we are equal here, if we were in England I would think scorne that this man (Smith) should be my companion'. See also p. 231 and n. 1.
[2] Passage marked in margin (see p. 219, n. 1, above).
[3] Passage again marked in margin.

that Came to my handes, whereof I could not discharge my self by wrighting, and that I should lye in prison vntill I had paid it /

The Cape Marchant had deliuered me our Marchantdize without any noat of the pertycularyties vnder my hand, for himself had receyued them in grosse; I like wise as occation mooued me spent them in Trade, or by guift amongst the Indians, so likewise did Cap*tay*n Newport take of them; when he went vp to discouer the kinges river, what he thought good, without any noate of his hand, mentioning the Certainty, and disposed of them as was fitt for him, of these likewise I could make no accompt, onely I was well assured I had neuer bestowed the valewe of three penny Whitles to my owne vse, nor to the private vse of any other, for I neuer carryed any fauorite over with me, or intertayned any thear, I was all one, and one to all[1] /

Vpon theis consideracions I answered M*aste*r President and the Councell that his M*ai*esties handes were full of mercy and that I did appeale to his M*ai*esties mercy, they then comytted me prisoner againe to the master of ye Pynnasse with theis words: looke to him well he is now the kinges prisoner[/]

Then M*aste*r Archer pulled out of his bosome an other paper [387] booke full of Artycles against me, desiring that he might reade them in the name of the Collony: I said I stood there ready to answere any mans Complaint whome I had wronged, but no one man spoke one word against me, then was he willed to reade his booke, whereof I complayned; but I was still answered if they doe me wrong they must answere it: I haue forgotten the most of the Artycles they were so slight (yet he glorieth much in his penn worke) I knowe well the last, and a speeche that he then made sauored well of a mutyny; for he desired that by no meanes, I might lye prysoner in the Towne, least boath he, and others of the Collony, should not

---

[1] 'All one, and one to all' is a play on the basic meaning of 'alone'. Wingfield had no favourites, so he was alone ('all one'); being alone, he was the same to all.

giue such obedience to their Comaund as they ought to doe, which goodly speech of his they easilye swallowed /

But it was vsuall, and naturall to this honest gent Master Archer to be allwayes hatching of some mutany, in my tyme, hee might haue appeered an author of 3 seuerall mutynies /

And hee (as Master Pearsie [Percy] sent me worde) had bought some Witnesses handes against me to diuers artycles with Indian Cakes (which was no great matter to doe after my deposall, and considering their hungar) perswations and threates; at an other tyme he feared not to saie openly, and in the presence of one of the Councell, that if they had not deposed me when they did, he hadd gotten twenty others to him self, which should haue deposed me, but this speech of his was likewise easily disiested [digested] /

[387ᵛ] Master Croftes feared not to saie that if others would ioyne with him, he would pull me out of my seate, and out of my skynn too; others would saie, (whose names I spare) that vnlesse I would amend their allowance, they would be their owne Caruers; for these mutin[o]us speeches, I rebuked them openly, and proceeded no further against them, Considering th'end of mens liues in the kinges service there; one of the Councell was very earnest with me to take a guard aboute me, I answered him I would no guard but gods loue, and my owne innocencie. in all theis disorders was Master Archer a Ring leader /

When Master President and Master Archer had made an end of their Artycles aboue menc*i*oned, I was againe sent prisoner to the Pynnasse, and Master Kendall taken from thence had his liberty, but might not Carry Armes¹ /

All this while the Salvages brought to the Towne such Corne and flesh as they could spare, Paspaheighe by Tapahanaes mediation was taken into freindshipp with vs, the Councellors (Master Smyth especially) traded vp and downe the River

---

¹ 'Kendall taken from thence' – 'taken' was originally written 'takeinge', and the '– inge –' clumsily corrected. Kendall was under arrest for little more than a fortnight.

with the Indyans for Corn, which releued the Collony well /

As I vnderstand by report I ame much charged with staruing the Collony; I did allwayes giue euery man his allowance faithfully, both of Corne, oyle, aquivite &c as was by the Counsell proportioned, neyther was it bettered after my tyme, vntill towards th'end of March [1608], a Bisket was allowed to euery workeing man for his breake-fast, by meanes of the prouision brought vs by Capt*ay*n Newport, as will appeere [388] here after: It is further said I did much banquit, and Ryot: I neuer had but one Squirell roasted, whereof I gaue p*ar*t to M*aste*r Ratcliff then sick; yet was that Squirell given me; I did never heate a flesh pott, but when the Comon pot was so vsed likewise; Yet how often M*aste*r Presidentes and the Councellors spittes haue night & daie bene endaungered to break their backes so laden with swanns, geese, duckes, &c, how many tymes their flesh pottes haue swelled, many hungry eies did behold to their great longing: and what great Theeues, and theeving thear hath bene in the Comon stoare since my tyme,[1] I doubt not but is all ready made knowne to his M*aies*ties Councell for Virginia /

The 17th daie of September I was sent for to the Court to answere a Complaint exhibited against me by Jehu Robinson, for that when I was president, I did saie, hee with others had Consented to runn awaye with the Shallop to newfound land, at an other tyme, I must answere M*aste*r Smyth, for that I had said hee did conceale an intended mutany; I tould M*aste*r Recorder those wordes would beare no actions, that one of the Causes was done without the lymites menc*i*oned in the Patent graunted to vs, and therefore prayed M*aste*r President that I mought not be thus lugged with theis disgraces and troubles; but hee did weare no other eies or eares then grew on M*aste*r Archers head; The Iury gaue the one of them 100^{li}, and the [388^v] other twoe hundred pound damages for slaunder,[2] then

[1] Passage marked in margin (see p. 219, n. 1, above).
[2] The £200 obviously were for Smith. If it is meant that Wingfield handed over

*Ma*st*e*r Recorder did very learnedly comfort me, that if I had wrong, I might bring my writ of error in London, whereat I smiled /

I seeing their lawe so speedie and cheape, desired Iustice for a Copper Kettle, which *Ma*st*e*r Crofts did deteyne from me, hee said I had giuen it him, I did bid him bringe his proofe for that; he Confessed hee had no proofe, Then *Ma*st*e*r President did aske me if I would be sworne I did not giue it him, I said I knew no cause whie to sweare for myne owne, hee asked *Ma*st*e*r Crofts if he would make oath, I did giue it him, which oath hee tooke, and wann my Kettle from me, that was in that place and tyme, worth half his waight in gold; yet I did vnderstand afterwards that he would haue given John Capper the one half of the Kettle to haue taken the oath for him, but hee would [have?] no Copper on that price[1] /

I tould *Ma*st*e*r President I had not knowne the like lawe and prayed they would be more sparing of law, vntill wee had more witt, or wealthe, that lawes were goode spies, in a populous, peaceable, and plentifull Cuntry, whear they did make the good men better, & stayed the badd from being worse, y^t wee weare so poore as they did but robb vs of tyme that might be better ymployed in service in the Collonye /

[389] The   daie of   the President did beat Iames Read the Smyth. the Smyth stroake him againe [back], for this he was condempned to be hanged, but before he was turned of[f] the Lather he desired to speake with the President in private, to whome he accused *Ma*st*e*r Kendall of a mutiny, and so escaped himself: What Indictment m*a*st*e*r Recorder framed, against the Smyth I knowe not, but I knowe it is familiar for the President, Counsellors, and other officers to beate men at

---

that sum to Smith in Jamestown, which is likely, it seems remarkable that a colonist would have such a sum with him. (For comparative value, note that the annual salary of the tutor for the heir to the wealthy Earl of Northumberland was £40 a year.)

[1] Capper is completely obscure. He is not listed as a gentleman, nor as a labourer.

their pleasures, one lyeth sick till death, an other walketh lame, the third cryeth out of all his boanes, which myseryes they doe take vpon their Consciences to Come to them by this their Almes of beating. Wear this whipping, lawing, beating, and hanging in Virginia knowne in England I feare it would driue many well affected myndes from this honorable action of Virginia /

This Smyth Comyng aboord the Pynnasse, with some others, aboute some busines 2 or 3 dayes before his arraignement brought me Comendacions from Master Pearsye, Master Waller, Master Kendall, and some others saieing they would be glad to see me on shoare: I answered him they were honest gentlemen and had carryed themselues very obediently to their gouernors, I prayed god that they did not thinck of any ill thing vnworthie [of] themselues; I added further that vpon Sundaie if the weathiar were faire, I would be at the sermon, lastly I said that I was so sickly, starued, lame, and did lye so could, and wett in the Pynnasse as I would be dragged thithere before I would goe thither any more, sundaie proued not faire I went not to the Sermon /

The   daie of   Master Kendall was executed being shott to death for a mutiny / [Added in small letters by the same hand:] In th'arrest of his Iudgment he alleaged to Master President y^t his name was Sicklemore, not Ratcliff: & so had no authority to pronounce Iudgment, then Master Martyn pronounced Iudgment[1] /

Some what before this tyme the President, and Councell had sent for the keyes of my Coffers, supposing that I had some Wrightinges Concerning the Collony, I requested that the Clearke of the Councell might see what they tooke out of my Coffers, but they would not suffer him or any other, vnder Cullor heereof they tooke my bookes of Accompt, and all my [389ᵛ] noates that concerned the expences of the Collony, and

---

[1] On Kendall, see Barbour, 'Captain George Kendall', *VMHB*, LXX (1962), 297–313.

instructions vnder the Cape Marchantes hande of the stoare of prouision, diuers other bookes & trifles of my owne proper goodes, which I could neuer recouer. Thus was I made good prise on all sides /

The   daie of   the President Comaunded me to Come on shore, which I refused as not rightfully deposed and desired that I mought speake to him and the Councell in the presence of 10 of the best sorte of the gentry,[1] with much intreaty some of them wear sent for, then I tould them, I was determined to goe into England to acquaint our Councell there, with our weaknes; I said further their lawes, and government was such as I had no ioye to liue vnder them any longer; that I did much myslike their triumverat, haueing forsaken his Maiesties instruccions for our government, and therefore praied there might be more made of the Councell: I said further I desired not to goe into England, if eyther Master President, or Master Archer would goe but was willing to take my fortune with the Collony, and did also proffer to furnish them with 100^{li} towards the fetching home the Collonye, if the action was given over; They did like of none of my proffers, but made diuers shott at mee in the Pynnasse: I se[e]ing their resolucions went a shoare to them, wheare after I had staied a while in conference they sent me to the Pynnasse againe[2]

Decem: The 10th of December Master Smyth went vp the Ryuer of the Chechohomynaies to trade for Corne, he was desirous to see the heade of that River, and when it was not passible with the Shallop, he hired a Cannow and an Indian to Carry him vp further, the river the higher grew worse and worse[;] then hee went on shoare with his guide, and left Robinson & Emmery, twoe of our men in the Cannow, which were presently slayne by the Indians Pamaonkes men; and hee himself taken prysoner,

---

[1] Passage marked in margin (see p. 219, n. 1, above). The '10 of the best sorte' must have comprised nearly half of all the gentlemen then living.

[2] There is no punctuation here, and the passage is marked in the margin, as above. For a conjectural explanation of what took place, see Barbour, *Smith*, 153-4.

and by the meanes of his guide his lief was saued, and Pamaonche
haueing him prisoner Carryed him to his Neybors wyroances [390]
to see if any of them knew him for one of those, which had
bene some twoe or three yeeres before vs in a River amongst
them Northward, and taken awaie some Indians from them,
by force, at last he brought him to the great Powaton (of
whome before wee had no knowledg) whoe sent him home to
owr Towne the viijth of Ianuary[1] /   Ianuary

During Master Smythes absence the President did swear
Master Archer, one of the Councell,[2] contrary to his oath
taken in the Artycles agreed vpon betweene themselues (before
spoken of[)], and contrary to the kinges instruccions, and without Master Martyns consent, whereas there weare no more but
the President and Master Martyn then of the Councell /

Master Archer being setled in his authority sought how to
Call Master Smyths lief in question, and had indited him vpon a
Chapter in Leuiticus for the death of his twoe men; hee had
hadd his tryall the same daie of his retorne, and I belieue his
hanging [was to have been] the same, or the next daie, so
speedie is our lawe thear, but it pleased god to send Captayn
Newport vnto vs the same eevening to our vnspeakeable com-
fortes; whose arryuall saued Master Smyths leif, and myne,
because hee tooke me out of the Pynnasse, an[d] gaue me leaue
to lye in the Towne: [added in much smaller writing:] Also by
his comyng was prevented a Parliament, which ye newe
Counsailor Master Recorder intended thear to summon;[3]
Thus error begot error /

Captayne Newport haueing landed, lodged, and refreshed
his men, ymploied some of them aboute a faire stoare house,
others aboute a stove, and his Maryners aboute a Church, all

---

[1] The date is clearly written, but must be mistaken, since the fire took place afterwards, and that is dated the seventh of January. Newport *arrived* the day of Smith's
return, which is clearly deducible from Perkin's letter as the second of January (see
pp. 159–60). Brown has guessed that the viijth should stand for the iiijth, but that is
the day Newport *landed* his men. Wingfield's memory must have been at fault.

[2] Passage marked in margin.   [3] Passage marked in margin.

JAMESTOWN VOYAGES

Ianuary

which workes they finished cherefully and in short tyme /
The 7 of Ianuary,[1] our Towne was almost quite burnt, with all our apparell and prouision; but Capt*ay*n Newport healed our wants to our great Comforts, out of the great plenty sent vs by the prouident and loving care of our worthie & most worthie Councell /

[390ᵛ]
This Vigillant Captayne slacking no opertunity that might advaunce the prosperity of the Collony haueing setled the Company vppon the former workes, tooke M*aste*r Smyth and M*aste*r Scrivener (an other Councellor of Virginia, vpon whose discretion liueth a great hope of the action) went to discouer the Ryver Pamaonche on the further side, whearof dwelleth the great Powaton, and to trade with him for Corne: This River lyeth North from vs, and runneth east and West, I haue nothing but by relation, of that matter, and therefore dare not make any discourse thereof least I mought wrong the great desart, which Capt*ay*n Newports loue to the action hath deserued, especially himself being present,[2] and best able to giue satisfacc*io*n thereof, I will hasten therefore to his retorne /

March
The 9th of Marche he retorned to Iames Towne, with his Pynnasse well loaden with Corne, Wheat, beanes, and Pease, to our great Comfort & his worthi Comendac*io*ns /

By this tyme the Counsell & Captaine haueing intentiuely looked into the Carryadge bothe of the Councellors, and other officers[,] remoued some officers out of the stoare; and Capt*ay*n Archer, a Councellor, whose insolency did looke vpon that litle in himself with great sighted spectacles, derrogating from others merrites by spueing out his venemous libells, and infamous Cronicles, vpon them; as doth appeere in his owne hand wrighting / [added in much smaller writing:] For which & other worse trickes he had not escaped yᵉ halter, but that Capt*ay*n Newport interposed his advise to the Contrarye /

[1] Perkin states that the fire was on a Thursday, and 7 January was a Thursday.
[2] If this means, as it seems to mean, that Newport was present, or expected to be present, at the examination of Wingfield, this must have taken place after 28 May and before Newport returned to Virginia (probably between 15 and 29 July).

Captayne Newport haueing now dispatched all his busines and sett the Clocke in a true course (if so the Councell will keepe it) prepared himself for England vpon the xth of Aprill, and arryued at Blackwall on Sunday the xxjth of Maye 1608 /[1]

Aprill

Maie

FINIS

[The following rider is in a similar, if not the same, hand, written more compactly, and with an average of two more lines to the page.]

I humbly craue some patience to answere many scandalus imputacions, which malice, more than malice hath scattered vpon my name, and those frivolous greevances obiected against me by the President and Councell, and though *nil conscire sibi*[2] be the onely maske that can well couer my blushes; yett doe I not doubt, but this my Appollogie shall easily wipe them awaie /

[391]

It is noysed that I Combyned with the Spanniards to the distruccion of the Collony: That I ame an Athiest because I Carryed not a Bible, with me, and because I did forbid the preacher to preache, that I affected a Kin[g]dome: That I did hide of the Comon prouision in the ground /

I Confesse I haue alwayes admyred any noble vertue & prowesse as well in the Spanniards (as in other Nations) but naturally I haue alwayes distrusted, and disliked their neighborhoode [/]

I sorted many bookes in my house to be sent vp to me at my goeing to Virginia, a mongst them a bible; They were sent me vp in a Trunk to London, with diuers fruite, conserues, &

---

[1] The date has been tampered with twice: The words 'on sunday' were added above the line, and the 'j' in 'xxjth' was clumsily inserted. Since Sunday fell on 22 May 1608, it may be that they arrived on that date, but the scribe could not find room for 'ii' or 'ij'. Van Meteren gave the date as 14 May, but this has been added also (see Document no. 52, p. 274 and n., below). Unfortunately, neither Wingfield nor van Meteren is infallible as to dates.

[2] 'Being conscious of nothing [wrong]' – the quotation is from Horace, *Epistles*, I, i, 61.

preserues, which I did sett in Master Crofts[1] his house in Ratcliff; In my beeing at Virginia I did vnderstand my trunck was thear broken vp [in Ratcliff], much of my sweete meates eaten at his Table, some of my bookes which I missid to be seene in his handes; and whether a mongst them my Bible was so ymbeasiled, or mislayed, by my servauntes; and not sent me I knowe not as yet /

Twoe or three sundayes morninges the Indians gaue vs allarums at our Towne, by that tymes they wear answered, the place aboute vs well discouered [reconnoitred], and our devyne service ended, the daie was farr spent: The preacher did aske me if it weare my pleasure to haue a sermon, hee said hee was prepared for it: I made answere that our men weare weary, and hungry, and that hee did see the tyme of the daie farr past (for at other tymes hee neuer made such question but the service finished he began his sermon) & that if it pleased him wee would spare him, till some other tyme: I never failed to take such noates by wrighting out of his doctrine as my Capacity could Comprehend, vnlesse some raynie day hindred my indeauour,

[391ᵛ]

My mynde never swelled with such ympossible mountebanck humors, as could make me affect any other Kingdome then the kingdome of heaven /

As truly as god liueth I gaue an ould man then the keeper of the private stoure, 2 glasses with sallet oyle which I brought with me out of England for my private stoare, and willed him to bury it in the ground, for that I feared the great heate would spoile it, whatsoeuer was more I did never Consent vnto, or knewe of it: And as truly was it protested vnto me, that all the remaynder before mencioned of the oyle, wyne &c[.] which

---

[1] Wingfield's quarrelsome relations with Crofte[s] are difficult to explain, but there probably was some remote tie through Wingfield's far-spreading family tree. Although Crofte's identity is far from certain, it is possible that he was the Richard Crofte, son of Edward of Crofte Castle, Hereford, who was admitted to the Middle Temple on 2 December 1587, and would thus have been about ten years younger than Wingfield (admitted to Furnival's Inn on 13 April 1576). The details need yet to be investigated.

the President receyued of me, when I was deposed, theye themselues poored into their owne bellyes /

To the Presidentes and Councelles obiections I saie, that I doe knowe Curtesey and Civility became a governor; no penny whitle was asked me but a kniffe, whereof I had none to spare, the Indyans had long before stoallen my knife, of Chickins, I never did eat but one, and that in my sicknes; Master Ratcliff had before that tyme tasted of 4 or 5: I had by my owne huswiferie bred aboue 37 and the most part of them of my owne Poultrye, of all which at my Comyng awaye I did not see three liueing: I never denyed him (or any other) beare [beer] when I had it, the Corne was of the same which wee all liued vpon /

Master Smyth in the tyme of our hungar had spred a Rumor in the Collony that I did feast my self and my servauntes, out of the Comon stoare, with entent (as I gathered) to haue stirred the discontented Company against me, I tould him privately in Master Gosnolds Tent, that indeede I had caused half a pinte of pease to be sodden, with a peese of porke of my owne prouision for a poore old man, which in a sicknes (whereof he died) he much desired, and said that if out of his malice he had giuen it out otherwise, that hee did tell a lye. It was proued to his face, that he begged in Ireland like a rogue, without lycence, to such I would not my name should be a Companyon[1] /

Master Martins payns during my Comaund never stirred [392] out of our Towne tenn scoare, and how slack hee was in his watching and other dutyes, it is too well knowne: I never defrauded his sonne of anything of his owne allowance, but gaue him aboue it, I belieue their disdainefull vsage, and threates which they many tymes gaue me, would haue pulled some distempered speeches out of farr greater Pacyence then myne; yet shall not any revenging humor in me befoule my penn with their base names and liues here and there, I did visit Master Pearsie, Master Hunt[,] Master Brewster, Master

[1] For suggestions as to Smith in Ireland, see Barbour, *Smith*, p. 145, and p. 436, n. 2.

Pickasse, Master Allicock, ould short ['old' Edward Short], the Bricklayer and diuerse others, at seuerall tymes, I neuer miscalled at a gent at any time /

Concerning my deposing from my place, I can well prooue that Master Ratcliff said if I had vsed him well in his sicknes (wherein I finde not my self guilty of the contrary) I had never bene deposed /

Master Smith said if it had not bene for Master Archers [libels?] I hadd never bene deposed: since his being heere in the Towne [since his return from the Chickahominy voyage?] he hath said that he tould the President, and Councell that they were frivolous obiections they had Collected against me, and that they had not doone well to depose me; Yet in my Conscience I doe belieue him the first & onely practizer in theis practises[1] /

Master Archers quarrell to me was, because hee had not the choise of the place for our plantation, because I misliked his leying out of our Towne in the pinnasse, because I would not sware him of the Councell for Virginia, which neyther I could doo or he deserue.

Master Smyths quarrell because his name was mencioned in the entended & Confessed mutiny by Galthropp /

Thomas Wootton the Surieon, because I would not subscribe to a Warrant (which he had gotten drawne) to the Treasurer of virginia to deliuer him mony to furnish him with drugges, and other necessaryes, & because I disallowed his living in the pinnasse, haueing many of our men lyeing sick, & wounded in our Towne to whose dressinges by that meanes he slacked his attendaunce /

[392ᵛ] Of the same men also Captayn Gosnold gaue me warning misliking much their dispositions, and assured me they would ley hold of me if they could, and peradventure many, because I held them, to watching warding, and workeing, and the

---

[1] This is odd, after the blame heretofore placed squarely on Archer. The text may be corrupt.

Collony generally because I would not giue my consent to starue them; I cannot rack [wrest] one word, or thought from my self, touching my Carryadg in Virginia other then is herein sett downe /

If I may now at the last presume vpon Your fauours; I ame an honourable suitor; that your owne loue of truth will vouchsafe to cleare me from all false aspertions happining since I embarked me into this affaire of Virginia, for my first worke (which was to make aright choise of a spirituall Pastor) I appeale to the remembraunce of my Lord of Caunterbury his grace; who gaue me very gracious audience in my request. And the world knoweth, whome I tooke with me [Hunt]; truly in my opinion a man not any waie to be touched with the rebellious humors of a popish spirit, nor blemished with ye least suspition of a facti[o]us scismatick. whereof I had a speciall Care. for other obiections if your worthie selues be pleased to sett me free, I haue learned to dispise ye populer verdict of ye vulgar. I euer chered vp my self with a confidence in ye wisdome of graue iudicious Senatours & was never dismayed in all my service by any synister event, though I bethought me of ye hard begininges which in former ages betided those worthy spirites, that planted the greatest Monarches in Asia & Europe, wherein I obserued rather ye troubles of Moses & Aron, with other of like History, then that venom in the mutinous brood of Cadmus or that harmony in ye swete consent of Amphion: And when with ye former I had considered that even the b[r]etheren [Romulus and Remus] at their plantacion of the Romaine Empire were not free from mortall hatred, & intestine garboile, likewise that both ye Spanish & English Records are guilty of like factions, it made me more vigilant in ye avoyding thereof: and I protest my greatest contencion was to prevent contencion, and my chiefest endeauor to preserve the liues of others, though with ye great hazard of my own[,] for I never desired to enamell my name with bloude: I reioyce that my trauells & daungers haue done somewhat for the behoof of Ierusalem in virginia. If it be obiected as my ouersight to put my self amongst such men, I can saie for my self there wear not any other for our consort. & I could not forsake ye enterprise of opening so glorious a Kingdome vnto ye king, wherein I shall ever be most ready to bestow ye poore remainder of my dayes, as in any other his Heighnes disignes according to my bounden duty with ye vtmost of my poore Tallent /

[Endorsed:] A Discourse of Virginia
   Per Ed*ward Maria* wingfilld

35. *1608* [*published in 1611*].
 News from Paris.[1]

[1608]

Gaultier Raleg [Walter Ralegh], during the reign of Queen Elizabeth of England, discovered Virginia, which is a country between Florida and Norombega.[2] Groups of English colonists had been brought there to live, but after 1587 because of dire necessity they came back to England with Drake. After that, no-one had been there to stay. Last year [1606 is meant] a number of English noblemen and merchants presented a petition to the King to establish two colonies; which was granted to them. The first colony was to be sent from London, and the other from Burgstov [Bristol], Excestre and Pleimuth. Ordinances were drawn up regarding the places where they were to live, with restrictions on some against going to live there, and permission [to the licensees] to expel by force those who wanted to try to. In brief, they [the licensees] were granted splendid privileges.

Colonies which the English have set up in Virginia in this year

[1] Extract, translated. *Le Mercure François, ou, La Suite de l'histoire de la Paix* . . . [1605–1610]. Paris, 1611. Sigs. Bb3 v–Bb4. First reprinted, in French, in Neill, *Virginia Company*, 17–18. Published, in English, in Brown's *Genesis*, I, 142, with the odd mistake of 'Western' for *Australe*.

[2] Norombega, with a wide variety of spellings, was a name applied to the northeast coast of North America as early as the 1520s (see Sigmund Diamond, 'Norumbega: New England Xanadu', *The American Neptune*, XI [1951], 95–107).

EVENTS IN ENGLAND

In the spring of this year [1607 is meant], the Colony (which was to inhabit the southern part of Virginia), which was composed of a hundred men, with their wives and children, under the charge of Vincfeld [Wingfield], set sail in a ship commanded by Neoport, who without any unlucky accident landed at the mouth of a river in Virginia and set up lodgings. Vincfeld and the new inhabitants (who tried to make friends with a handful of poor Indians) began to build a fort, and to explore for mines: they found some [rock-]crystal and some ore, which they gave to Neoport to take back to England, which he did, and he employed only five weeks in returning. But these minerals were found to be of little value.[1] Let us now see what happened at the weddings of the Prince of Savoy and the Infanta, his daughter....

36. *24 April 1608.*
    Resolution of the States General.[2]

At the request of [Sir] Thomas Gates, Knight, Captain of a company of English soldiers, commissioned by the King of Great Britain to be in command, along with three other nobles, in the land of Virginia, of the peopling of that land, the petitioner is permitted to that end to absent himself from his company for the period of one year, on condition that he first supply his company with good officers and soldiers wherewith to serve the country [the States General].

[1] Though it is somewhat garbled, this account is interesting, since it was the first published news of Virginia to appear on the Continent. The importance of the Jamestown voyages to French minds is shown by the speed with which the author turns to the politico-matrimonial affairs of the House of Savoy.

[2] Translated. St Gen., inv. nr. 33 (1608), fo. 57. Printed in translation by Brown, in *Genesis*, I, 148.

37. *7 July 1608.*
John Chamberlain to Dudley Carleton.[1]

... Here is a ship newly come from Virginia that hath ben long missing, She went out the last yeare in consort with captain Newport, and after much wandering found the port three or fowre dayes after his departure for England, I heare not of any nouelties or other commodities she hath brought more then sweet woode....[2]

38. [5/] *15 September 1608.*
Pedro de Zúñiga to Philip III.[3]

Sir:

It has occurred to me to send to Your Majesty a map of Virginia,[4] and another [a plan] of the fort which they have built there,[5] along with an account given me by a person who has been there.[6] I am still exercising every effort to learn more, and I will inform [you] of it [what I learn]. I have just received by way of Flanders the letter which Your Majesty was pleased to have written to me the 16th of the past [month] with the Account which is recommended [for me to use] of our reasons for throwing into the galleys the English who took part in this expedition in 1606 [which sailed to found a colony in Maine but was taken en route], and I will avail myself of it in con-

---

[1] Extract. P.R.O., S.P. Dom., S.P. 14/35. Printed in Arber, *Smith, Works*, p. xcii; Brown, *Genesis*, I, 180; and in full in McClure, *Chamberlain*, I, 259.

[2] The reference is obviously to Nelson's *Phoenix*, which arrived at Jamestown ten days after Newport had sailed. Since there is a break of seventeen months in Chamberlain's surviving correspondence immediately preceding this letter, it is not possible to establish how long before 7 July Nelson reached London. Since he was off Cape Henry on 2 June, it cannot have been many days. John Smith confirms that Nelson's cargo was 'Cedar wood' (Document no. 33, p. 208, above).

[3] Translated. Original, written by a secretary, signed by Zúñiga. Archivo General de Simancas, Legajo E 2586, 145 to 148. The letter is numbered 145.

[4] See Document no. 40, below.

[5] The plan of the fort, 'St Georges Fort' in the northern colony, on the Sagadahoc River, is evidently of English origin (Simancas, M y P: XIX–163).

[6] See Document no. 39, below.

Emanuel van Meteren recorded about that time that Captain John Smith sent 'letters and maps' to Hudson from Virginia (Document no. 52, p. 274, below). A result of this was Hudson's contract of 8 January 1609, with the Directors of the (Dutch) East India Company to search for the Northwest Passage, which resulted in his discovery of the river at New York City now named for him.

The map contains sixty-eight names of Indian villages in the region explored by Smith before 2 June 1608, and scattered additional names from hearsay – those to the south of Jamestown taken from Sir Walter Ralegh's people; those to the north of the Pamunkey River from his Indian informants.

The map is crudely drawn, for the simple reason that Smith had done very little careful exploring at the time he sketched it. (It is absurd to attempt to establish a 'scale of miles', as Alexander Brown did (*Genesis*, I, 184).) Nevertheless, despite the distortion, the general geography of the region through which Smith passed is fairly presented. The most noteworthy details are:

(1) Notable exaggeration of the size of Jamestown peninsula, identified by the triangular fort just below the centre of the map.
(2) The dotted line showing Smith's captivity-trail, 10 December 1607 to 2 January 1608, starting just left of top centre and zigzagging down until it reaches Jamestown.
(3) The descriptive annotations, detailed below, to the left of the James River and at the top of the map.
(4) The sweep of Chesapeake Bay toward the top of the map, due to confusion in Smith's information of the Bay and the Potomac River. Kuskarawaock, for example, at the lower right, was on Delmarva Peninsula, on the Nanticoke River, probably inside the State of Delaware; Moyoonces [Moyaones], the sixth village indicated above, was not far below Washington, D.C. This geographical jumble was undoubtedly due to Smith's lack of expertise in the language

JAMESTOWN VOYAGES

of the Indians coupled with the lack of knowledge of upper Chesapeake Bay on the part of the Indians themselves, and a certain amount of hope that the great river described to him would be the one which led toward the 'great salt water' which Smith identified with the South Sea (the Pacific Ocean).

While a list of the villages named on this map is out of place here, the annotations are worth some brief attention. On the left side of the map there are three, from left to right, as follows:

A. Pakerakanick. Here remayne the 4 men clothed that came from Roonock [Roanoke] Oconohowan. [Neither Pakerakanick nor Oconohowan is in the Roanoke accounts.[1]]
B. Here the king of paspahegh reported our men to be and went to se[e].
C. Here paspahegh and 2 of our men landed to go to panawiock.[2]

And at the top of the map are five additional notes:

D. [To the right] Hear the salt water beatethe into the riuer [to the left] amongst theis rocks [below] being the south sea.
E. Monacan. 2 days Iorney.
F. 20 miles aboue this C[aptain] S[mith] [word crossed out] was taken.
G. [A large cluster of dots] Rassaweck. 2 days Iorney.
H. Pocoughtawonauck. A Saluag people Dwelling vpon this seay beyond this mayne that eate the men & women.

[1] Both names were picked up by the Jamestown settlers, and both are mentioned in Strachey's *Historie*.
[2] This name appears (as Panauuaioc) in de Bry's engraving of John White's 'Map of Eastern North America' (see Quinn, *Roanoke*, facing I, 462).

41. *Between 10 September and early December, 1608.*
*Captain John Smith to the Treasurer and Council of Virginia,
London.*[1]

The Copy of a Letter sent to the Treasurer and Councell of Virginia from Captaine Smith, then President in Virginia.

Right Honorable, &c.

I Received your Letter, wherein you write, that our minds are so set vpon faction, and idle conceits in diuiding the country without your consents, and that we feed You but with ifs & ands, hopes, & some few proofes; as if we would keepe the mystery of the businesse to our selues: and that we must expresly follow your instructions sent by Captain Newport: the charge of whose voyage amounts to neare two thousand pounds, the which if we cannot defray by the Ships returne, we are like to remain as banished men. To these particulars I humbly intreat your Pardons if I offend you with my rude Answer.

For our factions, vnlesse you would haue me run away and leaue the Country, I cannot prevent them: because I do make many stay that would els fly any whether. For the idle Letter sent to my Lord of Salisbury, by the President and his confederats, for diuiding the Country &c.[2] What it was I know

[1] Extract. Captain John Smith, *The generall historie of Virginia, New-England, and the Summer Isles;* . . . (London, 1624) pp. 70–2. As to the dating, the letter was certainly written after Captain Smith was elected president of the council in Virginia (10 September) and before the departure of Newport for England (after 26 November) (see Document no. 42) but in time to reach London before 16 January 1609). It is not improbable that this is not a *literatim* copy of the letter Smith wrote. (See Barbour, *Smith*, pp. 233–4 and n. 2.) Alexander Brown has objected that the superscription to the letter was improper, in that the title 'Treasurer and Councell' was not mentioned before 1609. This seems of little importance, since Smith first printed the letter after the title had become customary, and in any event, since the council existed it must have had some officer responsible for administration, someone must have signed the letter sent to Jamestown, and there is no reason for precluding the possibility that the signer was, even officially, called the treasurer.

[2] The 'President' referred to must have been Ratcliffe. That he may well have written to Salisbury is hinted by a later letter from him to the same (Document no. 54, p. 283,

not, for you saw no hand of mine to it; nor euer dream't I of any such matter. That we feed you with hopes, &c. Though I be no scholer, I am past a schoole-boy; and I desire but to know, what either you, and these here doe know, but that I haue learned to tell you by the continuall hazard of my life. I haue not concealed from you any thing I know; but I feare some cause you to beleeue much more then is true.

Expresly to follow your directions by Captaine Newport, though they be performed, I was directly against it; but according to our Commission, I was content to be overruled by the major part of the Councell, I feare to the hazard of vs all; which now is generally confessed when it is too late. Onely Captaine Winne and Captaine Waldo I haue sworne of the Councell, and Crowned Powhatan according to your instructions.

For the charge of this Voyage of two or three thousand pounds, we haue not receiued the value of an hundred pounds. And for the quartred Boat to be borne by the Souldiers over the Falles, Newport had 120 of the best men he could chuse. If he had burnt her to ashes, one might haue carried her in a bag, but as she is, fiue hundred cannot, to a navigable place aboue the Falles. And for him at that time to find in the South Sea, a Mine of gold; or any of them sent by Sir Walter Raleigh: at our Consultation I told them was as likely as the rest. But during this great discovery of thirtie myles, (which might as well haue beene done by one man, and much more,[1] for the value of a pound of Copper at a seasonable tyme) they had the Pinnace and all the Boats with them, but one that remained with me to serue the Fort. In their absence I followed the new

below). The London council was amply fed with reports of factions and internal strife at Jamestown.

[1] Smith's meaning is probably that one man could have accomplished much more than Newport's hundred and twenty men, which, under the circumstances, seems likely. It must be remembered that the entire population of Powhatan village, at the point where Newport tried to carry his boat around the James River falls, was at most 140 to 170 souls, food was always a problem, and the burnt trails through the forest were certainly not designed for a 'task force' of such size.

begun workes of Pitch and Tarre, Glasse, Sopeashes, and Clapboord, whereof some small quantities we haue sent you. But if you rightly consider, what an infinite toyle it is in Russia and Swethland, where the woods are proper for naught els, and though there be the helpe both of man and beast in those ancient Common-wealths, which many an hundred yeares haue vsed it, yet thousands of those poore people can scarce get necessaries to liue, but from hand to mouth. And though your Factors there can buy as much in a week as will fraught you a ship, or as much as you please; you must not expect from vs any such matter, which are but a many of ignorant miserable soules, that are scarce able to get wherewith to liue, and defend our selues against the inconstant Salvages: finding but here and there a tree fit for the purpose, and want all things els the Russians haue. For the Coronation of Powhatan, by whose advice you sent him such presents, I know not; but this giue me leaue to tell you, I feare they will be the confusion of vs all ere we heare from you againe. At your Ships arrivall, the Salvages harvest was newly gathered, and we going to buy it, our owne not being halfe sufficient for so great a number. As for the two ships loading of corne Newport promised to provide vs from Powhatan, he brought vs but foureteene Bushels; and from the Monacans nothing, but the most of the men sicke and neare famished. From your Ship we had not provision in victuals worth twenty pound, and we are more then two hundred to liue vpon this: the one halfe sicke, the other little better. For the Saylers (I confesse) they daily make good cheare, but our dyet is a little meale and water, and not sufficient of that. Though there be fish in the Sea, foules in the ayre, and Beasts in the woods, their bounds are so large, they so wilde, and we so weake and ignorant, we cannot much trouble them. Captaine Newport we much suspect to be the Authour of those inventions. Now that you should know, I haue made you as great a discovery as he, for lesse charge then he spendeth you every meale; I haue sent you this Mappe of the

Bay and Rivers, with an annexed Relation of the Countries and Nations that inhabit them, as you may see at large.[1] Also two barrels of stones, and such as I take to be good Iron ore at the least; so devided, as by their notes you may see in what places I found them. The Souldiers say many of your officers maintaine their families out of that you send vs: and that Newport hath an hundred pounds a yeare for carrying newes. For every master you haue yet sent can find the way as well as he, so that an hundred pounds might be spared, which is more then we haue all, that helpe to pay him wages. Cap. Ratliffe is now called Sicklemore, a poore counterfeited Imposture.[2] I haue sent you him home, least the company should cut his throat. What he is, now every one can tell you: if he and Archer returne againe, they are sufficient to keepe vs always in factions. When you send againe I intreat you rather send but thirty Carpenters, husbandmen, gardiners, fisher men, blacksmiths, masons, and diggers vp of trees, roots, well provided; then a thousand of such as we haue; for except wee be able both to lodge them, and feed them, the most will consume with want of necessaries before they can be made good for any thing. Thus if you please to consider this account, and of the vnnecessary wages to Captaine Newport, or his ships so long lingering and staying here (for notwithstanding his boasting to leaue vs victuals for 12 moneths, though we had 89 by this discovery lame and sicke, and but a pinte of Corne a day for a man, we were constrained to giue him three hogsheads of that to victuall him homeward)

[1] Smith's map and relation cannot be identified with precision, but it may be assumed that the map was a copy of the sketch map later improved and used as the basis for his engraved map of 1612 (see Document no. 63, p. 374, below). The 'relation' probably consisted of the notes he was later to use in his 1612 book.
[2] Unless Ratcliffe was, like Kendall and Brewster, some sort of an agent of Salisbury's, it is difficult to understand why he enjoyed such favour with the Virginia Company. In one and the same document (the 'instructions to Sir Thomas Gates'), Ratcliffe is placed on the local council under Gates (section 4) and ordered to be examined in the matter of 'iniuries and insolences' (section 30) dating back to Ratcliffe's presidency (Kingsbury, *Records*, III, 13 and 22–3). In addition, Ralph Hamor, who arrived in Jamestown after Smith was gone and Ratcliffe was dead, went so far as to write, 'not worthy remembring, but to his dishonour' (Hamor, *True Discourse*, 7).

or yet to send into Germany or Poleland for glasse-men & the rest, till we be able to sustaine our selues, and relieue them when they come. It were better to giue fiue hundred pound a tun for those grosse Commodities in Denmarke, then send for them hither, till more necessary things be provided. For in over-toyling our weake and vnskilfull bodies, to satisfie this desire of present profit, we can scarce ever recover our selues from one Supply to another. And I humbly intreat you hereafter, let vs know what we should receiue, and not stand to the Saylers courtesie to leaue vs what they please, els you may charge vs with what you will, but we not you with any thing. These are the causes that haue kept vs in Virginia, from laying such a foundation, that ere this might haue given much better content and satisfaction; but as yet you must not looke for any profitable returnes: so I humbly rest.

42. *26 November 1608.*[1]
Peter Winne [Wynne] to Sir John Egerton.

Most noble knight

I was not so desirous to come into this Country, as I am now willing here to end my dayes: for I finde it a farr more pleasant, and plentifull country than any report made mencion of. vpon the River [vpon] which wee are seated I have gon six or seaven score miles, and so farr is navigable; afterward I travailed between 50 or 60 myles by land, into a Country Called Monacon who owe no subiection to Powaton; this land is very high ground and fertill, being very full of very delicate springes of sweet water: the ayre more helthfull than the place wher wee are seated, by reason it is not subiect to such fogges and

[1] Holograph. Huntington Library, Jamestown Colony, EL 1683. First printed in Charles M. Andrews, *The Colonial Period of American History*, I, 100 n. 4. Reprinted with a brief but useful introduction in Louis B. Wright, *Newes from the New-World*, Huntington Library, San Marino, 1946, pp. 9–11. Winne died early in 1609 (Barbour, *Smith*, p. 263). The letter was evidently written in time for Newport to take it to England when he sailed, toward the end of 1608 (see p. 241, n. 1).

mistes as we continually have. the people of Monacon speak a farr differing language from the subiectes of Powaton, theyr pronunciation being very like welch so that the gentlemen in our Company desired me to be theyr Interpretor. The Comodities as yet knowne in this Country whereof ther wilbe great store, is Pitch, Tarr, Sope ashes, and some dyes, wherof we have sent examples. As for thinges more precious I omit till tyme (which I hope wilbe shortly) shall make manifest proof of it. As concerning your request of Bloudhoundes, I cannot learne that ther is any such in this Country; only the dogges which are here are a Certeyne kind of Currs like our wariners hey dogges in England; and they keep them to hunt theyr land fowles, as Turkeys and such like, for they keep nothing tame about them. hereafter I doubt not but to give you at large a farther relacion then as yet I am able to doe, and doe therfore desire you to take theis fewe lines in good part and hold me excused for the rest vntill fitter oportunity. Thus Comending my service to your good love with many thankes for all favours and kindnesses received from you I doe ever remayne

Iames Towne in virginia   Your most devoted in all service
this XXVI of November
                        [Signed] Peter wyn

[Endorsed:] To the Honourable Knight Sir
            Iohn Egerton at Yorke
            House geve these

[Later endorsement:] Captain Peter Wynne
                     Virginia

43. *23 January 1609.*
    John Chamberlain to Dudley Carleton.[1]

... here is likewise a ship newly come from Virginia with some petty commodities and hope of more, as diuers sorts of woode

[1] Extract. P.R.O., S.P. Dom., S.P. 14/43. Printed in Arber, *Smith, Works*, xciii; Brown, *Genesis*, I, 205; and in full in McClure, *Chamberlain*, I, 283.

for wainscot and other vses, sope ashes, some pitch and tarre, certain vnknowne kindes of herbes for dieng, not without suspicion (as they terme yt) of Cuchenilla....[1]

44. *14 February 1609.*
John Chamberlain to Dudley Carleton.[2]

... newes here is none at all but that John Dun [Donne][3] seekes to be preferred to be secretarie of Virginia....

[1] Chamberlain states at the beginning of this letter that he would have written on 20 January but for troubles with a messenger. John Sanderson, however, gives a nearer date for Newport's return. On 16 January he wrote to Martin Calthorpe in Norfolk: 'Newes, a pinis, laden with cloves, arived frome the East India, and another pinis frome Virginia...' (*The Travels of John Sanderson in the Levant, 1584–1602*, edited by Sir William Foster, Hakluyt Society, 2nd ser., LXVII (1931), 258).

[2] Extract. P.R.O., S.P. Dom., S.P. 14/43. Printed Brown, *Genesis*, I, 237 (with reference to previous printing in Birch's *Court and Times of James I*); and in full in McClure, *Chamberlain*, I, 284.

[3] John Donne was the son-in-law of Sir George More of the Virginia Company, who had first been so infuriated over the marriage that he had Donne thrown into the Fleet prison, but who had become reconciled with the couple in the autumn of 1608. This apparently was the immediate cause of Donne's interest in Virginia. A year or so later Donne mentioned Virginia briefly ('We've added to the world Virginia...') in a verse letter to Lucy, Countess of Bedford (her brother was young Sir John Harington, Prince Henry's 'chief friend'), but London and poetry held him fast. Years later, when he was Dean of St Paul's, Donne wrote a complimentary verse for Captain John Smith's *Generall Historie* (Arber, *Smith, Works*, pp. 284–5).